MARTIN HOLLADAY

D1086930

MUSINGS OF AN ENERGY NERD

TOWARD AN ENERGY-EFFICIENT HOME

The Taunton Press

The Taunton Press
Inspiration for hands-on living®

The Taunton Press, Inc., 63 South Main Street
PO Box 5506, Newtown, CT 06470-5506
Email:tp@taunton.com

Editor: Peter Chapman
Copy Editor: Candace B. Levy
Indexer: Cathy Goddard
Jacket/Cover design: Guido Caroti
Interior design: Guido Caroti
Layout: Sandra Mahlstedt, Lynne Phillips

The following names/manufacturers appearing in *Musings of an Energy Nerd* are trademarks: #6 Mastic®,
3M®, AccuVent®, Air Conditioning Contractors of America®, AirCycler®, American Concrete Institute®,
Band-Aid®, Best Materials®, Blue Seal®, Broan®, Celotex®, CertainTeed®, Clima,Guard™, Cree® Delta®-Dry,
DensGlass® gold, Duct Blaster®, Elmer's®, Empire®, Energy Advantage™, Energy Star®, EnergyTrust™ of
Oregon, EnergyGauge®, Estwing®, Evergreen Solar®, Fantech®, FastenMaster®, FlexFix®, Florida Solar
Energy Center® (FSEC®), Foil-Grip™, Georgia-Pacific®, GFX™, Glenkote®, Goodman®, Guardian®, Habitat
for Humanity®, Hardcast®, Harvey®, Heat Mirror®, HERS®, HOBO®, Homasote®, Home Depot®, Home
Energy Saver™, Howard Johnson®, Hunter Panels®, Inex™, Insulweb®, Intercept®, International Bildrite®,
International Energy Conservation Code® (IECC), International Residential Code® (IRC), Intertape Polymer
Group®, Lennox®, Lifebreath®, Lima®, LoĒ²-270®, Marvin®, MemBrain®, Minneapolis Blower Door™,
Monitor™, Mr. Slim®, Nashua®, National Electrical Code®, National Fiber®, Navien®, Owens Corning®,
Panasonic®, Pella®, Ping-Pong®, Polyken®, Power-Pipe®, PPG IdeaScapes®, Quaternity™, RCD Corpora-
tions®, RecoupAerator®, REM/Rate™, RenewAire®, RESNET®, Right-D®, Right-J®, Rinnai®, Robur®,
Rosco®, Roxul®, Sheetrock®, Shurtape®, Solarban®, Sonotube®, Stanley®, Stiebel Eltron®, Styrofoam®,
SunDrum®, Sungate®, Super Spacer®, Superior Walls®, Swiggle Seal®, Thermax™, Thermoply®, Thermo-
tech®, Tigerflex®, Tremco®, Tremproof®, Tu-Tuf®, Tyvek®, Uni-Mastic™, Venmar®, Versa-Grip™, Walmart®,
WhisperGreen™, Wind-Lock™, Wrightsoft®, WUFI®, Zehnder®, ZIP System®

Library of Congress Cataloging-in-Publication Data

Names: Holladay, Martin.
Title: Musings of an energy nerd : toward an energy-efficient home / Martin
   Holladay.
Description: Newtown, CT : The Taunton Press, Inc., [2017] | Includes index.
Identifiers: LCCN 2016046598 | ISBN 9781631862564
Subjects: LCSH: Dwellings--Energy conservation. | Ecological houses.
Classification: LCC TJ163.5.D86 H63 2017 | DDC 696--dc23
LC record available at https://lccn.loc.gov/2016046598Printed in the United States of America
10 9 8 7 6 5 4 3 2 1

About Your Safety: Construction is inherently dangerous. Using hand or power tools improperly
or ignoring safety practices can lead to permanent injury or even death. Don't try to perform
operations you learn about here (or elsewhere) unless you're certain they are safe for you. If
something about an operation doesn't feel right, don't do it. Look for another way. We want
you to enjoy working on your home, so please keep safety foremost in your mind.

ACKNOWLEDGMENTS

I am indebted to a great many energy experts, physicists, engineers, and researchers who have generously taken time from their busy schedules to answer technical questions and clarify their research findings.

Among those who have been especially helpful are Robb Aldrich, Michael Blasnik, Terry Brennan, Rob Dumont, Gautam Dutt, Don Fugler, Bruce Harley, Pat Huelman, Achilles Karagiozis, Joseph Lstiburek, Chris Mathis, Neil Moyer, Gary Nelson, Harold Orr, Danny Parker, John Proctor, William Rose, Marc Rosenbaum, Armin Rudd, Andy Shapiro, Max Sherman, John Straube, Anton TenWolde, John Tooley, Iain Walker, and Kohta Ueno.

To those who belong on the list but whose names have been inadvertently omitted, I offer my sincere apologies.

I am also deeply grateful to my loving wife, Karyn Patno, without whose support this book would not have been possible.

If you're concerned about environmental deterioration and global climate change, you're probably attracted to so-called green products and lifestyles. You're not alone, and whole industries are now attempting to cater to your needs. Builders are no exception; hence the rise of the "green building movement."

I'm a builder and an environmentalist, but I'm not exactly sure what *green building* means. Even though I edit a website called Green Building Advisor, I try to avoid the use of the word *green*, because it has no technical definition and is often used to sell questionable products.

Now that the market is flooded with green products, it's important to distinguish true environmental responsibility from greenwashing. There is overwhelming evidence that the most effective way we can reduce our environmental impact is to reduce our energy consumption—especially our consumption of fossil fuels. North Americans, who now consume far more than our fair share of the earth's resources, are going to have to find ways to drastically reduce our energy use if we hope to avoid catastrophic climate change.

Spending $250,000 on a newly built "green" home is not going to help the planet. What the planet really needs is for all of us to buy less stuff, including so-called green building materials, and to strive, every year, to burn less fossil fuel than the year before. Of course, we may need to buy a few things to help us reduce our fossil fuel use, but our shopping list should be modest.

Because I was a builder for many years, I've spent a lot of time thinking about ways to build houses that use less energy than the typical American house. Since our new homes aren't very well built, they need more energy to operate than they should. The main problem with new homes is that they leak a lot of air. During the winter, warm air escapes from the typical home through all kinds of cracks in the floors, walls, and ceilings, and that escaping warm air is replaced by cold out-door air sneaking in through other cracks.

The good news is that relatively minor changes in construction practices—changes that are relatively inexpensive to implement—can result in much better homes. The tragic corollary, of course, is that even though we've known how to build tight buildings for 25 or 30 years, we have failed to do so. Our building codes don't require builders to pay much attention to air sealing, so most builders ignore these details.

Although the energy performance of new American homes has been dismal for decades, things are slowly starting to change. New homes are getting tighter. And the best American homes—those built by a small subset of builders who strive to build very tight, superinsulated homes—are among the best performing homes in the world.

At the time of new construction, it doesn't cost much to turn what might have been a bad house into a pretty good house. Unfortunately, once a house has been completed, occupied, and filled with furniture, it's much more expensive to turn an energy hog into an energy miser. That's why we need to improve our energy codes—so that all new homes are built with energy efficiency in mind.

Any builder involved with new construction needs to know how to build an energy-efficient house, and this book contains plenty of advice on how that can be done. Most of us aren't planning to build a new home, however, so this book also includes advice on fixing up the home you're living in now.

Although it's awkward and expensive to perform energy retrofit work on an existing house, I'm all in favor of such work. For one thing, we're not going to solve the current climate emergency by building millions of expensive new homes. Instead, like it or not, we're all going to have to figure out how to make the homes we now live in a lot more efficient.

Some builders compete to determine who can build the tightest house or the house with the most insulation or the house with the most sophisticated windows. Unfortunately, many of these superinsulated homes are extremely expensive. If your budget is unlimited, you can turn any house into a zero-energy house. (In fact, I know of a woman in New Hampshire who turned an old run-of-the-mill ranch house into a high-tech zero-energy house. The only problem: The project cost her a million dollars.)

Because most of us don't have million-dollar budgets—and it's probably good for the planet that we don't, since shopping isn't very environmentally friendly—we all need to figure out how far to go when we're fixing up a house or building a new one. How tight should we make our home? Should we aim for 2 air changes per hour at 50 Pascals (2 ACH50), or should we adopt the Passivhaus goal of 0.6 ACH50? How much insulation should

we put in our attic? Is R-49 enough, or should we install R-60?

There are no easy answers to these questions. However, almost every energy expert agrees that the best way for most homeowners to save energy is to invest in air sealing. Though unglamorous, the work yields high dividends. Once implemented, air-sealing measures are long-lived; unlike a fancy new furnace or ground-source heat pump, the caulk used to fill cracks in your attic is unlikely to need maintenance or replacement. Simple measures are best.

Once you move beyond air-sealing measures, however, decisions become trickier. Some energy experts recommend retrofit work that costs about $100,000 to implement in a typical home. Clearly, most Americans will never be able to afford that type of a deep-energy retrofit. And even the rare homeowner who can afford it has to decide whether thick insulation is overkill, especially when the price of photovoltaic modules is dropping precipitously. If your home already has pretty good insulation, a $15,000 investment in PV equipment may make more sense than a $15,000 investment in additional insulation.

This example shows how tricky it can be to distinguish the silly ideas from the wise investments. The more you learn, however, the easier these decisions will become.

As designers engage in an arms race to develop increasingly comfortable homes, green builders need to know when to say "enough is enough."

Buildings have had central heating for only about 140 years, and they have had air-conditioning for only about 80 years. For most of human history, people took comfort in winter from a stone fireplace—somewhere to heat up a kettle or warm one's hands. Once heating and cooling systems were developed, almost everyone wanted them. Why? Because people want to be comfortable.

COMFORT IS HARD TO PIN DOWN

What is comfort? Definitions vary. If you are camping and get caught in a rainstorm, you'll probably find that a dry sleeping bag in a dry tent is extremely comfortable. If you are spending the day ice fishing, you may find that a plywood shack equipped with a tiny propane heater is extremely comfortable—especially compared to the guy outside who is sitting on a drywall bucket in the wind.

The American Society of Heating, Refrigerating, and Air-Conditioning Engineers (ASHRAE℠) has developed a standard (ASHRAE Standard 55) that decrees heating and cooling systems should maintain a building's indoor temperature and relative humidity within a comfortable range: not too hot, not too cold, not too dry, and not too damp.

The Passivhaus standard takes a similar approach, while also noting that the interior of a building shouldn't be windy or drafty and that the temperature of all of the surfaces in a room (especially window panes) shouldn't be so cold in winter that radiational effects make people uncomfortable.

Standards that define a range of indoor conditions leading to human comfort are useful. All such standards note that not all people have the same ideas about comfort. Human comfort depends in part on whether the person is active or at rest, whether the person is fully clothed or naked, and whether the person is young or old.

Even if these factors are carefully controlled, however, humans differ. If two similarly clothed people of the same age are sitting in a room, one might say "I'm cold," while the other might say, "I'm hot." Because of this human variability, standard writers have to specify ranges for conditions leading to comfort.

A FAMILY HISTORY OF COMFORT

If I look back a couple of generations, I can easily document how comfort expectations have changed in my own family. My grandmother was born in 1904, and grew up in rural South Dakota in a leaky frame house that was so cold every winter that the family banked the foundation with manure in the fall. I imagine that her bedroom was often below freezing during the winter.

As far as I know, my parents both grew up in homes with central heating (although my mother's family had an icebox, not a refrigerator). If they wanted to experience air-conditioning, they went to the movies.

MOST PEOPLE WANT TO LIVE IN A HOME that feels like a safe refuge—a place where the family can relax and feel comfortable. Indoor relative humidity and indoor air temperature are only two of a long list of factors that contribute to our sense that a room feels comfortable.

My first memories date back to the late 1950s, when my family lived in a house with single-glazed windows in Boulder, CO. I remember waking up on winter mornings to admire the swirling, flower-like patterns of frost on the windows. Our eaves were often loaded with icicles—a sign that the attic didn't have much insulation—and when I was having a bath, my parents used to make me laugh by breaking off an icicle and putting it in the bathtub for me to play with. When I was growing up, cars didn't have air-conditioning. We would drive with the windows open, sticking our heads out like dogs.

NO ONE WANTS TO LIVE THE WAY WE DID IN THE 1930S

There is no turning back the comfort clock. It's perfectly understandable that people prefer their homes to be air-conditioned during the summer. But advances in comfort raise the question, When does the arms race stop?

Would any of us recognize a motel room from 1960? These days, when you walk into a hotel or motel room—assuming you're not staying in a hostel that caters to backpackers—you get more than a just a bed. You get a very wide bed—maybe two beds—with more pillows than a person could possibly use. In the bathroom you'll find enough towels for a football team. If the hotel offered you a bedroom like the one you have at home, you'd probably be insulted. That's the arms race in action.

PASSIVHAUS LEVELS OF COMFORT

I have written several articles noting that the Passivhaus standard often requires investments that aren't cost-effective—for example, investments in thick insulation, triple-glazed windows, and Zehnder® heat-recovery ventilators (HRVs). When I suggest that it might be possible to specify less subslab insulation, double-glazed windows, or a simpler ventilation system,

Passivhaus designers often respond, "You don't understand! It's not about cost-effectiveness! It's about comfort!"

Sometimes they're right—for example, when temperatures drop below 0°F, it's usually more comfortable to sit next to a triple-glazed window than a double-glazed window. Other times, they're simply wrong. There is no way that a human can tell the difference between 6 in. of subslab foam and 12 in. of subslab foam. But in all cases, these Passivhaus designers fail to ask an important question: How much money should we spend on comfort? If you get a chill when you sit next to a double-glazed window, maybe all you really need to do is put on a sweater.

If we establish a standard that insists that no surface in a house should ever be more than 7 F° cooler than the indoor air temperature, we are assuming (a) humans should never have to suffer the indignity of sitting next to a window that has a surface temperature that is 9 F° cooler than the air and (b) spending lots of money on very expensive windows to meet our comfort needs is a good use of the world's resources.

A ROOM THAT FEELS COMFORTABLE to people who are fully clothed may feel uncomfortable to people who are naked.

TWO KINDS OF ENVELOPE AND HVAC MEASURES

I love envelope measures (for example, air-sealing work and increased insulation levels) and HVAC solutions (for example, ductless minisplits) that are cost-effective. If investing in one of these measures saves enough energy over its lifetime to exceed the cost of the measure, it's a great investment. Everybody wins.

What about envelope measures that aren't cost-effective but increase comfort? These measures make sense for homeowners who want high levels of comfort and can afford to spend more money on their house than the average family. But

these measures shouldn't be considered "green." They are luxury features, not necessities.

SHOULD OCCUPANTS NEVER NOTICE ANYTHING?

Some Passivhaus designers and radiant-floor enthusiasts aim to create a house in which we never notice the temperature. The temperature and relative humidity of the air should always be perfect. The goal appears to be for the occupants to think, "I notice nothing."

In this vein, Mark Eatherton, the executive director of the Radiant Professionals Alliance, posted the following comment to a GBA article about radiant floors: "Being comfortable means that you are not aware of your surroundings . . . You are not hot, nor are you cold. You are not over-humidified nor are you under-humidified. Ideally, you do not hear your comfort being delivered. Simply stated, you are not thinking about it, and if you are, then you are not comfortable."

If this goal is achieved, it's far from clear that our lives have been improved. It turns out that there is a paradox at the heart of this quest for perfect comfort: Once it has been achieved, our lives feel somewhat empty. Most Buddhists have a fundamental understanding of this phenomenon.

If all human beings want is freedom from heat and cold, it would be hard to explain why children remember camping trips with so much joy. Kids seem especially to remember the exhilaration of camping trips when everyone got wet and cold—and then got so hot and sweaty that they couldn't wait to jump into a mountain lake.

There are two aspects to the phenomenon I'm describing. The first is that unchanging blandness seems to depress the human soul, in the same way that many nursing home residents are depressed by a diet without any hot peppers or garlic.

The second aspect to this phenomenon is more subtle; it was examined in depth by David Foster Wallace in his hilarious book *A Supposedly Fun Thing I'll Never Do Again*. When expectations are raised, as they are by Eatherton's attempt to deliver a house in which occupants are always perfectly comfortable, and as they are by the Passivhaus promise that indoor temperatures will be perfectly uniform, we are setting people up for dissatisfaction. Expecting perfection, homeowners notice the slightest draft, and the slightest draft becomes irritating.

WE CAN BE COMFORTABLE IF WE ARE WILLING TO ACCEPT THE WORLD AS IT IS

Designers and homeowners need to remember that it is sometimes OK to live in an imperfect house—one that feels a little hot in July and a little cold and drafty in January. In fact, this type of imperfect house might be more affordable (or even greener) than an expensive Passivhaus.

When you're hot, it might be time to drink a glass of lemonade. When you're cold, it might be time to put on a pair of fuzzy slippers and brew a pot of tea. After all, summer is supposed to be different from winter. If you take this approach, you might discover that your imperfect house is fine just the way it is.

A high-performance house has good water-management details, the right shape, the right orientation, and the right type of roof. If an architect or designer is set on imposing design features that are incompatible with good energy performance, it's hard to fix the bad features later with Band-Aids®.

A high-performance house is achievable only when everyone on the team—including the designer, the general contractor, and the owners—has agreed to certain design principles from day one.

1

CONSTRUCTION BASICS

Buying an inefficient refrigerator is an expensive mistake. But at least the solution is simple: You can always buy a new refrigerator. If you build an inefficient house, however, you may have an unfixable problem on your hands. Some newly built homes are so poorly designed, sited, and built that it would be cheaper to demolish them and start again than to correct all their flaws.

Assuming you get the details right from the start, the incremental cost of better energy features will be affordable, and you'll still be smiling when energy prices double. But if you get the details wrong— if you choose cheap windows or build a leaky ceiling—you may be stuck with a white elephant.

The great tragedy of poorly built new homes is that many details that would have been easy to include at the time of construction are notoriously difficult to retrofit. To be sure your new home is an energy miser, not an energy hog, follow these 10 important steps.

1. DESIGN A SMALL HOUSE

Avoid the temptation to build big, even if you think you can afford it. If you build a spare bedroom, remember that as long as you own the home, you'll be paying taxes on it, heating it, cooling it, ventilating it, and vacuuming it. Maybe all you really need is a fold-out couch.

If you've ever been lucky enough to visit friends in Paris, Madrid, or Rome, you know that it's possible to live a luxurious, civilized life in a small apartment. If it weren't for building code requirements, I'd advise you to design your next house

BUILDING SMALL is one of the best ways to keep energy bills low.

like a sailboat; failing that, at least use boat design principles for inspiration.

2. ORIENT THE HOUSE PROPERLY

Passive solar design principles aren't very complicated; a few simple steps can save significant amounts of energy. If you're building on a lot that is large enough to give you some flexibility, try to orient the house with the long axis aligned east–west. That provides the best orientation for rooftop solar panels, as well as the best orientation to take advantage of winter sunlight; it also makes it easier to avoid afternoon overheating. In a cold climate, it's best if your south elevation is unshaded. In a hot climate, however, you probably want to preserve as many trees as possible.

3. PLAN YOUR WINDOWS CAREFULLY

It's painful to see an otherwise well-designed home with bad windows. Unfortunately, such houses are extremely common. It's the designer's job to be sure that windows are properly sized, properly oriented, properly shaded, and properly glazed. Designers should always use energy modeling software (see p. 90) when sizing windows.

If you drive through a new residential development in Texas or Georgia, it's easy to tell which houses have oversize windows—just look for the curtains and shades. Many of these homeowners have paid for windows that might as well be covered with drywall; to avoid glare and overheating, the owners are forced to retreat behind curtains or blinds. If these homes had been properly designed, the windows would have been fewer, smaller, better shaded, and equipped with low-solar-gain glazing.

Windows in a hot climate—and west-facing windows in almost all climates—need glazing with a solar heat gain coefficient (SHGC) of 0.30 or lower (see p. 165). In a hot climate, east- and west-facing windows should be minimized.

In climates with a significant heating season, it makes sense to orient about half of a home's windows to the south. Cold-climate builders should seriously consider using triple glazing—at least for the north, east, and west windows and perhaps for the south windows too.

In all climates, south-facing windows should be protected by a roof overhang that shades the windows during the hottest time of the year. Finally, all windows in all climates should include low-e glazing.

If your house is small and tight, you may be able to specify heating and air-conditioning equipment that is smaller and simpler than the equipment found in most homes. Use those savings to upgrade your windows. Good windows cost more than run-of-the mill windows, and they're usually worth every penny.

4. DESIGN YOUR AIR BARRIER

A home's air barrier is like a three-dimensional balloon surrounding the home's conditioned space. A builder needs to know exactly where that balloon is located and exactly how it will be built. The details of your air barrier design need to be finalized before the excavator shows up to dig your foundation. An air barrier is too important for job-site improvising by head-scratching framers, roofers, and window installers.

It's not enough to say, "I'm using Tyvek® as an air barrier." If Tyvek is part of your air-barrier system, you should be able to answer all of these questions before you begin building:

- What happens at the base of the wall? How is the Tyvek tied in to your concrete foundation?

- What happens at Tyvek seams?
- What happens when Tyvek is cut for window installation?
- What happens when the plumber installs a sill cock?
- What happens at the top of the wall? How is the Tyvek tied to the ceiling air barrier?
- Do any electrical boxes interrupt the air barrier?
- How are floor and ceiling penetrations dealt with?

Of course, your air barrier may not include Tyvek—you might be using the airtight drywall approach or you might be depending on spray polyurethane foam. That's fine, as long as your air barrier system is designed ahead of time.

5. INSTALL ABOVE-CODE INSULATION

The building code describes the worst house that can legally be built. If you build a home any worse than code requirements, you can be arrested or fined. That's a pretty low bar, especially when it comes to insulation.

Architectural fads come and go, and many people live to regret certain choices—for example, a blue toilet or fake exterior plastic quoins on the corners of a Dallas "chateau." But nobody has ever regretted installing extra insulation. If you can find a way to build your foundation, walls, and ceiling with more insulation than the code minimum, you'll never regret it.

6. INSTALL A DRAIN-WATER HEAT-RECOVERY DEVICE

A drain-water heat-recovery device (for example, the GFX™ or Power-Pipe®) is a simple and cost-effective way to reduce the amount of energy used for domestic hot water. The typical unit consists of a 3-in.- or 4-in.-dia. copper drainpipe surrounded by a spiraling cocoon of ¾-in. copper tubing. When installed vertically in a plumbing waste line, such a device can transfer about 55% of the heat energy in the drain water to the incoming supply water.

In a home where the residents prefer showers to baths, this simple device with no moving parts can save between 15% and 22% of the energy used for water heating. The price for a 3-in.-dia. 6-ft.-long Power-Pipe unit is $850.

7. KEEP ALL DUCTS INSIDE THE THERMAL ENVELOPE

Putting ductwork in an unconditioned attic should be a criminal offense. An attic is almost as cold as the exterior in winter and can be much hotter than the exterior in the summer. During summer, the difference between the cool air in the ducts and the surrounding attic air is much greater than the difference in temperature between the indoor and outdoor air. So why is attic ductwork insulated to only R-4 or R-6, while the attic floor gets R-38 or more?

The air in a supply duct is at a much higher pressure than the air inside or outside a house. Most duct seams leak, so a significant portion of the air passing through attic ducts typically escapes into the attic. Moreover, leaks in return ducts allow hot, humid attic air to be pulled into the air handler.

Needless to say, installing a furnace or air handler in an attic causes even more problems than merely installing ductwork there. In an energy-efficient home, all of the HVAC equipment and all of the ductwork must be located within the home's conditioned space. No exceptions—end of story.

Lighting design is as much an art as a science. Here are some principles for effective lighting design.

- It's better to bounce light off the ceiling than aim light at the floor. Ceilings should be white.

- Include lots of task lighting; there's no need to light up the whole room like a baseball field if all you need is a reading light or work light.

- Avoid the temptation to control a group of fixtures with a single switch. Individual toggle switches, one per fixture, should be installed in several locations to provide lighting flexibility. Don't line up all of a room's light switches in a single location like ducks in a row.

- Avoid fixtures with elaborate shades or diffusers that limit the amount of light that leaves the fixture. It's crazy to hide a nice 70-lumen-per-watt CFL behind a heavy lamp shade.

Selecting the right appliances and equipment can save a significant amount of energy.

Keep in mind:

- Some appliances are optional. Instead of shopping for efficient equipment, you might want to consider omitting a dishwasher, clothes dryer, air-conditioner, automatic irrigation system, or swimming pool pump. Less is more.

- Elaborate heating equipment makes little sense in a small well-insulated house. If your heating bill is only $500 a year, you don't need to spend tens of thousands of dollars on a ground-source heat pump or a radiant floor system.

- Energy use is more important than energy efficiency. Energy Star® labels can be misleading because they usually compare an appliance only to other appliances of the same size. That's why a large Energy Star refrigerator can use more electricity than a small refrigerator without an Energy Star label. The same problem exists with labeled televisions. Ignore the Energy Star label; instead, compare wattage or kilowatt-hours per year.

8. UPGRADE THE VENTILATION SYSTEM

By now, most builders know that a tight home requires a mechanical ventilation system. If you're building a very good home, its envelope should be really, really tight.

Do yourself a favor and invest in a high-quality ventilation system. If you are building in a cold climate, investing in a HRV or energy-recovery ventilator (ERV) with dedicated ventilation ductwork

makes sense. The system should pull stale air from the bathrooms and laundry room and deliver fresh air to the living room and bedrooms. If you are building in a mixed climate or a hot climate, and your house has forced-air ductwork, the best ventilation system is probably a central-fan-integrated supply ventilation system. This type of ventilation system requires a duct that supplies outdoor air to the furnace's return air plenum; this duct should be equipped with a motorized damper controlled by a fan cycler device.

9. ADDRESS LIGHTING AND APPLIANCES

For any home, the most cost-effective energy upgrade is to replace all incandescent bulbs with compact fluorescent lamps (CFLs) or LED lamps. In recent years, the light output quality and dependability of CFLs and LEDs have significantly improved. So make sure that every home you build is incandescent free.

10. PERFORM A BLOWER DOOR TEST

Air sealing is too important to leave to guesswork. The only way to know a home's air leakage rate is to perform a blower door test; that test should be performed on every single home you build. If the test is performed before drywall is hung, and if you're standing by during the test with lots of caulk and cans of spray foam, it won't be too late to fix some of the defects revealed by the blower door.

It's challenging to build a house that meets the Passivhaus standard of 0.6 ACH50. But even if you reduce your air leakage rate only down to 1.6 ACH50 or 1.8 ACH50, your house will still be significantly tighter than most new homes.

MEASURE, DON'T GUESS. The performance of any new home depends on the integrity of the home's air barrier. Because the only way to determine a home's air leakage rate is to measure it, every new home should be tested with a blower door.

Some features and methods are so difficult to implement that designers might want to avoid them entirely

Is it possible to disassemble old shipping pallets and glue the pieces of lumber together to make furniture? Of course it's possible; some woodworkers have used this method to make beautiful tables and chairs. There's a fly in the ointment, however: While it's possible, it's not very easy. Many commonly used construction methods, design details, and materials fall into a category I would call "possible but not easy." I decided to create a list of items that fall into this category.

The unfortunate twist to this category of difficult methods is an apparent paradox: Though hard to do well, these methods are actually fairly easy to implement if you are willing to do a sloppy job. (That's why many of the methods are common.) The methods are difficult only for builders who want to build a tight, high-performance home.

My list is deliberately provocative. Some readers will respond, "I've used many of the methods on your list, and I always do a good job." To which I will answer, "That's great. But most builders aren't as conscientious as you are."

I'm addressing this list to architects and designers. Because these methods are hard to implement well, it's best to leave them off your plans and specifications. Use other methods.

MARTIN'S "POSSIBLE BUT NOT EASY" LIST

Look your client in the eye and just say no. It may take a little practice, but you can do it.

Crawl spaces. Most crawl spaces are damp, leaky, poorly insulated, and rarely visited. Creating a dry crawl space is possible, but it's rare for a builder to get all the necessary details right.

Basements can be damp, too—but at least they are easier to access. (Easy-to-access spaces are more likely to be frequently visited, and frequently visited spaces are less likely to have problems that go unnoticed for years.)

Slab foundations have drawbacks—but nowhere near as many pitfalls as crawl spaces.

Dormers. Occasionally, an architect will design a dormer for a vented unconditioned attic, in hopes of creating a roof that looks lively and exciting from the curb. (Needless to say, this is nuts. It's the kind of detail you would see on a Hollywood set.)

In most cases, however, dormers are specified when the space under the roof is conditioned space. The components of this type of dormer are part of the home's thermal envelope, and it's hard to get the details right. The thermal envelope has to be continuous. That means that you need to have insulation that follows the roof slope; when you pop a dormer, you need to make sure that all of the barriers—the

air barrier, the water management barrier, and the insulation barrier—are uninterrupted and that the barriers on the dormer cheeks are continuous with these barriers on the main roof.

Let's face it—the air barrier ends up like Swiss cheese. Moreover, the framing used for dormer cheeks and dormer rafters is never thick enough for an adequate insulation layer, and the roofer's step flashing details at the base of the dormer cheeks are often faulty.

So don't do dormers.

Bay windows. Bay windows are almost as difficult to detail well as dormers. In most homes, this type of bump-out is an energy nosebleed. If you insist on building a bay window, make sure you have developed good details to limit air leakage and to provide a thick layer of insulation.

Garrison overhangs. The second floor of a Garrison-style home has a greater area than the first floor. This magic is made possible by cantilevering the floor joists a foot or more, creating an exterior soffit. You can guess what's coming: I don't like Garrison overhangs. These bump-outs are

hard to seal, so they usually leak abundant quantities of air.

Fiberglass batt insulation. Yes, it's possible to install fiberglass batt insulation in such a way that it achieves the R-value advertised on the package—but it doesn't happen often. If you care about the thermal performance of the building you are designing, it's best to specify a different type of insulation.

Recessed can lights in insulated ceilings. Many builders have tried and failed to make recessed can lights airtight, using a combination of caulk, spray foam, and site-built covers. They've also tried to heap enough insulation on top of the fixture to meet minimum code requirements, only to be stymied by insufficient clearance to the roof sheathing or difficulties keeping the mounded-up insulation in place.

Fortunately, most designers who focus on energy efficiency have sworn off recessed cans. The biggest remaining problem is that designers are weak; they need to develop a backbone to better resist homeowners who plead for recessed lighting.

Brick veneer. Brick cladding is durable, low-maintenance, and attractive. Tradi-

NICE WINDOW, but it doesn't belong in the shower.

details are done right? Not really—not without a webcam.

Including brick veneer on this list is something of a stretch, I know—and I'm going to get pushback on this issue, especially from builders in Texas and Georgia. But designers and builders who specify brick veneer need to be aware of the pitfalls of this cladding and need to have a plan for supervising the work carefully.

Windows in showers. You want a window in your shower, don't you? Maybe you live in the country. You don't have neighbors, and you enjoy the little *frisson* of excitement you feel when you shower in front of your window. Or maybe you just want to look at the trees or enjoy the natural light.

Can you install a window in a shower in a way that keeps water out of your wall? Sure. With enough copper flashing, butyl gaskets, and peel-and-stick tape, you can do almost anything. Do most window installers get these details right? No.

tionally, however, bricks were not intended as a facing for structural wood framing. The idea of marrying masonry cladding to structural wood framing is a relatively recent development, and it is fraught with problems.

How many ways are there to screw up brick veneer? Lots. The builder can use the wrong wall sheathing, the builder can install the water-resistive barrier (WRB) with reverse laps, the mason can forget the weep holes at the bottom of the wall, the mason can fail to install durable flashing near the weep holes, the weep holes can end up below grade after landscaping work is completed, the mason can fail to install proper flashing and weep holes above a bay window, and the mason can clog up the drainage space behind the bricks with gobs of mortar.

Is there a good way for the architect and builder to make sure that all of these

Adhered manufactured stone cladding. Adhered manufactured stone cladding over oriented strand board (OSB) sheathing is probably the riskiest cladding option for a wood-framed building. Hundreds—perhaps thousands—of homes with this type of cladding have had serious problems with moisture intrusion and rot, dragging the homeowners, builders, designers, and their insurance companies into protracted construction-defect negotiations.

If a designer and builder can come up with details that include a ventilated rainscreen gap between the cladding and the OSB, along with bulletproof flashing details, this cladding option might work. If you want to go that route, you have a stronger stomach than I do.

Ground-source heat pumps. There are two hurdles that need to be crossed if you want a residential ground-source heat pump (GSHP) that performs well: system design and equipment installation. Both are difficult. Energy experts have learned that both steps are often muffed.

Every ground-source heat pump insulation is a custom-designed system that is site-assembled from components that are often purchased from a variety of suppliers. This approach is fraught with risk. Even when perfectly designed and installed, these systems are so expensive they rarely make sense for single-family homes.

Ducts. Most ducts are undersize. Most duct seams are leaky. Many ducts are convoluted and are located outside of a home's thermal envelope. To overcome a duct system's static pressure, furnace fans and ventilation equipment must expend a significant amount of energy.

If you are designing a home, one solution to these problems is to choose systems (for example, ductless minisplits or Lunos ventilation fans) that don't require ducts.

If you decide to install equipment that requires ducts, make sure that:

• The duct system is designed according to standard engineering principles.

• The ducts are installed as shown by the system designer.

• Duct seams are sealed with mastic or high-quality tape to make them as airtight as possible.

• All ducts are located inside the home's conditioned envelope.

CAN ALL OF THESE FEATURES BE AVOIDED?

It's perfectly possible to build a house that has none of the features on this list. Such a house will be easier to build and will be more likely to perform well than a house that includes several of them.

If you are an architect who wants to include some of the features on this list, my opinions are unlikely to dissuade you. Just make sure that you provide your builders with plenty of detail drawings. And it might be a good idea to stop by the job site frequently to make sure that everything is going according to plan.

For the best performance, build a simple roof shape over a vented unconditioned attic

Lots of things can go wrong with roofs: Bad flashing can cause leaks, a poorly designed valley can create a slow-moving ice field, and misplaced gutters can do more harm than good. Experienced roofers see a lot of stupid roofs.

Soon after I dropped out of college in 1974, I got my first construction job. I was hired by the Edward J. Thornton Roofing Company in Newtonville, MA. The company paid me $3.50 an hour. For the next 12 months, I installed countless bundles of asphalt shingles and mopped acres of tar-and-gravel roofs with hot asphalt. Every now and then, I also helped Ed, the company's sheet-metal worker, to install copper valleys and copper-lined cedar gutters on slate roofs.

Most of the time, I was installing asphalt shingles, back in the days before nail guns and portable compressors. We used heavy wooden extension ladders. My staging consisted of 2×12 planks laid on hardwood shingle brackets; each bracket was secured to the roof with three 16d nails. We never had any fall protection.

My tools were simple: a 16-oz. straight-claw Estwing® hammer, a Stanley® utility knife, a cat's paw, a chalkline, a measuring tape, a pair of metal snips, and a cotton nail bag. My toolbox was so light that I was able to commute to the roofing shop on my bicycle; I strapped my toolbox and my lunch box on the rack over the rear wheel. (Fortunately, my boss delivered the ladders, staging, and shingles to the job site.)

I really enjoyed shingling. I still remember the satisfaction I experienced every time I nailed the last few cap shingles on the end of a ridge—especially when the weather was sunny.

Once a roofer, always a roofer. I still shake my head when I drive by a house and see a classic, obvious mistake, like a brick chimney in the middle of a valley. But my eye also catches errors that others miss, like a shingle roof with a badly woven valley between roofs with different slopes. (When the roofer isn't paying attention, these woven valleys tend to drift to one side.)

I also hate to see asphalt shingle roofs where the slots don't line up, or a roof without drip edge at the rakes, or badly planned shingle courses. (A classic error happens when a ridge isn't parallel to the eaves; an inexperienced roofer is surprised by the discrepancy at the end of the job, and the lack of parallelism shows. An experienced roofer snaps lines to gradually correct the problem over 10 or 12 courses.)

I have strong opinions about roofs. Without apology, I hereby present my opinions.

1. AVOID VALLEYS

If you are designing the roof of a new house, try to design a roof without any valleys. Valleys concentrate water and often clog with ice. It's far more common to have leaks or ice dam problems near valleys than in the middle of a simple sloped roof.

Many valleys exist because of a designer's conceit rather than necessity. Often, these valleys trace back to the mistaken belief that a chopped-up, complicated, multi-plane roof looks better than a simple gable. It doesn't.

2. JUST SAY NO TO DORMERS AND SKYLIGHTS

There's no reason for a new house to have a dormer. When I see a dormer, I conclude that the designer or the architect made a mistake. They didn't include enough interior space, and the homeowner was forced to cut a hole in the roof because the ceiling was too low to stand up.

If you want to build a multistory house, that's fine. If you want two floors, build two floors. If you want three floors, build three floors. Then build a roof over the top floor. This roof shouldn't have any deliberate holes in it. The "no holes" rule covers both dormers and skylights.

3. AN UNCONDITIONED VENTED ATTIC IS BETTER THAN AN INSULATED ROOF

It makes more sense to put insulation on the attic floor than to try to insulate a sloped roof, for several reasons:

- Rafters usually aren't deep enough to hold a thick layer of insulation; on the other hand, it's usually easy to add a deep layer of insulation to the attic floor. Insulating the attic floor is also cheaper.
- If you leave your rafter bays uninsulated, it will be easier to locate roof leaks.
- It's easier to air seal the attic floor than a cathedral ceiling.

- Damp roof sheathing will dry out quicker if it faces an attic than if it is part of a cathedral ceiling.

4. THE BEST ROOF SHAPE IS A SIMPLE GABLE OR HIPPED ROOF

In a cold climate, the ideal roof is a simple gable. Because gables don't have any valleys or hips, they are easy to vent. It's a straight shot from the soffits to the ridge. That's good.

Chopped-up roofs with a variety of intersecting planes are hard to frame, hard to keep watertight, and hard to vent. Every nook and cranny creates somewhere for pine needles and ice to accumulate. You don't want any nooks and crannies on your roof.

In a hot climate, a hipped roof makes more sense than a gable, because a hipped roof makes it easier to provide shade on all four sides of the house. In a hot climate, shade is good. Fortunately, people in hot climates rarely have to worry about ice dams—in Florida, it doesn't really

A SIMPLE GABLE ROOF. This old brick house has wonderful lines; it has a simple gable roof with generous roof overhangs. And note that in the old days builders knew that the right location for chimneys is near the ridge.

EVERY HOUSE NEEDS ROOF OVERHANGS

Roof overhangs have several important functions: protecting exterior doors, windows, and siding from rain; shading windows when solar heat gain is undesirable; and helping keep basements and crawl spaces dry. A house with improper overhangs can overheat in the summer, can suffer from water entry problems at windows and doors, and can have premature siding rot.

The most common design error is to make roof overhangs too stingy. It's also possible (although much rarer) for roof overhangs to be too wide. A typical gable roof has two kinds of roof overhangs: eaves overhangs and rake overhangs. Because it's easier to frame a wide eaves overhang than a wide rake overhang, problems from stingy overhangs are more common at rakes than eaves.

Perhaps the most important function of wide roof overhangs is to help keep water off siding, windows, and doors. While it's impossible to stop all wind-driven rain from reaching your walls, wide roof overhangs make a big difference, especially if there is just one story under the overhang.

Walls with stingy roof overhangs get regularly soaked. These repeated wetting episodes cause a variety of problems. Although these problems are worse in high-rainfall climates than low-rainfall climates, almost all North American homes are built in regions where it makes sense to protect walls from rain.

- **Protecting siding.** A house without roof overhangs leaves siding unprotected and vulnerable. Unprotected walls suffer high rates of water entry, premature failure of any paint or stain, and premature siding failure.

- **Protecting windows and doors.** Windows and doors can be protected either by roof overhangs, by recessing windows and doors in thick walls, or by including head casing and head flashing that are designed to be significantly proud of the siding plane. If you look at older buildings, you'll often notice that the casing on window heads and door heads is substantial and is often capped by a protruding ledger. These features help deflect rain.

- **Getting rain to drip away from the foundation.** Another function of wide eaves overhangs is to ensure that roof water doesn't drip near the foundation. Keeping the eaves drip away from the house helps keep your crawl space or basement dry.

- **Reducing splash back.** Keeping the eaves drip away from the house also limits the damage caused by splash back. Splash back is a common cause of siding rot.

- **Shading your windows.** Roof overhangs can help shade your windows. In cold weather, any shade on your windows is probably unfortunate; in hot weather, shade is almost always welcome. Because shade is sometimes good and sometimes bad, window shading strategies are usually a balancing act.

matter if you choose a roof shape that is hard to vent.

In all climates, make overhangs generous. (Roof overhangs help shade south-facing windows in summer and help keep siding dry on all orientations. Remember: Every exterior door needs to be protected by a roof overhang or its own roof.) If you're building a gable roof, don't forget the rake overhangs; most rake overhangs are too stingy. If necessary, frame the rake overhang with full-depth ladder-style outriggers.

5. DON'T REDUCE THE SLOPE OF YOUR ROOF HALFWAY BETWEEN THE RIDGE AND THE EAVES

A good roof plane has a consistent slope from the ridge to the eaves. A roof that changes slope at midpoint is disturbing. Especially disturbing is a steep roof that suddenly switches to a shallow pitch (for example, when a porch with a shallow-pitched roof is affixed to a house with a steep roof). Such roofs hold snow and are susceptible to leaks.

6. ASPHALT FELT MAKES MORE SENSE THAN SYNTHETIC ROOFING UNDERLAYMENT

Unless you plan to leave your roofing underlayment exposed to the weather for several weeks, there's no reason to buy synthetic roofing underlayment, a product that costs much more than old-fashioned asphalt felt. I like to use #30 felt, which is heavier than #15 felt.

Besides being more expensive than asphalt felt, most brands of synthetic roof underlayment are vapor-impermeable, so they don't allow the roof sheathing to dry to the exterior. According to the manufacturers of synthetic roofing underlayment, these products should never be used on unvented roof assemblies.

7. PLUMBING VENT PIPES SHOULD PENETRATE THE ROOF NEAR THE RIDGE

Like chimneys, plumbing vents should penetrate a roof near the ridge rather than near the eaves, for two reasons:

• While ridges are dry, eaves are wet. Eaves see much more water over the course of a year than ridges, so any defect near the eaves will leak more water than a defect near the ridge.

• If you live up north, snow and ice can tear your plumbing vent right off your roof, especially if it is located near your eaves. It's much safer higher up the roof.

In a house with a vented unconditioned attic, it's easy to install a couple of 45° ells in the vent pipe so that the pipe penetrates the roof near the ridge. The same approach is also possible in a house with a cathedral ceiling, although the rafter bay in which the vent pipe is run will not be as well insulated as the other rafter bays.

8. CHOOSE METAL ROOFING OR ASPHALT SHINGLES

I'm just expressing my opinion here. Clay tiles and slate are expensive. Concrete tiles are fragile and tricky to walk on. Cedar shingles are beautiful, but they are time-consuming to install and (because of their flammability) are illegal in some jurisdictions. Imitation slate and imitation wood shingles look like they belong on a Howard Johnson®'s restaurant. EPDM membrane and roll roofing, if visible, are ugly.

My favorite type of roofing is ordinary through-fastened steel roofing. It's available in a wide variety of colors and can be ordered cut to any length. It goes on fast, lasts a very long time, and is recyclable. It costs less than standing-seam metal roofing.

My second favorite type of roofing is good old-fashioned asphalt shingles. They have their downsides, of course—they are made from petroleum, are susceptible to algae, and don't last very long. But they are affordable, easy to install, integrate well with all types of flashing, and adapt easily to new penetrations or changes to the roof. Asphalt shingle roofing is easier to repair than other types of roofing.

In most areas of the country, it makes sense to order algae-resistant shingles. Otherwise, install a galvanized steel or copper ridge cap; leachate from the ridge cap will keep your shingles algae-free.

9. GET FLASHING DETAILS RIGHT

Step flashing should be generously sized; the vertical leg should be at least 6 in. high, although 8 in. is better. Remember, you aren't going to be bringing your siding down to the roof, so at least 3 in. of step flashing will remain visible under your siding. Each piece of flashing should be bent from a piece of sheet metal measuring at least 8 in. by 12 in.; crease the flashing so that it has two 6-in.-wide legs.

Each piece of step flashing gets only one nail into the roof. Never nail step flashing to the wall—that just complicates the job

FLASHING DETAILS. Note the kickout flashing and step flashing. There's only one problem: Step flashing should be nailed only to the roof, never to the wall.

of replacing the step flashing in the future. If your step flashing begins at the eaves, don't forget to install kick-out flashing at the eaves.

When I install step flashing on an asphalt shingle roof, I like to add a sideways course of cedar shingles under the step flashing, installed at 90° to the usual shingle orientation, with the butt end of each cedar shingle facing the sidewall and the tapered edge blending into the field of the roof. (The cedar shingles are later hidden by the asphalt shingle roofing.) These imperceptible shims direct water away from the vulnerable sidewall flashing, and lighten the load of water that the kickout flashing has to deal with.

Chimneys always get two types of flashing to allow the roof to settle without breaking the flashing. I was taught to flash chimneys with 16-oz. copper flashing and lead counterflashing. These days, however, many roofers are avoiding lead because of its toxicity; it's possible to counterflash chimneys with copper instead of lead, but the copper isn't as flexible.

Unless the chimney bisects a ridge, every chimney needs a cricket. Make the cricket oversize, so the two cricket valleys terminate away from the chimney.

Installers of steel roofing often do a sloppy job with flashing. When I install steel roofing, I always plan carefully for any roof penetrations like vent pipes, chimneys, or skylights. Ideally, you want to lap the steel panels at the penetration. One sheet of metal roofing runs from the eaves to a few inches above the penetration; then the penetration is flashed. Next, a second sheet of metal roofing is installed from the ridge down to a few inches below the penetration, so that the steel roofing laps at the penetration.

At this point, many readers are probably thinking that my rules are arbitrary. I'm willing to make several stipulations:

- Yes, I know that it isn't that hard to install roofing and flashing details that keep valleys and dormers leak free.

- Yes, I know that my worries about ice dams and roof glaciers apply in only certain climates.

- Yes, I know that skylights can provide welcome daylighting to dark interior spaces.

- Yes, I know that many home buyers think dormers are charming.

- Yes, I know one reason designers include dormers is because zoning height restrictions preclude unconditioned attics.

- Yes, I know that design imperatives sometimes prevent chimneys from penetrating the roof at the ridge.

I have provided design rules from the perspective of a roofer. These rules, of course, are not set in stone, but they are useful principles to keep in mind. Break the rules if you must, but break them consciously and only for good reasons.

10. ANTICIPATE ICE DAMS

If you're building in a climate that gets snowy winters, your roof should include details to minimize the likelihood of ice dams:

- Frame your roof with raised-heel trusses.

- Make sure your ceiling is as airtight as possible.

- Install a very deep layer of insulation on your attic floor. The insulation needs to cover the top plates of the home's exterior walls.

- Make sure there is adequate blocking between your trusses to keep the insulation from spilling into the soffit and to prevent wind washing.

- Install ventilation baffles to maintain a ventilation channel from your soffit to the attic.

- Install two or more courses of self-adhering rubber roof membrane, so the membrane extends from the eaves to a point at least 3 ft. higher than the plane of your exterior wall.

- If possible, make sure your roof has no valleys.

- If possible, don't install gutters; if gutters are necessary, make sure they are installed below the plane of the roofing so they won't prevent ice from sliding off the roof.

If there is any takeaway to this list of rules, it's this: Designers who gussy up their roofs with flourishes and do-dads are often insecure. Apparently, they think a few more Christmas ornaments will wow their clients. In contrast, classic Japanese and Shaker designers had the self-confidence and restraint to recognize there is no shame in choosing simple, elegant shapes. In my opinion, such Zen or Shaker principles should govern roof design.

Whether you decide to make it vented or unvented, get the details right—because every cathedral ceiling offers opportunities to make big mistakes

nsulated cathedral ceilings are a relatively recent phenomenon. The craze for insulated cathedral ceilings (and great rooms) really took off in the 1970s and 1980s, when examples began popping up like mushrooms after a warm rain. In those days, most builders stuffed cathedral ceiling rafter bays with fiberglass batts. Sometimes they included flimsy Proper-Vents between the fiberglass and the roof sheathing, but often they just specified thin batts to ensure there would be an air space above the batts for ventilation.

The cathedral ceilings of the 1970s and 1980s were thermal disasters. In most cases, these ceilings leaked air, leaked heat, created monumental ice dams, and encouraged condensation and rot. In many cases, roofers tried to solve these problems by improving ventilation openings in the soffits and at the ridge; these "improvements" often made every symptom worse. Fortunately, most builders have learned a few lessons from these disasters.

DOES A CATHEDRAL CEILING NEED TO BE VENTED?

Until recently, building codes required that insulated sloped roofs include ventilation channels directly under the roof sheathing. Many builders still follow this time-tested technique. As building scientist Bill Rose has shown, code requirements for roof venting were never based on research or scientific principles. In a well-documented *Journal of Light Construction* article on roof venting ("Roof Ventilation Update"), he explained, "For the most part, the focus of codes, researchers, designers, and builders on roof ventilation is misplaced. Instead, the focus should be on building an airtight ceiling, which is far more important than roof ventilation in all climates and all seasons . . . . Once this is accomplished, roof ventilation becomes pretty much a nonissue."

Because of their unscientific origins, code requirements for venting roofs are often misunderstood. It's worth establishing a few basic facts:

- Roof ventilation cannot be used to lower indoor humidity levels.

- Builders should not encourage the migration of water vapor through a cathedral ceiling.

- During the summer, roof ventilation does not significantly lower the temperature of asphalt shingles or other types of roofing.

- While roof ventilation can lower the risk of ice damming, it's essential for builders to limit the flow of heat into roof ventilation channels by including one or more ceiling air barriers and by installing thick insulation, so that as little heat as possible escapes from the home.

- While roof ventilation can help dry out damp roof sheathing, it's essential to limit the flow of water vapor escaping from the home so that the roof sheathing never gets damp in the first place.

- In the absence of an airtight ceiling, roof ventilation can do more harm than good because air movement in rafter bays can encourage indoor air to leak through ceiling cracks.

HOW DO I BUILD A VENTED CATHEDRAL CEILING?

A vented cathedral ceiling makes sense only if the geometry of your roof is simple. You need a straight shot from the soffits to the ridge. That's relatively easy on a gable roof without any dormers or skylights, but if the geometry of your roof is complicated—with features like hips, valleys, and dormers—it's impossible to ensure air flow through all of your rafter bays. If you're trying to insulate a roof like that, consider building an unvented roof.

Ventilation channels are created by installing a material that can maintain a separation (an air gap) between the insulation and the roof sheathing. This building component is known by a variety of confusing names, including a ventilation (or vent) baffle, a ventilation (or vent) chute, a ventilation (or vent) channel, or a Proper-Vent (a brand name).

The first vent baffles to hit the market—the classic Proper-Vent of the 1970s and 1980s—were inexpensive, flimsy items made of thin polystyrene. Polystyrene baffles have several disadvantages: Being thin and flexible, they can't resist the pressures from dense-packed cellulose or blown-in fiberglass, they don't ventilate the entire width of the rafter bay, and as usually installed, they allow air to leak out the top of the insulated assembly.

Eventually, manufacturers began offering stiffer alternatives that are better able to resist the pressures of dense-packed insulation. These products come and go, and many are no longer available. At one time or another, it was possible to buy baffles made of polystyrene, cardboard, vinyl, and compressed cellulose fibers. These days, the best available vent baffle is probably the AccuVent® baffle, which is made from stiff vinyl.

Some builders aren't satisfied with commercially available vent baffles, so they make their own site-built baffles. According to section R806.3 of the 2006 International Residential Code® (IRC), "A minimum of a 1-inch space shall be provided between the insulation and the roof sheathing and at the location of the vent." Such a vent space can be created by installing 1-in. by 1-in. "sticks" in the upper corners of each rafter bay, followed by stiff cardboard, thin plywood, OSB, fiberboard sheathing, or panels of rigid foam insulation.

If you use rigid foam for your baffles, it probably makes more sense to choose thin expanded polystyrene (EPS) or extruded polystyrene (XPS) rather than foil-faced polyisocyanurate, to allow a bit of outward drying, however slow, by diffusion. A thin layer of EPS or XPS is somewhat vapor-permeable, whereas foil facing is a vapor barrier.

Many experts advise that 2-in.-deep vent cavities are even better than 1-in.-deep cavities; if that's the route you want to go, size your spacers accordingly.

As with all types of vent baffles, it's a good idea to pay attention to airtight construction methods, especially if you will be installing air-permeable insulation in the rafter bays. Seal the edges of each panel with caulk, and tape the seams between panels with a high-quality tape.

If you prefer, you can locate your ventilation channels on top of the roof sheathing rather than under the roof sheathing, as long as you specify roof sheathing and roofing underlayment that is somewhat vapor-permeable. You can create 1½-in.-high ventilation channels above the roof sheathing with 2×4s installed on the flat and located above the rafters, 16 in. or 24 in. on-center. Although this approach is less fussy than installing vent baffles underneath the sheathing, it usually costs more because most types of roofing require a second layer of plywood or OSB on top of the vent channels.

In some cases, these ventilation channels are installed above a layer or two of rigid foam. It's also possible to purchase nail-base (a type of structural insulated panel [SIP] with OSB on one side instead of two) that includes integrated ventilation channels between the OSB and the rigid foam; one brand of these panels is Cool-Vent from Hunter Panels®.

If you are choosing to build a vented roof assembly, don't forget to include soffit vents and ridge vents.

ARE MY RAFTERS DEEP ENOUGH?

Most rafters aren't deep enough to accommodate the insulation needed to meet minimum R-values required by code, especially if the rafter bays include a ventilation channel. For example, 2×10 rafters are 9¼ in. deep, so they provide room for only about 8¼ in. of insulation—in other words, about R-30 of fibrous insulation—if the rafter bay is ventilated. This is less than the minimum code requirement in colder climates.

Builders solve this problem by furring down or scabbing on additional framing below the rafters to deepen the rafter bays. Another technique is to add a layer of cross-hatched 2×4s, 16 in. on-center, installed beneath the rafters. It's also possible to specify deep open-web trusses or to use deep I-joists for rafters.

Another way to add R-value to your roof assembly is to include one or two layers of rigid foam in the roof assembly—either above the roof sheathing or below the rafters. In addition to improving the R-value of the roof assembly, a layer of rigid foam has another benefit: It interrupts thermal bridging through the rafters.

Remember: If you choose to install rigid foam on top of your roof sheathing, don't install ventilation channels under the roof sheathing; these two practices are incompatible.

CAN I BUILD AN UNVENTED ROOF ASSEMBLY?

In recent years, most building codes have begun to allow the construction of unvented insulated sloped roof assemblies. Many such roofs have failed over the years, however, so it's essential to get the details right.

First of all, you can't use air-permeable insulation (for example, fiberglass batts, mineral wool batts, dense-packed cellulose, or blown-in fiberglass) to insulate an unvented roof assembly unless the roof assembly also includes a layer of air-impermeable insulation (either spray polyurethane foam or rigid foam panels) directly above or directly below the roof sheathing.

The IRC defines air-impermeable insulation as "an insulation having an air permeance equal to or less than 0.02 L/s-m² at 75 Pascals (Pa.) pressure differential tested according to ASTM E 2178 or E 283." Although spray foam insulation and rigid foam insulation meet this standard, fiberglass batts and dense-packed cellulose do not.

If you want to use just one type of insulation in unvented rafter bays, you are limited to spray polyurethane foam. Another possibility, of course, is to build your roof with SIPs.

The code restrictions on the use of air-permeable insulation between rafters were developed to prevent the roof sheathing from rotting. When fiberglass batts are installed in unvented rafter bays, the batts allow moist indoor air to reach the cold roof sheathing. That leads to condensation or moisture accumulation in the sheathing, followed eventually by sheathing rot. Because spray foam prevents air movement, it almost eliminates this problem.

It's important to note, however, that recent research suggests that closed-cell spray foam is much less risky than open-cell spray foam in this location.

To summarize, there are three ways to build an unvented roof assembly:

• Install closed-cell spray foam against the underside of the roof sheathing, and no other type of insulation. Be sure that the thickness of the spray foam is adequate to meet minimum code requirements. Remember that open-cell spray foam is risky in all climate zones, and if open-cell spray foam is installed in this location in a cold climate, the underside of the cured foam must be covered with gypsum drywall that has been painted with vapor-retarder paint. Vapor-retarder paint is ineffective if it is sprayed directly on the cured foam.

• Install rigid foam insulation above the roof sheathing and air-permeable insulation between the rafters. If you choose this method, it's possible to install vent channels between the top of the rigid foam and the top layer of roof sheathing by installing a series of parallel 2×4s— one above each rafter—extending from soffit to ridge.

• Install a layer of closed-cell spray foam against the underside of the roof sheathing and fill the rest of the rafter cavity with an air-permeable insulation.

If I use a combination of foam and fluffy insulation, how thick should the foam be?

If you want to install a combination of rigid foam on top of your roof sheathing and air-permeable insulation between your rafters, you need to be sure that your rigid foam is thick enough to keep your roof sheathing above the dew point. Guidelines to achieve that goal are included in the 2009 and 2012 IRC.

According to section R806.5 of the 2012 IRC, "Unvented attic assemblies (spaces between the top-story ceiling joists and the roof rafters) and unvented enclosed rafter assemblies (spaces between ceilings that are applied directly to the underside of roof framing members/rafters and the structural roof sheathing at the top of the roof framing members/rafters) shall be permitted" as long as a number of conditions are met.

If you want to combine air-permeable and air-impermeable insulation, there are two possible ways to proceed. One option (according to the code) requires: "In addition to the air-permeable insulation installed directly below the structural sheathing, rigid board or sheet insulation shall be installed directly above the structural roof sheathing as specified in Table R806.5 for condensation control."

Table R806.5 specifies the minimum R-value for the foam installed on top of the sheathing (not the R-value for the whole roof assembly). The table calls for a minimum of:

• R-5 foam for climate Zones 1–3.

• R-10 for climate Zone 4C.

• R-15 for climate Zones 4A and 4B.

• R-20 for climate Zone 5.

• R-25 for climate Zone 6.

• R-30 for climate Zone 7.

• R-35 for climate Zone 8.

After you have installed at least the code-mandated thickness of rigid foam above your roof sheathing, you're free to install enough fluffy insulation to meet code requirements between the rafters.

If you want to install a combination of closed-cell spray-foam on the underside of the roof sheathing and air-permeable insulation between your rafters—an

DETAILS FOR A THICK ROOF

If you want to install fluffy insulation between the rafters of an unvented cathedral ceiling, you must also install enough rigid foam insulation on top of the roof sheathing to keep the sheathing above the dew point. The only other acceptable approach would be a flash-and-batt installation using closed-cell spray foam on the underside of the roof sheathing.

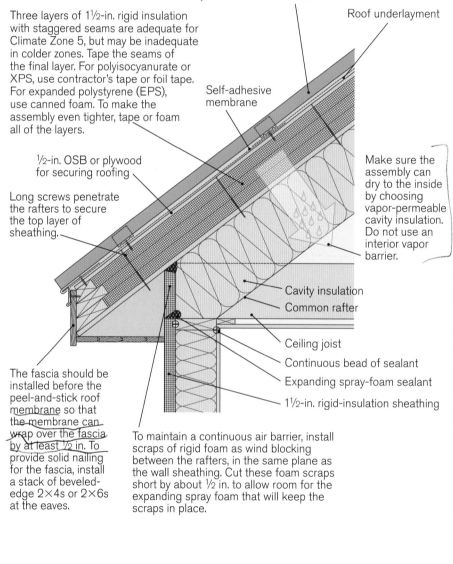

Metal roofing is shown here. Other types of roofing work as well. Check asphalt-shingle warranties to make sure hot roofs are acceptable to the manufacturer.

Three layers of 1½-in. rigid insulation with staggered seams are adequate for Climate Zone 5, but may be inadequate in colder zones. Tape the seams of the final layer. For polyisocyanurate or XPS, use contractor's tape or foil tape. For expanded polystyrene (EPS), use canned foam. To make the assembly even tighter, tape or foam all of the layers.

Roof underlayment

Self-adhesive membrane

½-in. OSB or plywood for securing roofing

Long screws penetrate the rafters to secure the top layer of sheathing.

Make sure the assembly can dry to the inside by choosing vapor-permeable cavity insulation. Do not use an interior vapor barrier.

Cavity insulation

Common rafter

Ceiling joist

Continuous bead of sealant

Expanding spray-foam sealant

1½-in. rigid-insulation sheathing

The fascia should be installed before the peel-and-stick roof membrane so that the membrane can wrap over the fascia by at least ½ in. To provide solid nailing for the fascia, install a stack of beveled-edge 2×4s or 2×6s at the eaves.

To maintain a continuous air barrier, install scraps of rigid foam as wind blocking between the rafters, in the same plane as the wall sheathing. Cut these foam scraps short by about ½ in. to allow room for the expanding spray foam that will keep the scraps in place.

approach sometimes called "flash and batt"—the building code requires that spray foam (or, arguably, rigid foam insulation) be "applied in direct contact with the underside of the structural roof sheathing" and that the foam insulation meet the requirements "specified in Table R806.4 for condensation control." These are the same minimum R-value requirements listed on p. 27, ranging from R-5 in zone 1 to R-35 in zone 8. Moreover, "The air-permeable insulation [for example, fiberglass batts or cellulose insulation] shall be installed directly under the air-impermeable insulation."

CAN I USE DENSE-PACKED CELLULOSE AS THE ONLY INSULATION FOR AN UNVENTED ROOF ASSEMBLY?

In a word, no, you cannot use only dense-packed cellulose in an unvented roof; the code explicitly forbids this method. Cellulose can be used in an unvented roof assembly only if there is an adequate layer of rigid foam above the roof sheathing or an adequate layer of closed-cell spray foam under the roof sheathing. Cellulose alone won't work.

However, in some areas of the country, especially in the Northeast, insulation contractors have been dense-packing unvented rafter bays with cellulose for years. Because the method has deep roots in New England, many building inspectors accept such installations.

If you're building a new house, however, here's my advice: If you want to insulate with cellulose, make it a ventilated roof by including ventilation channels under your roof sheathing. Leaving out the ventilation channels is risky.

DO I NEED TO INSTALL AN INTERIOR VAPOR BARRIER?

While vented roof assemblies are designed to dry to the exterior, unvented roof assemblies are designed to dry to the interior. That's why an unvented roof assembly should never include interior polyethylene.

If a building inspector insists that you install some type of interior "vapor barrier," you can always install a smart vapor retarder like MemBrain® to satisfy your inspector. For more information on the theory behind roof assemblies and wall assemblies with exterior rigid foam,

---

A GOOD ROOF HAS AIRTIGHT DETAILS AND THICK INSULATION

Now you know how to build an insulated sloped roof. To sum up:

- Make sure the roof assembly is as close to airtight as you can make it. If you are using fluffy insulation, you need two air barriers: one below the insulation and one above the insulation.

- Make sure to install insulation that provides at least the minimum code requirement for ceiling R-value. Insulation that exceeds the minimum code requirement is even better.

- If possible, include a ventilation channel above the top of your insulation layer. The ventilation channel will provide cheap insurance against moisture buildup, and will lower the chance of ice damming.

- Remember, an insulated sloped ceiling isn't always a good idea. Sometimes a good old-fashioned unconditioned attic is the best way to cap your house.

A LEAKY CEILING doomed the roof sheathing. The ceiling of this 10-year-old house was cut for an electrical box, and the sloppy oversized hole was never caulked. The cracks around the electrical box allowed moisture-laden air to enter the roof assembly. When the moisture encountered cold roof sheathing, it condensed, leading to moisture accumulation and rot. The rubberized membrane seen in the photo was used as a temporary patch for a hole in the roof, and did not contribute to the failure mechanism.

see "Calculating the Minimum Thickness of Rigid Foam Sheathing" on p. 155.

DO I NEED TO INSTALL AN AIR BARRIER UNDER THE INSULATION?

Of course you need to install an air barrier, especially if you are using fluffy insulation like fiberglass batts, blown-in fiberglass, or dense-packed cellulose. (If you insulate your ceiling with spray foam, the spray foam should create an air barrier, as long as the installer does a good job.)

If you are building a cathedral ceiling insulated with fluffy insulation, the biggest air-barrier blunder is to install tongue-and-groove boards as your finish ceiling without first installing taped gypsum drywall. A board ceiling is notoriously leaky, and this type of ceiling is often associated with roof sheathing rot.

WHAT ABOUT RECESSED CAN LIGHTS?

Recessed can lights should never be installed in insulated rafter bays. Period, full stop, end of story. Recessed can lights take up room that should be filled with insulation; they give off heat, creating thermal hot spots in your insulated roof; and they leak air. They should be removed from your ceiling and deposited in front of a moving steam roller.

How ice dams form, how to prevent ice dams, and what to do if you have an ice dam right now

What do you call the weeks between Valentine's Day and Easter? It's ice dam season, of course. During snowy winters, tens of thousands of northern homes are plagued by ice dams. If your house suffers from wet ceilings during the winter, you may be ready to call up a contractor. Be careful, though: Because most contractors don't understand the causes of ice dams, they often suggest the wrong solution.

HOW ICE DAMS FORM

Ice dams form when a home's escaping heat warms the roof sheathing and melts the underside of the snow layer on the roof. Water trickles down the roof until it reaches the cold roofing over the eaves, where it freezes. After a while, the ice at the eaves gets thicker, forming an ice dam. If the water reservoir behind the ice dam is large enough, water can back up under the roof shingles and damage ceilings.

The most common cause of ice dams, by far, is air leakage. Warm interior air leaks through ceiling defects or recessed can lights as well as through hidden passages in wall assemblies and roof assemblies, and this warm air contacts the underside of the roof sheathing. The second-most common cause of ice dams is thin or missing insulation.

Bad roof design can make ice dams worse. Because ice can form in gutters, roofs with gutters (especially gutters that extend higher than the plane of the roof) are more susceptible to ice dams than

ICE CAN FORM a lip that traps water. This ice dam probably includes a hidden ice "tongue" extending far up the roof.

roofs without any gutters. Roofs with valleys are more susceptible to ice dams than roofs without any valleys. Low-slope roofs are more susceptible to ice dams than steeply pitched roofs.

HOW TO PREVENT ICE DAMS

Scandalously, builders in snowy climates are still building new homes without testing the homes for airtightness. Many of these new homes have leaky ceilings and

HOW ICE DAMS FORM

1. Warm interior air entering an attic (or roof assembly in a cathedral ceiling) raises the temperature of the roof sheathing, causing the underside of the snow to melt.

2. Water trickles down the roof until it reaches the eaves—which are significantly colder than the rest of the roof—where it refreezes.

3. This recurring process causes the ice at the eaves to get thicker and thicker, forming an ice dam.

4. Eventually, water from melting snow backs up behind the ice dam. If the water reservoir is large enough, it can seep up under the roof shingles, leak through the roof sheathing, and cause damage.

will soon develop ice dams. If you are building a new house, the following steps should eliminate ice dams.

• If possible, design a roof without any valleys. If you install gutters, make sure that the outer lip of your gutter is below the plane of the roofing.

• If the house has a vented unconditioned attic, make sure that no ducts, water heaters, air handlers, furnaces, or other types of HVAC equipment are located in the attic.

• Make sure that the ceiling above the uppermost story of the home is as airtight as possible. Verify airtightness with a blower door test.

- Install ceiling or roof insulation that meets or exceeds minimum code requirements. In areas of the country where ice dams are a problem, that usually means that you need a minimum of R-49 insulation. The insulation should extend to the outer edge of the top plates of the perimeter walls. Choose insulation with a reputation for good performance; avoid the use of fiberglass batts, which perform worse than any other type of insulation on the market. Make sure the insulation is carefully installed and the performance of the insulation is not undermined by thermal bridging.

- If you are designing an insulated sloped roof assembly (that is, a cathedral ceiling), the most robust design will include a generously sized ventilation channel above the insulation.

- If you are worried about ceiling leaks due to ice dams, choose a type of roofing—for example, a membrane roofing like EPDM or standing-seam metal roofing—that does a better job of resisting leaks from ice dams than asphalt shingles.

WHAT TO DO RIGHT NOW IF YOU HAVE AN ICE DAM

Remember, many roofers and general contractors don't have a good understanding of how ice dams form or how these problems should be fixed.

- As long as you don't have a great deal of water entering your home—so much water that you have a major disaster on your hands—it's usually better to wait until spring before you begin implementing ice dam solutions.

- Almost every expert warns homeowners that they shouldn't climb up on the roof to try to remove ice. While this "safety first" advice is understandable, it is sometimes necessary to remove roof ice, especially

if you have a major leak. Use common sense. You can either hire a contractor (one who has adequate insurance) to do this work, or you can take the risk yourself. The two biggest risks are falling off the roof—a risk that may be lessened by that enormous pile of fluffy snow that you will land in when you fall—and putting holes in your roofing or flashing because you stupidly decided to break up the ice with a hatchet. Again, common sense is very useful here; start with a wooden mallet or a baseball bat before you graduate to sharper tools. If you are unsure of yourself, don't do it.

- When removing ice at the eaves is difficult or unwise, it may still make sense to remove as much snow as possible from the area above the ice dam to reduce future melting. This can be done with a shovel (if it's possible to get on the roof safely) or a long-handled roof rake.

- Some people sprinkle road salt or calcium chloride tablets on their ice dams. You can fill old socks with rock salt, tie the open ends of the socks closed with a knot, and throw the socks onto the roof, aiming for the ice dams. This effort might help, especially if the weather ever warms up into the 20s, but the salt may not be very good for the vegetation below.

- In the spring, ignore the contractors who talk about roof repair and ventilation improvements. Find a home performance contractor who knows how to seal air leaks, using such tools as a blower door test, an infrared camera, or a theatrical fog machine. Remember: In most cases, adding insulation or changing the way a roof is vented will not solve an ice dam problem, especially if no attempt is made to seal air leaks first.

Fortunately, most HVAC contractors in cold climates know better than to install ducts or HVAC equipment in a vented unconditioned attic. If you are one of the unlucky homeowners with this problem—ducts or HVAC equipment in your unconditioned attic—the equipment and ducts should either be moved to a new location inside your home's thermal envelope, or your attic should be modified to turn it into an unvented conditioned attic. Trying to address this problem by leaving the ducts where they are, and merely improving the thickness of the duct insulation or sealing the duct seams, usually results in disappointment.

Once air leaks in your home's thermal envelope have been sealed, it may be useful to increase the R-value of the insulation between your ceiling and the underside of the roof sheathing. Aim for a minimum of R-49 insulation. An effective but expensive solution to ice dam problems is to install thick layers of rigid foam or nailbase above the existing roof sheathing, along with a "vented over-roof" above the rigid foam. Ideally, the vent channel above the rigid foam will be at least 1½ in. high.

While changes to roof ventilation details rarely solve an ice dam problem, such changes may improve matters—but only if you have conscientiously finished your air sealing work and your R-value improvements.

Solving ice dam problems in an older building is often difficult. Air leaks can be tricky to track down; attic areas that need work are often impossible to access without opening up holes in a ceiling or roof; and undersize rafters often provide insufficient room for the required insulation. Most of these problems have solutions, but the solutions aren't cheap.

There are many more contractors pushing bad ice dam solutions—for example, electric-resistance heating cables—than there are contractors pushing good ice dam solutions.

Homeowners who bite the bullet and do a thorough job of addressing their ice dam problems—perhaps by installing a thick layer of rigid foam above their roof sheathing, followed by above-foam ventilation channels, a second layer of sheathing, and new roofing—can look forward to feelings of satisfaction next winter.

If all goes according to plan, your house will stay icicle-free—even when every other house on the block is loaded with 5-ft. icicles. You'll also enjoy a useful side benefit: lower energy bills.

Is your basement a damp hole in the ground or a delightful place to retreat and tinker at your workbench?

Foundation discussions can get heated. For some reason, builders often dig in their heels when the topic of slabs versus crawl spaces versus basements comes up. It's time to declare a truce.

It's perfectly possible to build a great house on any one of these three foundation types, as long as everything is properly detailed. Each type of foundation has advantages as well as disadvantages. If you have a foundation type that you prefer, that's great. I'm not going to try to change your mind.

BASEMENTS ARE HANDY

Before the development of central heating systems and the electrical grid, most cold-climate homes in North America included a basement or cellar. Why? Because a cellar was the only room in the house where temperatures wouldn't drop below freezing during the winter. Homeowners could store potatoes, carrots, and turnips there without the risk that these foods would be spoiled by frost.

Of course, most of us no longer have to worry that the food stored in our kitchen cabinets will freeze. However, basements still have virtues:

• Plumbing repairs and plumbing changes that accompany remodeling are much easier in a home with a basement than in a home with a slab.

• A basement is an excellent location for mechanical equipment like a furnace, water heater, or HRV. If the basement is properly detailed, equipment located here will be inside the home's thermal envelope, where it belongs.

• A basement is an excellent location for ducts. Unlike a vented crawl space or a vented attic, a basement is inside a home's thermal envelope. When HVAC contractors install ducts in a basement, they can stand upright rather than crouch; for most contractors, easy access usually leads to higher-quality work.

• If a house has a basement, it's easier to put the water heater and the furnace near the center of the house than if the house is built on a slab. This keeps distribution lines (ducts or hot water tubing) short, improving the energy efficiency of these systems.

• Basements are useful in areas where the tornado risk is high. If you plan to install a safe room to help your family ride out the next tornado, the best place for the room is in a basement.

• If you need to build a frost wall that extends below the frost line, an 8-ft.-high frost wall—one high enough to create a basement—provides more usable space for homeowners than a 4-ft.-high or 5-ft. high frost wall that merely creates a crawl space.

• Most homeowners find that basements provide a useful location for frost-proof storage of rarely used possessions.

• If you are building on a small lot in a neighborhood with height restrictions, a finished basement can provide needed square footage that can't be designed into the house any other way.

IF YOU'RE PLANNING TO BUILD A BASEMENT

Let's assume you're familiar with the pros and cons of basement foundations and you've decided to include a basement. Here are some issues to consider.

Q. How should I build my walls?

A. In most areas of the country, concrete block (concrete masonry units, CMU) basement walls have gone the way of the dodo, and that's a good thing. Poured concrete walls are preferable in all respects to CMU walls.

If you want a basement wall system that includes insulation, you may want to specify the use of insulated concrete forms (ICFs) or a precast system like Superior Walls®. Either of these options is likely to cost more than a site-insulated poured concrete wall, however, so they make sense only if you have a compelling reason to prefer them.

Q. How tall should the walls be?

A. Basement walls are usually 8 ft. high, but they often feel shorter. Most basements have pipes and ducts that are installed below the floor joists. If a homeowner ever wants to finish the basement, these ducts and pipes dictate a low ceiling. That's why it often makes sense to specify 9-ft. basement walls for a new house.

Q. How can I keep water out of my basement?

A. Fixing a wet basement is expensive—especially if the repair work calls for excavation of the soil on the outside of your foundation. In general, it's better to spend a few hundred dollars on waterproofing details during new construction than thousands (or tens of thousands) of dollars on future repairs.

If you are building a new home on a basement foundation, you should specify:

- Wide roof overhangs to keep rain away from the foundation.

- Gutters at the roof eaves; these gutters should be connected to solid (non-perforated) conductor pipes that convey the roof water far from the house (either to daylight or a dry well).

- A 4-in.-thick layer of crushed stone under the basement slab as a capillary break; the crushed stone layer needs to be vented through the roof to help control radon.

- A layer of horizontal rigid foam on top of the crushed stone to insulate the slab from the cold soil below.

- A layer of polyethylene above the rigid foam (directly under the concrete slab) to act as a vapor barrier.

- At least one 4-in.-dia. drainpipe running horizontally through the footing, to connect the crushed stone layer under your basement slab with the exterior footing drain.

- A capillary break (for example, an asphaltic dampproofing compound, Tremco® Tremproof® 250 GC or elastomeric paint) between the top of the concrete footing and the foundation wall.

- A ring of perforated drainpipe on the outside of the footing, surrounded by crushed stone and wrapped with filter fabric to make a "burrito," drained to daylight, to a distant drywell, or to an interior sump.

- An application of dampproofing compound or waterproofing compound on the exterior side of the concrete foundation walls.

- A layer of dimple-mat drainage board installed on the exterior side of the foundation walls; failing that, the foundation should be backfilled with coarse, free-draining material like crushed stone, topped with an 8-in. layer of dirt (ideally, dirt with a high clay content).

- Closed-cell foam sill seal between the top of the foundation walls and the mudsill, to reduce air leakage and to act as a capillary break.

Q. Do basements need to be air sealed?

A. Absolutely. Common air leakage sites include the crack between the slab and the walls (yes, air can migrate through soil and crushed stone); unsealed sumps (all sumps need an airtight lid); and the rim joist area.

Q. Where should I put the wall insulation?

A. Either interior or exterior wall insulation can work, but it's important to get the specs and details right. If you're installing insulation on the interior of a basement wall, specify rigid foam or closed-cell spray foam, not fiberglass or cellulose.

Q. Can I skip the horizontal layer of rigid foam under the basement slab?

A. Some builders omit the layer of rigid foam under basement slab, arguing that homes don't lose enough heat through below-grade slabs to justify the expense of the foam. They forget that the main reason to include the rigid foam under the slab—at least in cold climates—has nothing to do with energy savings; the foam is there to keep the slab warm enough during the summer to avoid condensation or moisture accumulation in the slab. If the slab stays dry during the summer, the basement is less likely to smell damp and moldy. That's why it makes sense for builders in climate Zones 4 through 8 to install horizontal rigid foam under a basement slab.

Q. Do basements need to be actively conditioned?

A. If your basement is unfinished, there is usually no need to include any supply air registers connected to your furnace (or baseboard radiation connected to your boiler). If a furnace, boiler, or water heater is located in the basement, the incidental heat given off by these appliances is usually more than enough to take the chill off the basement in winter.

If your home is heated with ductless mini-splits (see p. 215), you may have no heating appliances in your basement. In that case, your basement may get cool during the winter—especially if there is a heat pump water heater in the basement. (Heat pump water heaters lower the air temperature of the room where they are located.) Under these circumstances, your basement may need a little bit of space heat, depending on the types of activities that occur there.

Q. When calculating air changes per hour at 50 Pascals (ACH50) via a blower door test, is the volume of the basement included in the house volume?

A. Yes. The conventional way to calculate ACH50 for houses with basements is to include the basement in the volume calculation.

Q. Should I install a dehumidifier?

A. If you are building a new house with a well-detailed basement, your basement should be dry, and you shouldn't need a dehumidifier. That's good, because dehumidifiers are energy hogs. However, if you live in an older home with a damp basement, you may find yourself between a rock and a hard place, with two unpleasant choices: hiring a contractor to make very expensive basement repairs or operating a dehumidifier. (You have my sympathy.) In such a case, you may find it necessary to install a dehumidifier as a stop-gap measure.

BASEMENTS ARE OFTEN WET

Even though basements have advantages, plenty of people still hate basements. Here are some of the reasons:

• Basements tend to be damp. The reason is simple: When you dig a big hole in the ground, nature likes to fill it up with water.

• Although there are construction details that you can use to keep water out of your basement, the required details are somewhat fussy and expensive.

• The easiest way to ensure that soil moisture doesn't enter your house is to make sure that every room is above grade. If your house design requires a mechanical room or a big walk-in closet to store rarely used possessions, there's no reason that you can't build these rooms above grade. Because most homeowners think that above-grade space is more desirable and versatile than below-grade space, why waste money on a basement?

• Basements are much more likely to have high radon levels than above-grade rooms.

• Crawl space foundations and slab-on-grade foundations cost less than basement foundations.

IS IT A GOOD IDEA TO TURN MY BASEMENT INTO FINISHED SPACE?

Below-grade rooms always carry a risk of possible water entry. If you are building a new house, and you want the house to include a home theater or a bar, it's usually best to design your house so that these rooms can be above grade. If you live in an older home, and you know that your basement stays dry, you may be tempted to transform your basement into finished space. As long as you understand the expense and the risks of this approach, you can certainly turn your basement into almost any type of room you want.

When it comes to the advisability of transforming a basement into finished space, opinions differ. Here's my opinion: Basements are different from above-grade space, and that's OK. In many homes, the basement is an informal space where people can retreat when they want to relax or make a mess. A basement is a good place for a Ping-Pong® table, for a sturdy shelf to hold homemade jam and pickles, or for a workbench to tinker on small projects.

If the basement is finished into a carpeted home theater and the workbench is banished to the garage, the house hasn't necessarily been improved. In my opinion, the trade-off probably isn't worth it. An honest, unfinished basement with a concrete floor is preferable in all respects to a finished room with damp carpeting.

Sealed crawl spaces have less mold and stay dryer than vented crawl spaces—and they often save energy

Residential foundations vary widely from one corner of the United States to another. Builders in some regions love basements, while builders in other regions swear by slabs on grade. Although most builders have a theory to explain these regional preferences, the main reason for these variations is habit, not logic. In areas of the country where basements are rare, there usually aren't any technical barriers to building basements; and up north, where basements rule, it's perfectly possible to build on a slab.

Slabs have several virtues: They are inexpensive and they keep all of a home's living area above grade, away from dampness and mold. Basements also have their virtues: They keep plumbing pipes from freezing, provide a good place to install a furnace and run ductwork, and provide a useful area for storage.

CRAWL SPACES COST ALMOST AS MUCH AS A BASEMENT, WITH NONE OF A BASEMENT'S ADVANTAGES

Crawl spaces are more of a puzzle, and it's hard to come up with a reason to like them. I don't have a dog in this fight, however, so if you really want a crawl space, go ahead and build one. Just be sure you get the details right.

If you're perverse, and you want to build a damp, moldy, nasty crawl space, just do two things: insulate the crawl space ceiling with fiberglass batts, and vent the crawl space to the exterior. If you live in the Southeast, within a few short years the fiberglass batts will begin to hang down at odd angles like drunken stalactites. Every summer, the open vents will introduce

SEALING A CRAWL SPACE. Close the vents and install a heavy-duty vapor barrier on the floor to keep moisture, mold, and radon out of the living space.

huge amounts of moisture into the crawl space. You'll end up with a classic moldy crawl space—one that represents a significant source of moisture for the house above.

In a hot, humid climate, venting a crawl space is counterproductive. During the summer, the outdoor air in North Carolina holds more moisture than the cooler crawl space air. When humid outdoor air enters the crawl space vents, it soon hits cool surfaces—concrete blocks, water pipes, and air-conditioning ducts. Condensation forms and begins to drip. The more you ventilate, the wetter the crawl space gets. If you set up a fan to double the ventilation rate, you'll just make the pipes drip faster.

Crawl space vents can also cause problems during the winter, when they introduce outdoor air that can cause pipes to freeze.

UNVENTED CRAWL SPACES ARE PERMITTED BY BUILDING CODES

In most areas of the United States, sealed crawl spaces work much better than vented ones. Most building codes permit the construction of unvented crawl spaces. In the most recent versions of the IRC (including the 2012 IRC), requirements for unvented crawl spaces can be found in Section R408.3. If an unvented crawl space has a dirt floor, the code requires exposed earth to be covered with a continuous vapor retarder with taped seams: "The edges of the vapor retarder shall extend at least 6 in. up the stem wall and shall be attached and sealed to the stem wall."

The code lists two options for conditioning unvented crawl spaces; both options require the installation of a duct or transfer grille connecting the crawl space with the conditioned space upstairs. Option 1 requires "continuously operated mechanical exhaust ventilation at a rate equal to 1 cfm for each 50 sq. ft. of crawl space floor area." In other words, install an exhaust fan in the crawl space that blows through a hole in the rim joist or an exterior wall; make sure that the fan isn't too powerful. (The makeup air entering the crawl space is conditioned air from the house upstairs; because this conditioned air is drier than outdoor air, it doesn't lead to condensation problems.)

Option 2 requires that the crawl space have a forced-air register delivering 1 cfm of supply air from the furnace or air handler for each 50 sq. ft. of crawl space area. (Assuming the house has air-conditioning, this introduction of cool, dry air into the crawl space during the summer keeps the area dry.)

A CRAWL SPACE CAN WORK WELL IN A DRY CLIMATE

According to researchers who conducted a careful study of vented and unvented crawl spaces in North Carolina, homes with sealed crawl spaces with insulated foundation walls use 18% less energy for heating and cooling than identical homes with vented crawl spaces with insulation between the floor joists.

However, similar energy savings cannot necessarily be expected in dry climates. Researchers comparing the energy performance of homes with different crawl space designs in Flagstaff, AZ, found that homes with insulated floors used less energy than homes with sealed crawl spaces and insulated foundation walls. According to a report on the research, "This seemed counterintuitive; ducts are a notorious source of heat loss. With all the Flagstaff homes' ductwork in the crawl space, one would expect better performance from the warmer, wall-insulated crawl spaces. But according to Cyrus Dastur, the Advanced Energy building scientist who directed the research, those homes' lack of floor insulation let heat radiate from the first floor to the crawl space, robbing more heat from the house than was saved by keeping the ductwork warm."

While vented crawl spaces often perform poorly in the humid states of the Southeast, they perform well in most Western states. According to an article in *Home Energy* magazine, "In the drier regions of the West, and even—surprisingly—in the marine climates of the Northwest, vented crawl spaces work acceptably most of the time. The hot-dry conditions in summer and the cold-moist conditions in winter do not cause the same problems that hot-humid conditions cause in the rest of the country . . . . The Washington State University Extension Energy Program (WSU-EEP), as part of its work for Building America, monitored four test houses in Vancouver and Moses Lake, Washington, for over a year and found that the vented crawl spaces rarely, if ever, reached dew point and that they remained above 80% RH only for brief periods of time."

CREATING AN UNVENTED CRAWL SPACE

If you live in a humid climate, and you still want to build a crawl space—or if you are trying to correct problems in an existing moldy crawl space—here's how to go about it.

- To help keep the crawl space dry, correct any grading problems on the exterior so that the grade slopes away from the foundation.

- Remove all rocks and debris from the crawl space floor and rake the dirt smooth. Ideally, the floor will be higher than the exterior grade, although keeping the grade high in the interior of a crawl space is not always possible.

- If the home is located in an area where radon is common, install a passive radon collection system in the crawl space floor.

- If the crawl space is subject to water entry, be sure to slope the floor to a sump equipped with a drain or a sump pump.

- Install a durable vapor barrier—for example, a 20-mil pool liner or Tu-Tuf® poly—over the floor and extending up the crawl space walls, to within 3 in. of the top of the wall. Leave a 3-in.-wide termite inspection strip at the top of the wall.

- Attach the top of the vapor barrier to the wall with horizontal battens, secured to the wall with masonry fasteners.

- Seal the seams of the vapor barrier material with a compatible tape or mastic; many builders use duct mastic embedded in fiberglass mesh tape.

- Consider installing a 2-in.- or 3-in.-thick concrete slab (a "rat slab") to protect the vapor barrier.

- If this is a new-construction crawl space, and you can't afford a rat slab, you may want to install a temporary (sacrificial) second vapor barrier—usually a layer of 6-mil poly—on top of the permanent vapor barrier; once construction is complete, this temporary poly is rolled up and discarded.

- Insulate the interior of the walls and rim joists with rigid foam—many builders use Thermax™, a polyisocyanurate foam that does not require a thermal barrier or ignition barrier—or spray polyurethane foam. Another option: Insulate the exterior of the foundation walls. If your crawl space has stone-and-mortar walls, you can't insulate the walls with rigid foam; the only type of insulation that makes sense for stone-and-mortar walls is closed-cell spray polyurethane foam. Install at least as much insulation as required by the 2012 IRC for basement walls—namely R-5 for climate Zone 3; R-10 for Zone 4 (except Marine Zone 4); and R-15 for Marine Zone 4 and Zones 5, 6, 7, and 8.

- Install a floor register in the floor above to allow air to flow between the living area and the sealed crawl space below.

- Install an exhaust fan or a forced-air register to meet code requirements for conditioning the crawl space. Be sure the fan does not exceed air flow requirements for the size of the crawl space because exhaust fans carry an energy penalty.

- Install good lighting—most crawl spaces will benefit from at least six fixtures, spaced evenly across the ceiling—controlled by a switch located near the entry door.

New-construction crawl spaces often require temporary dehumidification to remove construction moisture. Once the home is dried in, it's a good idea to install a stand-alone dehumidifier in the crawl space and run it for three or four months until the interior relative humidity stabilizes. Any combustion appliance (for example, a water heater or furnace) in a sealed crawl space should be a sealed-combustion unit.

EVEN WELL-DETAILED CRAWL SPACES MAY NOT MAKE SENSE

A well-detailed crawl space is a thing of beauty. (Perhaps such crawl spaces aren't beautiful to all eyes, but they are to mine. I used to work as a home inspector, and I have spent far too many hours crawling under houses, in damp caves littered with debris and animal droppings.)

That said, it's important to emphasize that even a well-detailed crawl space represents a problematic foundation design. Bill Rose, a building scientist and a research architect at the Building Research Council at the University of Illinois, remained skeptical of crawl spaces. "I'm very cautious about crawl space construction—maybe it ought to be abandoned," said Rose. "It would cost as much as a basement to get a crawl space right."

One problem with sealed crawl spaces: The air quality in such a space may be poor unless an installed exhaust fan runs continuously. Of course, such a fan can be part of a whole-house exhaust ventilation system; but when (not if) the fan eventually conks out, the homeowner is unlikely to notice. That raises concerns over air quality in the crawl space and in the home above.

According to the previously cited *Home Energy* article, "Additional radon testing showed that radon levels in the closed crawls—with a relatively low dilution rate—were roughly 10 times the levels measured in the vented crawls."

If a builder chooses to condition a sealed crawl space using Option 2 from the two code-approved options—that is, by installing a forced-air register rather than an exhaust fan in the space—it's easy for any radon or moisture in the crawl space to circulate throughout the house.

The more you think about crawl space problems and crawl space remedies, the better a slab on grade begins to look.

Does the poly vapor barrier belong above the rigid foam or below the rigid foam?

What goes under the concrete in a slab-on-grade home? In the old days, not much—just dirt. Eventually, contractors discovered that it made sense to include a 4-in.-thick layer of crushed stone under the concrete. The crushed stone provides a capillary break that reduces the amount of moisture flowing upward from the damp soil to the permeable concrete.

Because the crushed stone layer provides a fairly uniform substrate, it may also reduce the chance that a concrete slab will be poorly supported by random pockets of soft, easily compressible soil.

Eventually, polyethylene was invented. Concrete contractors learned that a layer of poly helps keep a slab dry, because it stops upward vapor diffusion from the soil. Finally, some contractors in cold climates began installing a continuous horizontal layer of rigid foam insulation under their concrete slabs. The foam layer isolates the room-temperature slab from the cold soil under the slab.

GETTING THE SANDWICH LAYERS IN THE RIGHT ORDER

At this point, we've got a sandwich with three or four layers, and questions arise, Does the order of the different layers matter? What goes down first, and what goes down last? According to most building scientists, here's how the layers should go, from the bottom up: crushed stone, rigid foam, polyethylene, concrete.

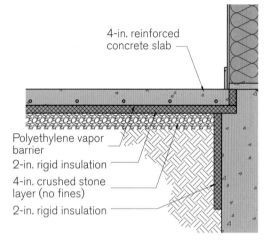

4-in. reinforced concrete slab

Polyethylene vapor barrier

2-in. rigid insulation

4-in. crushed stone layer (no fines)

2-in. rigid insulation

GET THE LAYERS RIGHT. From the bottom up, here's how the layers should go: crushed stone, rigid foam, polyethylene, concrete.

CAN I STILL USE BLOTTER SAND?

Some contractors may ask, Is it a mistake to put the polyethylene lower down in the sandwich? The answer is yes. To understand why, it's useful to study the history of blotter sand. Beginning in 1989, the American Concrete Institute® (ACI) recommended the installation of a 4-in. layer of granular material between a subslab vapor retarder and a concrete slab. ACI standard 302.1 R-96, *Guide for Concrete Floor and Slab Construction*, included this recommendation in Section 4.1.5: "If a vapor barrier or retarder is required due to local conditions, these products should be placed under a minimum of 4 in. (100 mm) of trimable, compactable, granular fill (not sand)."

Although the ACI specified "granular fill," most residential builders found it

more convenient to use sand. This layer became known as the "blotter sand" layer.

After a rash of flooring failures, the standard was revised

Because a layer of blotter sand between the polyethylene and the concrete allows for faster slab finishing and tends to reduce slab curling, especially if the concrete has a high water-to-cement ratio, many residential builders readily adopted the ACI recommendation. The use of blotter sand became particularly common in California.

In the late 1990s, however, some builders of slab-on-grade homes began receiving regular reports of flooring failures. Investigators discovered that many of these failures could be blamed on the inclusion of blotter sand above the poly.

Finally bowing to the evidence, the ACI eventually reversed the long-standing but controversial recommendation. In the April 2001 issue of *Concrete International* magazine, the ACI advised that for slabs with vapor-sensitive coatings (that is, virtually any kind of flooring), the vapor retarder should be installed directly under the slab, with no intervening layer of granular fill. In November 2001, the ACI included the updated recommendations in a new edition of ACI standard 302.1R-96.

Concrete contractors love blotter sand

Contractors used blotter sand because it provided certain undeniable benefits. Sand helps protect the polyethylene vapor retarder from abuse. With a layer of blotter sand, excess water can drain out of the fresh concrete, making it easier to place concrete with a high water-to-cement ratio. In contrast, when polyethylene is installed directly under the slab, bleed water dissipates more slowly and concrete finishing is delayed. When excess water leaves the

slab from the top side only, the slab may cure unevenly, in some cases resulting in slab curling, shrinkage, or cracking.

When I wrote an article on the topic of blotter sand for the May 2002 issue of *Energy Design Update*, I interviewed Howard Kanare, who at that time was a senior principal scientist at Construction Technology Laboratories in Skokie, IL. "On one side are the folks concerned with construction practices; they don't want to see a plastic sheet directly under the slab," Kanare told me. "On the other side are the people who have investigated failures. We almost never see a failure due to moisture infiltrating concrete when the concrete is directly on the plastic sheeting."

A subslab sponge that stays wet

While a sponge under the floor may help contractors during construction, it will probably be a headache for those who have to live in the house. "The problem is that the blotter layer needs some moisture to be compacted," Kanare said. "It might be at a moisture content of 7%, and if the layer is 4 in. thick you have a couple of pounds of water under each square foot. You are essentially forming a bathtub. It's a long-term source of moisture to recharge the concrete."

Water added for compaction is just one of many possible sources of moisture keeping blotter sand damp. Another is rain, as I learned when I spoke with Kelley Roberts, a water-intrusion consultant at Construction Forensics in Huntington Beach, CA. "At one home I investigated, they put down a bulletproof vapor barrier with 2 in. of sand on top, and then poured a 6-in. slab," said Roberts. "During the 30 days between the slab pour and when they got the building dried in, there was $4\frac{1}{2}$ in. of rain. But they went ahead and installed the flooring, and then they cranked the air-conditioner up. The VCT (vinyl construction tile) blew off in just 45 days."

Water can also reach the sand layer by capillary action from the edges of the slab, especially if homeowners have lawn sprinklers. In some cases, it may be able to come up from below through rips in the poly. "When you have sand with a moisture content of 18%, you are talking about waiting years, not months, for the slab to dry out," said George Donnelly, a concrete and flooring consultant in Hemet, CA.

Building scientist Joe Lstiburek agreed with Donnelly. Lstiburek wrote, "The sand layer is wetted by liquid phase wetting in a time frame measured in minutes. Whereas the sand layer can only dry upwards by vapor phase drying in a time frame measured in years."

In most cases, damp blotter sand eventually dries, but it may not dry as fast as the flooring contractor would like. "Everyone wants to get the flooring down in a hurry, and no one wants to take the time for a calcium box test," said Roberts.

THE FLOORING JUST POPPED

Until recently, homeowners with slab problems were mostly upset about their ruined flooring. But some homeowners have begun to notice that their failed flooring has mold on the underside, adding a whole new dimension to flooring litigation.

"Flooring failures over damp slabs are a huge issue in these class-action suits against builders," said Donnelly. When flooring pops off a slab, repairs aren't cheap. Once the flooring is demolished, the slab is usually shot-blasted in preparation for topside sealing.

After the sealer has cured, new flooring can be installed. "We just finished investigating a failure in a 1,200-sq.-ft. room," Roberts told me in 2002. "It cost $10,000 to seal the slab. That's not including

$30,000 it cost to remove and replace the flooring."

All kinds of flooring have been known to fail over damp slabs, including vinyl, carpet, and wood flooring. "The sheet vinyl flooring discolors, and a wood floor will swell," said Donnelly. "Sometimes you lift an object like a child's toy box, and underneath the carpet is damp." The common denominator in all of these failures is a damp slab. "With VCT, the first thing you see is the white glue oozing out of the joints," says Roberts. "With a wood floor, you can get cupping and buckling. If they find mold on the underside of the floor, now it turns into tens of thousands of dollars."

CONCRETE SPECIFICATIONS MATTER

Many residential builders pay little attention to concrete slab specifications, at least until they have flooring problems. But "anyone who has been successfully sued starts to pay attention," said Donnelly. With the recommendations of the ACI 302 committee now in line with most building science experts, there seems to be a firm consensus that the vapor retarder belongs immediately under the concrete slab.

Lstiburek tells contractors, "Repeat after me: don't ever, ever, put a layer of sand between a plastic vapor barrier and a concrete slab—don't even think about it." Still, some concrete contractors may be reluctant to abandon blotter sand, fearing problems with excess bleed water, slab curling, and cracking. But by switching to higher-strength concrete, reducing the water-to-cement ratio, and using adequate steel to prevent curling, these problems can be controlled. "The water-to-cement ratio should not exceed 0.45," said Kanare. "You should specify a five-sack mix, and the largest possible size aggregate. For a 4-in. slab, you should be using 1-in. aggregate."

In an article on blotter sand, Lstiburek imagined the objections of a concrete contractor from California: "'Yeah, but if I don't put the sand layer in there it will take too long to finish the floor.' Yes, that's true if you use crappy concrete with too much water in it. The easy answer is: don't use crappy concrete."

Some builders who have long used blotter sand may be tempted to substitute a layer of crushed stone for the blotter sand layer. According to Lstiburek, however, this won't work. "Large quantities of water are still held in the pea gravel—think surface area of the gravel and the fines in the pea gravel. Pea gravel does drain, but it retains huge amounts of water even though it drains."

Test the concrete

If you are worried about flooring failures, it makes a lot of sense to perform a calcium chloride test before you install the flooring. This test will verify that the slab's moisture level has dropped to within the specifications of the flooring manufacturer. After all, the cost of the test is a lot cheaper than litigation.

CAN I PUT THE POLYETHYLENE UNDER THE RIGID FOAM?

Some builders like to install polyethylene under a layer of rigid foam, so that the sandwich looks like this (from the bottom up): crushed stone, polyethylene, rigid foam, concrete. Is that OK? Well, it's not as bad a sandwich as one that includes a layer of blotter sand above the poly. But it's still not optimal. If it rains after the rigid foam is installed but before the concrete is placed, the polyethylene can hold hidden puddles. It's always best to install the polyethylene on top of the rigid

foam, so that it ends up directly under the concrete.

Is it important to make sure there are no holes in the polyethylene?

Some energy-efficient builders misunderstand the purpose of the polyethylene under a slab. They evidently think that the polyethylene is an air barrier, so they go to great lengths to seal every seam with expensive tape and to tape all pipe penetrations. These builders stay up at night worrying that the concrete contractors will put a little hole in their precious polyethylene. They should stop worrying. The polyethylene is a vapor barrier, not an air barrier. It's perfectly OK for the polyethylene to have a few holes.

The concrete slab is your air barrier. If you want an airtight floor—and there are several reasons you should, including radon worries—then you need to seal cracks at the perimeter of the slab with high-quality caulk, and you need to seal penetrations through the slab. This work is performed after the concrete has cured.

A vapor barrier can have a few holes and still perform perfectly well. If 5% of the surface area of a vapor barrier is missing entirely, the vapor barrier performs 95% as well as a vapor barrier that is intact.

Here's what Lstiburek had to say about polyethylene under a slab: "You can poke holes in it, you can puncture it, you can tear it, you can leave gaps in it, and pretty much have your way with it as long as it is in direct contact with the concrete . . . . Air barriers need to be continuous and free from holes, but vapor barriers do not need to be. Lots of vapor moves by air movement, not a heck of a lot of vapor moves by vapor diffusion. The concrete slab is the air barrier, and the ripped and torn and punctured polyethylene sheet is the vapor barrier . . . . I could wear golf shoes and march around the plastic vapor barrier and not do much damage."

Commonsense advice for people who can't decide how to build their walls

uilders love to talk about walls. Almost all of us are willing to argue about the best way to build a high-R wall, and we love to debate whether certain wall details are environmentally friendly enough to be considered green.

Although these conversations can be fun, our obsession with wall details is often misplaced. Details that inflame our passions are often irrelevant. In most cases, we should just choose a relatively airtight easy-to-build wall with good flashing details—one with an R-value in the range of R-20 to R-40—and be done with it.

TWO POPULAR APPROACHES

For readers who don't have time to get bogged down in details, here's the short version of my wall advice:

• In most of the United States and Canada, there are two cost-effective ways to build a wall with an R-value that exceeds minimum code requirements. The first approach is to build a double-stud wall. The second approach is to build a 2×6 wall with a continuous layer of insulation (usually rigid foam or mineral wool) on the exterior side of the wall sheathing.

DOUBLE-STUD WALLS interrupt thermal bridging through the studs by providing room for insulation between two parallel stud walls.

- Either of these approaches works very well, as long as the builder understands a few basic principles of moisture management.
- Other types of wall assemblies, including walls using ICFs, SIPs, Larsen trusses, straw bales, or adobe, can be made to work, and in some cases have a few advantages for certain locations or applications. But these approaches tend to cost more than a double-stud wall or a 2×6 wall with insulation on the exterior side of the wall sheathing.

DOUBLE-STUD WALLS

Energy-conscious builders in North America have been building double-stud walls for at least 40 years. Double-stud walls have two parallel framed walls—either two 2×4 walls, or one 2×4 wall and one 2×6 wall. The total wall thickness is variable; while 12-in.-thick walls are common, it's also possible to build a double-stud wall that is 9 in. thick or 14 in. thick.

If you plan to build a double-stud wall, you need to decide which of the two walls will be your bearing wall: the inner wall or the outer wall. Either approach can work, as long as you have a continuous load path from the bearing wall down to the foundation.

Experts advise that the most robust double-stud walls include the following features:

- Any type of exterior sheathing material other than OSB—for example, plywood, diagonal boards, fiberboard, or fiberglass-faced gypsum panels.
- A ventilated rain-screen gap between the siding and the WRB.
- A smart vapor retarder (for example, MemBrain) or vapor-retarder paint on the interior side of the wall—or (for builders who are following Joseph Lstiburek's specifications) a layer of OSB or plywood sandwiched between the two 2×4 walls.

Double-stud walls are considerably more expensive than walls with a single row of studs, so builders in warm climates (Zones 4 and warmer) should probably stick with a conventional 2×4 or 2×6 wall, with or without exterior insulation.

2×6 WALLS WITH EXTERIOR RIGID FOAM

Energy-conscious builders began switching from 2×4 wall framing to 2×6 framing in the 1970s. There are two problems with most 2×6 walls.

- The nominal R-value of the insulation is limited by the depth of the stud space.

Minimum Thickness of Exterior Rigid Foam			
Climate Zone	Minimum R-value of rigid foam layer for 2×6 wall	Foam thickness (assuming EPS)	Whole-wall R-value (assuming that the 2×6 wall has an R-value of R-14)
Marine Zone 4	R-3.75	1 in.	R-18
Zone 5	R-7.5	2 in.	R-22
Zone 6	R-11.25	3 in.	R-26
Zones 7 and 8	R-15	4 in.	R-30

WHAT DO I NEED TO KNOW ABOUT VAPOR DRIVE AND VAPOR PERMEANCE?

Many green builders think that a wall has to "breathe." While breathing is a poorly defined concept, it usually refers to a wall that is vapor-permeable.

The classic example of a vapor-permeable wall is a straw-bale wall. During winter, water vapor moves from the warm, humid interior of the building toward the cool, dry exterior. In the case of a straw-bale wall, the water vapor moves right through the bales. As long as the water vapor doesn't encounter an exterior vapor barrier, it will eventually evaporate. During summer, the direction of the vapor flow reverses. Water vapor will move from the hot, humid exterior toward the cool, dry interior.

This type of vapor flow can sometimes cause problems. For example, the wall sheathing on a double-stud wall is cold during winter. Plywood wall sheathing isn't as vapor-permeable as straw, so moisture can accumulate at the cold wall sheathing. Whether this type of moisture accumulation is a problem depends on how quickly the wall sheathing can dry to the exterior in spring.

Similarly, inward vapor flow during summer can be a problem if an air-conditioned home has walls with an interior layer of polyethylene. In some cases, water vapor that is driven inward by the sun shining on damp siding can condense on the cool polyethylene, leading to puddles at the base of the wall.

Builders use a variety of techniques to limit problems arising from vapor drive. Here are a few important points:

- There is no truth to the belief that vapor-permeable walls perform better than walls that include a vapor barrier. In fact, limiting the flow of vapor through floors, walls, and ceilings is often essential. (A wall with a vapor barrier can perform very well or very poorly. In general, vapor barriers that provide R-value—for example, foil-faced polyisocyanurate—usually cause fewer problems than vapor barriers that have no R-value—for example, polyethylene sheeting.)

- Wood-framed walls with an adequate layer of exterior rigid foam do an excellent job of preventing problems associated with vapor drive. The exterior rigid foam keeps the wall sheathing warm and dry during winter, so moisture can't accumulate in the sheathing. Moreover, the rigid foam prevents inward solar vapor drive during summer. Everything on the exterior side of the rigid foam dries to the exterior; everything on the interior side of the rigid foam dries to the interior.

- As noted earlier, the sheathing in a double-stud wall is far more likely to get damp during winter than the sheathing in a wall with exterior rigid foam. This wintertime moisture accumulation won't necessarily lead to problems, however, as long as the builder remembers to include good details. Double-stud walls should include a ventilated rain-screen gap between the siding and the WRB as well as a smart vapor retarder or vapor-retarder paint on the interior side of the wall. Builders should also consider installing a type of wall sheathing that is more vapor-permeable than OSB.

In most cases, 5½ in. of fluffy insulation has an R-value of R-20 or less. In cold climates, that's not much.

- Because of thermal bridging through the studs, the whole-wall R-value of a 2×6 wall insulated with R-20 insulation isn't R-20—it's R-12 to R-17, depending on

ALL ABOUT WALL ROT

Here's the most important advice for any homeowner with a wet-wall problem: Before beginning any repairs, be sure you know the source of the moisture that caused the rot. Once you have determined the source of the moisture, be sure to implement corrective action to ensure the same problem doesn't recur.

There are only two sources of moisture: It either comes from the exterior—in other words, it's rain—or it comes from the interior. Of these two sources, by far the most common is rain. Rain (or melted ice) can enter a wall through many mechanisms: bad window flashing, missing kickout flashing, bad roof flashing, ice dams, splashback, and inward solar vapor drive. Although the phenomenon is rare, it's also possible for a wall to get wet when interior moisture that is piggybacking on exfiltrating air gets trapped in a wall.

Take off the siding and WRB

If you are investigating a wet-wall problem, you'll need to remove the siding and housewrap or asphalt felt to get a good look at the sheathing. Keep removing siding until you're sure that you have reached solid sheathing.

Once the sheathing is exposed, you can look at the pattern of rot. Because water flows downward under the influence of gravity, you want to look at the uppermost area of rot to help determine what's going on. The pattern of the rot is the best clue to the water entry mechanism.

- **Rot due to bad window flashing.** This type of rot shows up at the lower corners of the windows and spreads out from there. In extreme cases, the entire area under the window is rotten. To solve this problem, the window has to be removed and the entire rough opening needs to be properly flashed. Simply slapping some peel-and-stick tape over the window flanges won't prevent future problems.

- **Rot due to splash back.** This type of rot occurs in a horizontal band along the bottom of a wall. In most cases, the siding is rotten as well as the sheathing. Rot due

to splash back occurs under the eaves of a roof, so it usually doesn't show up on the gable end of a house. The cause of this problem is simple: The grade is too high. While the traditional minimum distance between the grade and the lowest wooden components of the building is 8 in., I think 12 in. makes more sense.

- **Rot due to missing kickout flashing or missing step flashing.** If the roof of a one-story addition or an attached garage runs alongside a two-story wall, it's usually necessary to install kickout flashing at the eaves of the lower roof. If the builder left out the kickout flashing, water can dribble down the siding and lead to rot. A similar problem occurs if the roofer omitted the lowest piece of step flashing. If sheathing stains originate near the eaves of such a roof, you've probably discovered the source of the water.

- **Rot due to missing flashing at a deck ledger.** This common problem leads to rot under the deck. If it's a second-floor deck, the wall sheathing under the deck is often rotten.

- **Rot due to ice dams.** When ice dams lead to rotten wall sheathing, you'll notice that the water has entered at the top of the wall under the eaves. In many cases, the signs of water entry occur directly under a valley. If you suspect this mode of water entry, ask the homeowners whether the house has a history of ice dams.

Why did the wall rot?

Walls get wet all the time, but they don't always rot. So, if you are looking at a rotten wall, you may be wondering, "Why did this wall rot?" There is just one answer to this question: "Because the rate of wetting exceeded the rate of drying."

A little bit of moisture won't destroy a wall, as long as the wall is built in such a way that it can dry rapidly. The best way to be sure that wall sheathing can dry rapidly is to include a ventilated rain-screen gap between the siding and the sheathing.

So if you don't want to come back in a few years and fix more rotten sheathing at the same house, here's what you have to do: Fix all those flashing problems, lower the exterior grade, seal the air leaks on the inside of the house, and be sure to install the siding over a rain screen.

the wall's framing factor and how well the insulation is installed.

The R-value of a 2×6 wall can be greatly enhanced by adding a continuous layer of rigid foam on the exterior side of the wall sheathing. Builders who install rigid foam on the exterior of a wall need to make sure the rigid foam is thick enough to keep the wall sheathing above the dew point during winter. The table on p. 48 shows the minimum R-value and rigid foam thickness for walls in a variety of climate zones.

Builders in climate zones that are warmer than the zones shown in the table on p. 48 can install any thickness of exterior rigid foam they want, without worrying about moisture accumulation or condensation problems. In these warmer zones, many builders choose to install 1½-in.-thick ZIP System® R sheathing—a type of sheathing that combines OSB with R-6.6 of rigid foam.

While the table shows the minimum recommended thickness of exterior rigid foam in a variety of climate zones, nothing prevents a builder from installing rigid foam that is thicker than the examples. Walls with exterior rigid foam are designed to dry to the interior, so builders should never install an interior polyethylene vapor barrier or vinyl wallpaper on this type of wall.

Of course, in warmer climate zones, where walls don't require the high R-values sought by cold-climate builders, 2×4 framing may be perfectly adequate. The thermal performance of a 2×4 wall (like the thermal performance of a 2×6 wall) is greatly enhanced by the addition of a layer of exterior rigid foam.

What if I want to install exterior mineral wool?

Mineral wool insulation can be substituted for rigid foam insulation on the exterior side of wall sheathing. One advantage of mineral wool over rigid foam: Because mineral wool is vapor-permeable, it doesn't inhibit wall sheathing from drying to the exterior. That means that builders can install mineral wool of any thickness on the exterior side of their walls. You don't have to worry whether exterior mineral wool meets any minimum R-value requirement. (Of course, thicker insulation always does a better job of resisting heat flow than thinner insulation.)

What type of insulation should I install between the studs?

Double-stud walls are always insulated with an air-permeable insulation—for example, fiberglass batts, blown-in fiberglass, cellulose, or mineral wool—rather than spray polyurethane foam. (Spray foam insulation is too expensive to install in such a thick wall.)

If you're building a 2×6 wall with exterior rigid foam, it's also best to avoid using spray polyurethane foam between the studs. When I hear that a builder wants to install spray foam between the studs of a wall with exterior rigid foam, here's what I advise: If you want to use foam insulation, you have to choose where you want the foam to be located. Either it can be located between the studs or it can be located on the exterior side of the sheathing, but it shouldn't be installed on both sides of the sheathing. Why? Because if you enclose the OSB or plywood sheathing with foam insulation on both sides, the foam can inhibit drying. If the sheathing ever gets damp, it won't be able to dry out very quickly.

If a builder asks, Where's the best place to put the foam? I always answer, On the exterior side of the sheathing. There are three reasons this makes sense:

• Spray foam insulation is more expensive than rigid foam.

• Most brands of closed-cell spray foam insulation are manufactured with a blowing agent that has a very high global warming potential.

• Exterior rigid foam addresses thermal bridging through the studs, while spray foam insulation between the studs does nothing to reduce thermal bridging. The thermal bridging penalty is so great that it makes the high cost of spray foam insulation hard to justify compared to less-expensive types of insulation.

If a builder insists on using spray foam between the studs as well as rigid foam on the exterior side of the sheathing, I advise the builder to use open-cell spray foam (which is vapor-permeable) rather than closed-cell spray foam (which has a very low vapor permeance). That way, the sheathing will be able to dry inward if necessary.

No matter what type of air-permeable insulation (cellulose, fiberglass, or mineral wool) you choose to install between the studs, it's important to make sure the insulation fills all of the wall's nooks and crannies, without leaving any voids. This is easier to achieve with a blown-in insulation than a batt insulation.

If you decide to install cellulose insulation—a good choice, in my opinion—it needs to be installed using the dense-pack method. (For more information on dense-packed cellulose, see "How to Install Cellulose Insulation" on p. 144.) Dense-packing a double-stud wall is trickier than dense-packing a 2×6 wall; special techniques are used to make sure every part of the wall is insulated to the same density.

While experienced cellulose installers usually aim for a density of 3.5 lb. per cubic foot for 2×6 walls, a double-stud wall needs to be insulated to a density of 4 lb. per cubic foot to eliminate any possibility of settling.

Every wall needs a water-resistive barrier

Building codes require, and building scientists recommend, that every wall include a WRB. This WRB is usually located between the siding and the sheathing. Examples of WRBs are asphalt felt, Grade D building paper, plastic housewrap, liquid-applied barriers, rigid foam, and ZIP System sheathing.

Flashing details and rain-screen gaps

The most common way walls get wet is when rain leaks past defective wall flashing. Typical problems occur at windows—especially at the two lower corners of windows that lack sill pan flashing—and at penetrations like cantilevered joists or porch railings secured to the wall. If you want your wall to stay dry, you need to have a thorough understanding of flashing techniques, and these techniques need to be carefully executed. (For more information on this topic, see "All about Wall Rot" on p. 50).

Wall flashing must always be integrated with the wall's WRB—so if you don't know where the WRB is, you can't flash the wall. If you're using asphalt felt, Grade D building paper, or plastic housewrap as your WRB, all horizontal WRB seams (and all seams between the WRB and flashing) must be lapped shingle-style to shed water away from the house.

In addition to paying close attention to flashing details, it's important to include a ventilated rain-screen gap between the back of your siding and your WRB. This rain-screen gap adds a lot of forgiveness to your wall: Even if your wall has a flashing problem, the rain-screen gap can often save the wall by allowing the water to drain and by accelerating evaporation.

Pay attention to airtightness

If you care about your home's energy performance, you need to focus on airtightness. Exterior walls are part of your home's thermal envelope, so it's important that walls be built to be as airtight as possible.

Most energy-conscious builders now realize that the easiest way to create an air barrier for your wall is to tape the seams of the OSB or plywood wall sheathing with a high-quality tape.

Of course, if you decide to create an air barrier at the wall sheathing, taping the sheathing seams is just one aspect of the job. All of the wall penetrations, including windows and doors, need to be sealed to limit air leakage. Pay attention to tricky areas that have traditionally been missed, including the gap between the bottom plate of your wall and the subfloor. (This crack can be sealed with an EPDM gasket installed before the wall is raised, or with caulk or tape after the wall has been raised.)

Conscientious builders often install two air barriers: one on the exterior side of the wall and one on the interior side of the wall.

WHICH TYPE OF WALL IS BEST?

People who are planning to build a home sometimes ask me, "I can't decide between a double-stud wall and a 2×6 wall with exterior rigid foam. Which type of wall is best?" I answer, "Either type of wall works fine. The best type of wall is the one your builder prefers."

What is building science? The simplest definition is the one proposed by William Rose: "The study of the hygrothermal performance of buildings."

Most building scientists are physicists. Aided by engineers, building scientists study how air, heat, and moisture flows affect buildings. Their research and calculations inform designers and builders who need to know how to keep moisture from damaging buildings, how to control air flow in and through buildings, and how to improve the insulation layers that separate the comfortable interiors of our buildings from the mercurial forces of nature outdoors.

2

BUILDING SCIENCE

▶ Do I Need a Vapor Retarder?
Forget Vapor Diffusion—Stop the Air Leaks!
When Sunshine Drives Moisture into Walls
How Risky Is Cold OSB Wall Sheathing?
Monitoring Moisture Levels in Double-Stud Walls

Someday, builders will stop asking this recurring question— but unfortunately, that day has not yet come

Every couple of weeks, someone sends me an e-mail with a description of a proposed wall assembly and an urgent question, "Do I need a vapor retarder?" Energy experts have been answering the same question, repeatedly, for at least 30 years. Of course, even though I sometimes sigh when I read this recurring question, it's still a perfectly good one. The short answer is, If your wall doesn't have a vapor retarder, there is probably no need to worry. Builders worry way too much about vapor diffusion and vapor retarders. It's actually very rare for a building to have a problem caused by vapor diffusion.

WHAT IS WATER VAPOR?

Water vapor is water in a gaseous state— that is, water that has evaporated. It is invisible. It is present in the air we inhale, and (in even greater concentrations) in the air we exhale. When this invisible water vapor moves through building materials, the phenomenon is called vapor diffusion.

In the 1970s and early 1980s, builders were taught that it was important to install a vapor barrier (usually, polyethylene sheeting) on the warm-in-winter side of wall insulation and ceiling insulation. Many textbooks and magazines explained that a vapor barrier was needed to keep the walls dry during the winter, and that walls without vapor barriers would get wet.

This was bad advice, for several reasons. First of all, outward vapor diffusion through walls during winter almost never leads to wet walls. When interior moisture causes moisture damage in walls or ceil-

ings, the problem is almost always due to air leakage (exfiltration), not vapor diffusion. Second, because an interior polyethylene vapor barrier prevents wall assemblies from drying inward during summer, a layer of poly can actually make the wall wetter than it would be without the poly.

WHAT'S THE DIFFERENCE BETWEEN AIR LEAKAGE AND VAPOR DIFFUSION?

Water vapor can diffuse through vapor-permeable materials (for example, gypsum drywall) even when there are no air leakage pathways. If the air on one side of the drywall is hot and humid and the air on the other side of the drywall is dry and cold, the drywall absorbs moisture from the humid side. Once the drywall is damp, some of its moisture evaporates from the other side (the side facing dry air). This process of vapor transport through the drywall is called vapor diffusion. It happens even when the wall assembly is perfectly airtight.

Air leakage is a different phenomenon. If there is a hole in the drywall—at an electrical box, for example—then warm interior air can enter the wall cavity through the hole and escape through cracks in the wall sheathing, especially if there is a strong driving force, like the stack effect or a fan that is pressurizing the house. If the interior air is warm and humid and the wall sheathing is cold, it's possible for some of the moisture in the air to condense on the wall sheathing. (Although this phenomenon is often called condensation, it is more accurately referred to as sorption. What happens is that the cold, dry sheathing becomes damp as the moisture from the indoor air is transferred to the sheathing.) In the typical (somewhat leaky) wall, far more moisture is transported by air leaks than by vapor diffusion.

AIR BARRIERS VS. VAPOR BARRIERS

An air barrier is a material that stops air leakage. A vapor barrier is a material that stops vapor diffusion. Some building materials—for example, insect screening—allow the flow of air and water vapor. Insect screening is neither an air barrier nor a vapor barrier. Other building materials—for example, gypsum drywall or plastic housewrap—are vapor-permeable but are still air barriers.

It's also possible to have a building material—for example, a layer of vapor barrier paint on a leaky plaster wall, or the kraft facing on fiberglass batts—that meets the legal definition for a vapor barrier (or vapor retarder) without being an air barrier. Finally, it's possible to have a building material—for example, polyethylene sheeting with taped seams—that acts as both a vapor barrier and an air barrier.

How did requirements for vapor retarders get enshrined in our building codes?

William Rose, a research architect at the Building Research Council at the University of Illinois, investigated the question of code and vapor retarders and reported his findings in a landmark book, *Water in Buildings* (Wiley, 2005). According to Rose, there were three main players in this drama:

• Larry V. Teesdale, a senior researcher at the USDA Forest Products Laboratory;

• Tyler Stewart Rogers, a Harvard-trained architect; and

• Frank Rowley, a professor of mechanical engineering at the University of Minnesota.

During the 1930s, Teesdale, Rogers, and Rowley each contributed research or published articles that, directly or indirectly, responded to complaints of peeling paint on the exterior of recently insulated buildings. Rose wrote, "When insulation was introduced into wood-frame houses in the late 1920s and early 1930s, the paint began to peel. House painters often refused to paint insulated houses. The painters developed a pithy expression to describe what happens: 'Insulation draws moisture.'"

Insulation manufacturers, insulation contractors, and many researchers (who, because of its obvious benefits, often promoted the increased use of insulation) took exception to the conclusion drawn by these complaining house painters. Rogers was particularly offended by the idea that insulation might make sheathing and siding wetter than they would otherwise be. In a seminal article, "Preventing Condensation in Insulated Structures," published in the March 1938 issue of *Architectural Record*, he wrote, "Architects, owners and research technicians have observed, in recent years, a small but growing number of buildings in which dampness or frost has developed in walls, roofs or attic spaces. Most of these were insulated houses .... The erroneous impression has spread that insulation 'draws' water into the walls and roofs .... Obviously, insulation is not at fault—at least not alone."

Rose's analysis differed from Rogers's, however. Rose wrote, "Does insulation 'draw' moisture? Yes, insulation draws moisture to exterior materials. Insulation lowers the temperature of exterior materials. At the same vapor pressure, lower tem-

CAN I JUST IGNORE VAPOR DIFFUSION?

You can't ignore vapor diffusion totally. There are a few circumstances where builders need to pay attention:

- Vapor diffusion can be a significant moisture transport mechanism in certain rooms with high humidity—for example, greenhouses, rooms with indoor swimming pools, and rooms that are deliberately humidified—especially in a cold climate. If your building includes a greenhouse or indoor pool, get expert advice on your wall and ceiling details before proceeding with the project.

- In a very cold climate (the colder sections of climate Zone 7 as well as Zone 8), the traditional use of interior polyethylene vapor barriers is often beneficial. That said, interior polyethylene can occasionally cause problems even in these climates, especially in buildings that are air-conditioned during summer. When in doubt, a "smart" retarder with variable permeance is always safer than polyethylene.

- When open-cell spray foam is used on the underside of roof sheathing to create an unvented conditioned attic in a cold climate (Zones 5 and colder), outward vapor diffusion during winter can lead to damaging water accumulation in the roof sheathing. For this reason, it's best to use closed-cell spray foam for this application in Zones 5, 6, 7, and 8. If you insist on using open-cell spray foam, it must be protected on the interior with a layer of gypsum wallboard painted with vapor-retarder paint.

- Inward vapor diffusion during summer months can lead to problems in homes that include a "reservoir" siding (for example, brick veneer) and a vapor-permeable sheathing (for example, fiberboard). Details that limit this type of inward vapor drive include the use of rigid foam sheathing and the use of a ventilated rain-screen gap between the siding and sheathing.

- It's important to remember that diffusion can be a builder's friend. During summer, inward vapor diffusion through drywall can help dry a damp wall assembly. That's why the use of materials that limit inward drying, like interior polyethylene and vinyl wallpaper, often leads to problems.

---

peratures means higher relative humidity and higher moisture content. The painters were right. Paint holds more poorly on an insulated building, in general."

Like it or not, physics provides an explanation for the observation that paint doesn't last as long on an insulated building as it does on an uninsulated building. Adding insulation to a wall tends to make the sheathing and siding colder, and cold materials tend to be wetter than warm materials. When siding is cold, it draws moisture from the surrounding (exterior) air; the dampness is a function of its tem-

perature. Rose wrote, "Deciding to insulate has the direct and immediate effect of causing those exterior materials (in cold weather) to be wetter. Historically, those advocating for insulation did not want to be seen as being responsible for additional wetness."

Teesdale, Rogers, and Rowley promoted the idea that siding was getting damp because moisture was traveling through the wall assembly by diffusion from the interior. While this diffusion does occur, the amount of moisture transported via diffusion isn't that significant; the governing factor determining the moisture content of the siding is its temperature, not the rate of diffusion through the wall.

Rose wrote, "They produced prescriptive recommendations that later became code requirements, and these prescriptions embodied the incomplete and biased nature of their analysis . . . . They and their followers left a legacy of consumer fear of ill-defined moisture effects in buildings and of designers assigning excessive importance to prescriptive measures."

The "prescriptive measures" that have caused so many headaches for builders were vapor barrier requirements in building codes. According to Rose's research, in January 1942, the Housing and Home Finance Agency established a requirement for an interior vapor barrier with a minimum permeance rating of 1.25 perm. This requirement was incorporated into the BOCA code—an early residential building code—in 1948.

The building code requirements for vapor barriers were the result of politics and technical errors, not scientific research. Rose wrote, "The authors of the condensation paradigm created a framework, a way of analyzing moisture conditions in buildings, that was distorted. It promoted vapor control, with a prescriptive requirement for vapor barriers in all buildings. At the same time, it masked an important physical principle—how materials at cold temperatures are wetted, and how, once wetted, the possibilities for vapor control mitigation are severely limited."

HOW DO I FIGURE OUT IF A MATERIAL IS VAPOR PERMEABLE?

Published tables listing vapor permeance values for many common building materials are available online. For example, you can search for "Info-500: Build-

ing Materials Property Table" posted on the Building Science Corporation website (buildingscience.com).

Vapor permeance is measured in a lab; the relevant tests are governed by ASTM E96. There are two test procedures described by ASTM E96: procedure A (the dry-cup test) and procedure B (the wet-cup test). The IRC specifies that the permeance of a vapor retarder should be determined by procedure A, not procedure B.

It's fair to say that procedure A measures the vapor permeance of a material when it is dry, procedure B measures the vapor permeance of a material when it is damp. The permeance of many materials (including asphalt felt, plywood, and OSB) is variable: When these materials are dry, they have a relatively low permeance, when they are damp, their permeance rises. (Some people refer to materials with a variable permeance as "smart retarders.")

Is there any reason I have to know the exact perm rating for the materials I use?

You do not have to know the exact perm rating, but it's sometimes useful to know whether a material falls into a broad category—in other words, whether the material is vapor permeable, vapor impermeable, or somewhere in between. To simplify the situation, I'll list a few materials that are considered vapor permeable—that is, with a perm rating over 10 perms. These materials include gypsum drywall, plastic housewrap, fiberglass batts, cellulose insulation, asphalt-impregnated fiberboard sheathing, and 5 in. or less of open-cell spray foam.

Next, let's list examples of materials that are considered Class III vapor retarders — that is, with a perm rating between 1.0 perm and 10 perms. These materials aren't vapor barriers, but they slow down the flow of water vapor somewhat.

Examples include stucco, one or two coats of latex paint, 1 in. of EPS foam insulation, and more than 5 in. of open-cell spray foam. (Note that the greater the thickness of a piece of foam insulation, the lower its permeance.)

The next category is a group of materials that are considered Class II vapor retarders—that is, with a perm rating between 0.1 perm and 1.0 perm. These materials slow down the flow of water vapor to a greater extent than materials that are considered Class III vapor retarders. Examples include plywood, OSB, the kraft facing on fiberglass batts, 1-in.-thick XPS foam insulation, and one coat of vapor retarder paint applied to drywall.

Finally, the most impermeable materials are called Class I vapor retarders or vapor barriers. There materials include glass, sheet metal, aluminum foil, and polyethylene.

THE SHORT VERSION

- Most buildings don't need polyethylene anywhere, except directly under a concrete slab or on a crawl space floor.

- The main reason to install an interior vapor retarder is to keep a building inspector happy.

- If a building inspector wants you to install a layer of interior polyethylene on a wall or ceiling, see if you can convince the inspector to accept a layer of vapor retarder paint or a "smart" retarder (for example, MemBrain or Intello Plus) instead.

- Although most walls and ceilings don't need an interior vapor barrier, it's always a good idea to include an interior air barrier. Air leakage is far more likely to lead to problems than vapor diffusion.

VAPOR RETARDERS AND VAPOR BARRIERS

Answers to persistent questions about vapor diffusion

Although building science has evolved rapidly over the last 40 years, one theme has remained constant: Builders are still confused about vapor barriers. Any energy expert who fields questions from builders will tell you that, year after year, the same questions keep coming up: Does this wall need a vapor barrier? Will foam sheathing trap moisture in my wall? How do I convince my local building inspector that my walls don't need interior poly?

To begin a discussion of vapor retarders and vapor barriers, I'll answer a few of these persistent questions.

Q. Why would I want a vapor retarder in my wall or ceiling?

A. Vapor retarders help slow the diffusion of water vapor through a building assembly. During winter, a vapor retarder on the interior of a wall will slow down the transfer of water vapor from the humid interior of the home into the cool stud bays. During summer, a vapor retarder on the exterior of a wall will slow down the transfer of water vapor from damp siding toward the cool stud bays.

However, a vapor retarder is a double-edged sword: While under some circumstances it can have the beneficial effect of helping keep a wall or ceiling dry, under other circumstances it can have the undesirable effect of preventing a damp wall or ceiling from drying out.

Q. How often does water vapor diffusion through walls and ceilings cause problems?

A. Very rarely. In many cases, in fact, an interior vapor retarder does more harm than good. The most common way for moisture to enter

a wall is from the exterior (usually due to flashing defects that admit wind-driven rain). The second most common way for moisture to energy a wall is by means of air leaks (exfiltration) carrying piggybacking interior moisture that condenses in a wall cavity. Vapor diffusion is a relatively insignificant cause of moisture problems in walls.

Q. Under what circumstances can vapor diffusion cause problems?

A. Although vapor diffusion problems are rare, they can occur. Dangers of vapor diffusion problems are higher:

- In very humid rooms (for example, greenhouses or rooms with an indoor pool).

- In homes with humidifiers.

- In homes located in extremely cold climates.

Even in a home with one of the characteristics listed above, the mechanism for moisture transport into walls and ceilings is much more likely to be air leakage (exfiltration) than vapor diffusion.

Q. What's the difference between a vapor barrier and a vapor retarder?

A. A vapor barrier stops more vapor transmission than a vapor retarder. A vapor barrier is usually defined as a layer with a permeance rating of 0.1 perm or less, while a vapor retarder is usually defined as a layer with permeance greater than 0.1 perm but less than or equal to 1 perm.

Q. What does the code say about vapor retarders?

A. Codes vary; older versions of model building codes often included more sweeping requirements for vapor retarders than more recent versions. The 2006 IRC and the 2006 International Energy Conservation Code® (IECC) both define a vapor retarder as a material having a permeance of 1 perm or less. This definition includes such materials as polyethylene sheeting, aluminum foil, kraft paper facing, and vapor-retarder paint.

In section R318.1, the 2006 IRC requires: "In all framed walls, floors, and roof/ceilings comprising elements of the building thermal envelope, a vapor retarder shall be installed on the warm-in-winter side of the insulation." It should be emphasized that this code requirement makes no mention of poly-ethylene; vapor retarder paint fulfills this code requirement.

The 2006 IRC includes three exceptions to the vapor-retarder requirement. It allows a vapor retarder to be omitted:

- In climate Zones 1 through 4 (an area including most of the West Coast and the South).

- In walls, floors and ceilings made of materials (like concrete) that cannot be damaged by moisture or freezing.

- "Where the framed cavity or space is ventilated to allow moisture to escape"—an apparent (although poorly worded) reference to vented attics and walls with rain-screen siding.

In section 402.5, the 2006 IECC requires: "Above-grade frame walls, floors and ceilings not ventilated to allow moisture to escape shall be provided with an approved vapor retarder. The vapor retarder shall be installed on the warm-in-winter side of the thermal insulation."

In the 2006 IECC, the exceptions to the vapor retarder requirement are very similar to the exceptions listed in the 2006 IRC but with an additional exception: "Where other approved means to avoid condensation are provided." This last exception gives broad latitude to local building officials—and places a heavy burden on any builder intent on convincing a local official that a certain building assembly complies with this exception.

The 2007 supplement to the IRC introduced a new vapor retarder definition. Vapor retarders are now separated into three classes:

- Class I: Less than or equal to 0.1 perm (polyethylene);

- Class II: Greater than 0.1 perm but less than or equal to 1.0 perm (kraft facing);

- Class III: Greater than 1.0 perm but less than or equal to 10 perm (latex paint).

Since 2007, the IRC has required that walls in climate Zones 5 (Nevada, Ohio, Massachusetts), 6 (Vermont, Montana), 7 (northern Minnesota), 8 (northern Alaska), and Marine Zone 4 (western Washington and Oregon) have a Class I or Class II vapor retarder—in other words, a material like kraft facing or polyethylene. This requirement can be found in section R702.7 of the 2012 IRC, which notes three exceptions: Vapor retarders are not required on a basement wall, on the below-grade portion of any wall, or on a wall constructed of materials that cannot be damaged by moisture or freezing.

Further exceptions are allowed in section R702.7.1, which states that in climate zones where a Class I or Class II vapor retarder would normally be required, a less stringent vapor retarder—a Class III retarder like latex paint—can be used under the conditions listed in Table R702.7.1 (an in-depth discussion of this table is on pp. 155–157). Only certain types of wall assemblies are worthy of this exception; they must have either an adequate layer of exterior foam sheathing or "vented cladding"—an undefined phrase that apparently refers to siding installed over a vented rain-screen gap.

Q. Clearly, I can get in trouble with my building inspector if I omit a vapor retarder in certain climates. Are there any situations where the inclusion of a vapor retarder could cause problems?

A. Yes. Although it's perfectly legal to install interior polyethylene or vinyl wallpaper in any climate, these products can lead to moisture and mold problems in most of the United States. Unless you're building in Canada, Alaska, or somewhere close to the Canadian border, you don't want interior polyethylene or vinyl wallpaper—especially in an air-conditioned house.

Interior polyethylene and vinyl wallpaper prevent a wall from drying to the interior during summer, when inward solar vapor drive (a phenomenon associated with so-called reservoir claddings—for example, brick veneer and stucco—that absorb and hold moisture) can cause condensation on the exterior side of the wallpaper or poly. Unless the moisture introduced into the wall by inward solar vapor drive is able to dry to the interior, wall damage can result.

Q. When it comes to vapor retarders, what do the experts recommend?

A. Here's a sampling of statements by leading building scientists on the subject of vapor retarders:

- Anton TenWolde: "In practice it doesn't matter what the permeance of the vapor retarder is, because the air leakage will go around it for moisture transfer. I came to the conclusion that the idea that we need a vapor barrier to keep our walls dry doesn't hold a lot of water, so to speak."

- John Straube: "The whole reason we're talking about vapor barriers is not because vapor diffusion control is so important, but because people believe it is so important. The question comes up, have we seen diffusion-related building failures? And the answer is, very few—maybe in rooms with a swimming pool. Assuming that the vapor came from the inside, you would have to have a very high load before you would see a problem. I think that solar-driven vapor is much more important. The moisture is coming from the other side of the assembly."

- Joseph Lstiburek: "In North Carolina, for whatever reason, they build their walls with fiberglass insulation and with poly on the inside. Depending on the cladding—brick and stucco being the worst—the walls rot like crazy."

- Achilles Karagiozis: "It's all related—the vapor control strategy, airtightness, and whether or not there is a ventilation cavity behind the exterior cladding. If you have a ventilation cavity behind the cladding, it doesn't matter what kind of vapor retarder strategy you use."

- Bill Rose: "In the South, no vapor barrier. In the North, as long as you have insulated sheathing that meets the dew-point test, also no vapor barrier."

- Anton TenWolde: "When you put enough foam sheathing on the wall you get away from the cliff rapidly, and there's no reason to worry about vapor barriers anymore."

Building codes are finally beginning to recognize that air barriers matter more than vapor barriers

While building codes have historically shown a curious and unjustified obsession with vapor barriers, they have (until recent years) almost entirely ignored the need for air barriers. Unfortunately, this means that code officials got it exactly backward.

These days, things are looking up, and codes are belatedly beginning to address the need for residential air barriers. In section 402.4.2, the 2009 IECC required for the first time that some new homes be tested with a blower door test. (Under this version of the code, builders who don't want to arrange for blower door testing can instead comply with new air-sealing requirements by an alternate method that requires visual inspection of 17 areas known to contribute to air leakage.)

The 2012 IRC and IECC ratcheted up airtightness requirements. Blower door testing became mandatory and more stringent; the 2009 threshold of 7 ACH50 was changed to 5 ACH50 for climate Zones 1 and 2, and 3 ACH50 for homes in all other zones. The 2012 code requires builders to comply with both the checklist requirements in Table R402.4.1.1 and the requirement to conduct a blower door test.

So we're now in an interesting period of transition. Pressured by building scientists to eliminate nonsensical vapor retarder provisions, code officials have partially relented by expanding the climate zones where vapor retarders can be omitted and by providing more flexible ways to comply with vapor retarder requirements in cold climates. At the same time, code officials are taking steps toward logical air-sealing requirements. If this welcome trend continues, we may see increasingly stringent airtightness standards and the eventual elimination of vapor retarder requirements.

LOOKING BACK AT OLDER CODES

Builders with gray hairs may remember the early 1990s, before the advent of the international codes. Today's IRC was adapted from its precursor, a regional model code known at the CABO (Council of American Building Officials) One- and Two-Family Dwelling Code. I recently pulled out my copy of the 1992 CABO code to refresh my memory on the book's requirements. Back then, vapor retarder requirements were almost identical to those in the 2006 IRC. Like the 2006 IRC, the 1992 CABO required a vapor retarder rated at 1.0 perm or less on the warm-in-winter side of thermal insulation in walls, floors, and ceilings. (The exception for hot, humid climates was fairly limited.)

As far as I can determine, the 1992 CABO included no requirements whatsoever for air sealing—no section comparable to section N1102.4 in the 2006 IRC, which requires that "the building thermal envelope shall be durably sealed to limit infiltration." Although the 1992 code required the use of asphalt-saturated felt as a WRB under some types of siding, including brick veneer and shingles, the code specifically noted that no asphalt felt was required under horizontal fiberboard siding or wood bevel siding (clapboard).

Interestingly, code requirements for duct tightness predate code requirements for envelope air sealing measures. The 1992 CABO not only required ducts to be designed according to Manual D but also required that "joints of duct systems shall be substantially airtight by means of tapes, mastics, gasketing, or other means." Unfortunately, these requirements—just like similar requirements in the current versions of the IRC—were rarely enforced.

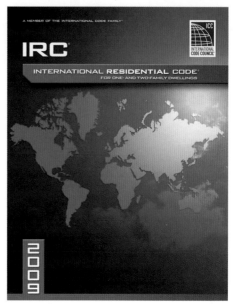

SLOWLY MOVING in the right direction. Recent versions of model building codes have loosened vapor retarder requirements and tightened air-barrier requirements. Older versions of the code were unjustifiably obsessed with vapor retarders and silent on air barriers.

Because of inward solar vapor drive, vapor diffusion from the outside inward is often more worrisome than vapor diffusion from the inside outward—so you need a good vapor control strategy

uilders have worried about wintertime vapor diffusion ever since 1938, when Tyler Stewart Rogers published an influential article on condensation in the *Architectural Record*. Rogers's article, "Preventing Condensation in Insulated Structures," included this advice: "A vapor barrier undoubtedly should be employed on the warm side of any insulation as the first step in minimizing condensation." Rogers's recommendation was eventually incorporated into most model building codes, and was considered dogma for over 40 years. Eventually, though, building scientists discovered that interior vapor barriers were causing more problems than they were solving.

Interior vapor barriers are rarely necessary because wintertime vapor diffusion rarely leads to problems in walls or ceilings. A different phenomenon—summertime vapor diffusion—turns out to be a far more serious matter.

SOMETHING IS ROTTEN IN DENMARK

During the 1990s, summertime vapor diffusion began to wreak havoc with hundreds of North American homes. This epidemic in rotting walls was brought on by two changes in building practice: The first was the widespread adoption of air-conditioning, while the second was one unleashed by Rogers himself: the use of interior polyethylene vapor barriers.

Rogers conceived of interior vapor barriers as a defense against the diffusion of water vapor from the interior of a home into cold wall cavities. Rogers failed to foresee that these vapor barriers would eventually be cooled by air-conditioning —thereby turning into condensing surfaces that began dripping water into walls during the summer.

ZARING HOMES GOES BANKRUPT

As with many scientific discoveries, it took a series of disasters to fully illuminate the phenomenon of summertime vapor diffusion. One early victim of this type of diffusion was Cincinnati builder Zaring Homes. In the mid-1990s, Zaring Homes was a thriving midsize builder that completed over 1,500 new homes a year. But the company's expansion plans came to a screeching halt in 1999 when dozens of its structures developed mold and extensive rot.

The first signs of the disaster surfaced in July 1999, when homeowners at Zaring's Parkside development in Mason, OH, first began complaining of wet carpets. These moisture problems emerged only 10 weeks after the first residents moved in to the new neighborhood. When inspection holes were cut into the drywall, workers discovered 1/4 in. of standing water in the bottom of the stud cavities. "We were able to wring water out of the fiberglass insulation," said Stephen Vamosi, a consulting architect at Intertech Design in Cincinnati.

problems would probably cost $60,000 to $70,000 per home. It was a spectacular failure, and they are out of business."

INWARD SOLAR VAPOR DRIVE PROBLEMS REQUIRE FOUR ELEMENTS

The phenomenon that destroyed Zaring's walls came to be known as inward solar vapor drive. The classic disaster requires four elements:

- A "reservoir" cladding—that is, siding that can hold significant amounts of water.
- Permeable wall sheathing like Celotex or Homasote®.
- A polyethylene vapor barrier on the interior of the wall.
- An air-conditioned interior.

Reservoir claddings include brick veneer, stucco, manufactured stone, fiber-cement siding, and (to a lesser extent) wood siding. Although wall failures with permeable sidings like Celotex are particularly spectacular, inward solar vapor drive is also a factor in the failure of walls sheathed with less permeable types of sheathing, especially OSB. Problems with inward solar vapor drive show up first on elevations that get the most sun exposure; north walls are usually immune to the problem.

Whenever a wall separates environments at different temperatures and moisture conditions, the direction of the vapor drive is from the hot, moist side toward the cool, dry side. After a soaking rainstorm, the sun eventually comes out to bake the damp siding. When it comes to driving vapor, the sun is a powerful motor.

The heat of the sun easily drives the moisture in damp siding through housewrap and permeable wall sheathing. The first cold surface that the vapor encounters is usually the polyethylene behind the dry-

FORGETTING THE AIR SPACE behind the bricks didn't help. After only 10 weeks of occupancy, some new homes built by Zaring of Cincinnati were so wet that most of the brick veneer, sheathing, insulation, and drywall had to be removed and demolished. A portion of the defective walls were sheathed with Celotex fiberboard, which is so vapor-permeable that moisture held in the brick veneer was easily driven into the wall cavity when sun shone on the bricks.

Consultants concluded that water vapor was being driven inward from the damp brick veneer through permeable fiber-board wall sheathing (Celotex®). During the summer months, when the homes at Parkside were all air-conditioned, moisture was condensing on the back of the polyethylene sheeting installed behind the drywall.

"Zaring Homes went out of business because they had a $20 to $50 million liability," explained building scientist Joseph Lstiburek. "Hundreds of homes were potentially involved. To fix the

AVOIDING PROBLEMS CAUSED BY INWARD SOLAR VAPOR DRIVE

If the components of a wall assembly are poorly chosen, as they clearly were at the Parkside development built by Zaring Homes, there may be no faster mechanism for destroying a house than inward solar vapor drive. After only 10 weeks of occupancy, some of the Zaring homes were so wet that most of the brick veneer, sheathing, insulation, and drywall had to be removed and demolished.

But once you understand inward solar vapor drive, it's relatively easy to choose building details to avoid problems. Here are a variety of ways to reduce risks; of course, you'll probably need to adopt only one or at most two of the following measures to avoid problems.

- Never include interior polyethylene or vinyl wallpaper in an air-conditioned home. If your building inspector insists on a vapor retarder that comes in a roll, choose a smart retarder like MemBrain.

- Avoid high-permeance sheathings like Homasote or Celotex. Instead, specify foam sheathing—especially behind brick veneer, stucco, or manufactured stone.

- Homes with asphalt felt experience fewer problems with inward solar vapor drive than homes with plastic housewrap.

- Consider the use of a WRB that is impermeable to water vapor. The best-known vapor-impermeable WRB is Delta®-Dry, which is made of stiff high-density polyethylene formed into a 5/16-in.-thick egg-carton configuration. The three-dimensional WRB creates two air spaces: one between the siding and the WRB and the other between the WRB and the sheathing. Unlike high-permeance housewraps, Delta-Dry depends on air movement (ventilation) to dry the gap between it and the sheathing.

- Walls with a rain-screen gap between the siding and the sheathing experience much less inward moisture transfer than walls without a gap.

- Ventilated rain-screen gaps are more effective at limiting inward moisture transfer than unventilated gaps.

- More vapor drive problems occur in homes with dark-colored siding than light-colored siding.

- When specifying stucco, choose a traditional stucco formulation without modern polymeric admixtures because stuccos with these admixtures dry much more slowly than traditional stucco formulations.

- Choose a siding (like vinyl siding) that is not a moisture reservoir.

wall. That's where the moisture condenses; it runs down the poly and pools at the bottom of the wall cavity. It doesn't take long before mold begins to grow and the walls begin to rot.

MOISTURE AND TEMPERATURE PROBES CONFIRM THE PHENOMENON

Data from a 2003–2004 wall-drying study by building scientists John Straube, Eric Burnett, and Randy Van Staaten confirmed the phenomenon of inward solar vapor drive. "Inward vapor drive redistributes moisture quite dramatically," said Straube. "Some people have said, 'Summer condensation on the interior does not occur.' But summer condensation does happen, even in Ottawa."

For decades, builders have worried about vapor diffusion into walls from the indoors during winter. But if a home has air-conditioning, vapor diffusion into walls from the outdoors is a much bigger problem.

AIR-CONDITIONING COOLED the polyethylene. Polyethylene vapor barriers should never be used on the interior of an air-conditioned home. During summer, moisture driven into a wall by inward solar vapor drive can easily condense on the back of the cold poly.

The thicker the wall, the colder the sheathing. If you build a very thick wall, will your sheathing stay cold and wet?

During the winter months, wall sheathing is usually cold. Cold sheathing is risky because it tends to accumulate moisture during the winter. Unless the sheathing can dry out during the summer months, damp sheathing can rot.

Cold sheathing can get wet from two directions. It can get wet from the exterior, due to leaks through defective flashing or a poorly detailed WRB. It can also get wet on the interior, due to a phenomenon traditionally called condensation, but more accurately called sorption. (As building scientist William Rose likes to say, "Capillary materials do not exhibit condensation at the dew point.")

Most wood-framed walls are somewhat leaky. Interior air can leak into wall cavities through cracks around electrical boxes and cracks between the drywall and the wall's bottom plate. When the warm air reaches the cold wall sheathing, one of two things usually happens: Frost can form on the sheathing or, at temperatures above freezing, the sheathing (which is hygroscopic or sorptive) can gain moisture from the air. (The source of the moisture taken on by sorption can be either interior or exterior.)

WHY DOESN'T EVERY COLD-CLIMATE WALL HAVE ROTTEN SHEATHING?

Most cold-climate homes have wall sheathing that gains moisture every winter. Usually, however, the wall sheathing doesn't rot because (1) wood doesn't rot when it's cold, and (2) the sheathing dries out every summer.

Building components can survive occasional wetting, as long as the rate of drying exceeds the rate of wetting. If, on an annual basis, the wall dries more than it gets wet, it will probably be OK. Probably—but not necessarily. In many areas of the United States, OSB-sheathed walls have failed at an alarming rate. A combination of factors—poorly installed WRBs, air leaks through drywall, and the use of claddings (like stucco) that dry very slowly—have caused the OSB on thousands of homes to turn to oatmeal.

Even if the builder gets all the details right, there are still a few reasons to worry about new OSB-sheathed walls, especially if the wall is unusually thick. These days, builders are experimenting with thicker and thicker walls. In some parts of the United States and Canada, an increasing percentage of new homes have double 2×4 walls that are 12 in. thick—a design that makes the OSB sheathing colder than ever.

At least in theory, there are two reasons thick walls are riskier than thin walls:

• Thicker insulation makes the OSB slightly colder—admittedly, less than 2 F° colder in most cases, but colder nevertheless—and therefore slightly wetter.

• Thicker insulation means that less heat is flowing through the wall to help dry the OSB when it does get wet.

"By doubling the R-value of the wall, we get half the energy available from the interior to drive the evaporation from wet wood," explained building scientist John Straube, a principal at the Building Science Corporation.

LOWERING THE RISK FACTORS

What factors make walls riskier?

Air leaks are bad. Leaks that allow interior air to enter a wall cavity are obviously risky because these leaks allow moisture to piggyback on the exfiltrating air. So it's important to create an air-tight wall.

Air-permeable insulation is risky. Fiberglass batts do little to slow air movement. Switching from fiberglass batts to dense-packed cellulose raises the risk slightly (by keeping the sheathing colder), but more important on balance, it lowers the risk by reducing the chance of air movement through the insulation.

The thicker the wall, the colder the sheathing. The thicker the insulation on the interior side of the OSB, the colder the OSB. If you build a double 2×4 wall with a total thickness of 12 in., you've made your sheathing colder than it used to be.

Sheathing temperature matters. Colder sheathing is at greater risk than warmer sheathing. (To quote Rose again: "Cold, wet. Warm, dry.") The more insulation you have on the exterior side of your sheathing—and the less insulation you have on the interior side of your sheathing—the warmer (and therefore dryer) your sheathing will stay. So an easy way to reduce the risk that your OSB sheathing will accumulate moisture is to install rigid foam on the exterior side of the sheathing. That keeps the sheathing warm. However, the foam also reduces the ability of the sheathing to dry to the exterior, so it's important to be sure that the foam is thick enough to keep the sheathing above the dew point during winter. Thick foam is better than thin

foam because thick foam keeps OSB or plywood sheathing warm and dry.

Rain-screen gaps are good. If there's a reason to believe your sheathing is getting damp every winter, you want to be sure that it can dry quickly during summer. One way to encourage faster drying: Include a ventilated rain-screen gap between the sheathing and the siding. That reduces the risk of rot.

Avoid OSB. OSB is more susceptible to rot than plywood. So if you're worried about the durability of your sheathing, choose plywood (or diagonal board sheathing) over OSB. Other possible (vapor-permeable) sheathing choices include structural fiberboard sheathing, which is available from International Bildrite® and Georgia-Pacific®, or DensGlass® gold.

Get your flashing details right. Although it should go without saying, remember to install proper flashing at all wall penetrations, windows, and doors, and remember to integrate your wall flashing with the WRB. Upper courses of your WRB should be properly lapped over lower courses.

JOHN STRAUBE'S ADVICE

After I mulled the issues raised here, I sent an e-mail to Straube, asking him about the riskiness of using OSB on a very thick double-stud wall and about whether my advice is on target. Straube's answer follows.

"We don't know the full significance of this question, but the basic physics of wood and humidity tells us that OSB sheathing on a thick wall is risky, and experience has shown us that it is risky. By risky, I mean riskier than historical practice.

"Anything we can do to reduce risk is therefore good. A major improvement is adding a ventilated gap over the sheath-

If you're planning to build a double-stud wall, you may want to switch from OSB sheathing to plywood sheathing. Because cold sheathing can accumulate moisture, be sure to include a ventilated rain-screen gap to encourage drying.

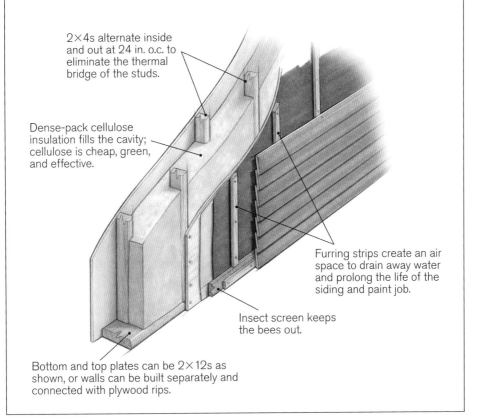

2×4s alternate inside and out at 24 in. o.c. to eliminate the thermal bridge of the studs.

Dense-pack cellulose insulation fills the cavity; cellulose is cheap, green, and effective.

Furring strips create an air space to drain away water and prolong the life of the siding and paint job.

Insect screen keeps the bees out.

Bottom and top plates can be 2×12s as shown, or walls can be built separately and connected with plywood rips.

ing: This allows for much better control of rain moisture (biggest concern) and encourages drying of the sheathing (particularly useful for air leakage condensation moisture). Switching to plywood adds more safety by further increasing the ability of interior moisture to dry outward.

"Your advice is good. I would differ by letting people know that it is more important to ventilate than switching from OSB to plywood—but both together are powerful allies.

"The presence of cellulose (rather than fiberglass batts) in the cavity is very help-ful as it reduces any air leaks, stops convection loops, and add moisture storage and mold resistance (via borate).

"So, when you add the three components—ventilated cladding, plywood, and dense-packed cellulose—you have reduced risk tremendously. Are you back to the same safety that we had in the past? I don't know. I don't think so—but you're likely really close.

"All of this assumes you have done a good job on the air barrier (tighter is better of course) and that rain control is managed (window subsill flashing, etc.)."

Is there any evidence that double-stud walls have damp sheathing?

Most wood-framed buildings have no insulation on the exterior side of the wall sheathing. That means that the wall sheathing gets cold and wet during the winter. Whether this common situation is a problem depends on whom you talk to. Monitoring studies show that the moisture content of the OSB or plywood sheathing on some homes with 2×6 walls rises in February (especially on the north side of the house); fortunately, however, the sheathing dries out in March or April. As long as the sheathing stays dry for most of the year, it can usually endure a few weeks at an elevated moisture content without developing mold or rot. In most cases, sheathing won't rot as long as the wall's drying rate exceeds its wetting rate on an annual basis.

Not all builders are comfortable with this analysis, however. Some builders prefer to install rigid foam or mineral wool insulation on the exterior side of their wall sheathing, to keep the OSB or plywood above the dew point during winter. Warm sheathing is dry and happy, so installing an adequate thickness of exterior rigid foam is one possible solution to cold sheathing worries. (The extreme version of this approach is called PERSIST. PERSIST homes put all of the wall insulation—usually rigid foam—on the exterior side of the wall sheathing, and leave the stud bays empty.)

In theory, a very thick wall with lots of insulation on the interior side of the wall sheathing—for example, a double-stud wall—is riskier than an ordinary 2×6 wall, because the high-R insulation reduces heat flow through the wall, making the sheathing colder and wetter than ever. Some hygrothermal modeling programs, including WUFI®, show that wall sheathing on a 12-in.-thick double-stud wall insulated with cellulose can have an elevated moisture content under certain conditions. (The sheathing moisture content shown by WUFI varies, of course, depending on the inputs made by the software user; variables include inputs for climate, wall orientation, and the interior relative humidity.)

DOUBLE-STUD WALLS.
Builders looking for affordable R-40 walls are increasingly turning to double-stud walls insulated with dense-packed cellulose. The only fly in the ointment for this type of wall assembly concerns allegations that double-stud walls may have damp sheathing in cold climates.

COLD SHEATHING WARNINGS

These computer modeling results have made some builders and designers nervous. Here are samples of warnings about cold sheathing on double-stud walls:

• The Building Science Corporation website warns that a highly insulated double-stud wall "will work in extreme climates, but still has significant risks to moisture related durability issues and premature enclosure failure."

• Jesse Thompson, an architect in Portland, Maine, posted the following comment on a GBA forum: "A double-stud wall with any type of batt insulation is a high-risk wall system in a cold climate, due to the cold sheathing issue."

• A Building America study that used WUFI to model several high-R walls noted, "Previous hygrothermal modeling conducted by CARB [Consortium for Advanced Residential Buildings] and others of high R-value walls has indicated a serious potential for moisture damage to the wood sheathing if located on the exterior of the wall just beneath the cladding, especially in cold, moist climates."

Having read these warnings for years, I set out to answer an important question, Are these warnings based on actual measurements of the moisture content of installed sheathing or are they based only on computer modeling?

MODELING STUDIES SHOW WORRISOME MOISTURE LEVELS

One modeling study that included somewhat worrisome findings, "Moisture Research—Optimizing Wall Assemblies," was authored by Lois Arena and Pallavi Mantha. Arena and Mantha both work at Steven Winter Associates in Norwalk, CT, where Arena is a senior building systems engineer and Mantha is a building sys-

tems analyst. Most of the research conducted by Arena and Mantha is funded by the U.S. Department of Energy, through its Building America program.

Some of the researchers' findings sound alarming. Arena and Mantha used WUFI to calculate the moisture content of several components of various wall assemblies, including 12-in.-thick cellulose insulated walls. The researchers wrote, "Results from WUFI indicate that condensation potential for the double [stud] cellulose walls is extremely high because the OSB in those wall assemblies is entirely outside of the insulation."

Delving deeper, I realized that some of their warnings rested on a shaky foundation. The authors noted, "WUFI offers several different methods for generating interior temperature and RH [relative humidity] levels. For this study, the interior conditions for all three wall types were generated using the ASHRAE 160-2009 method.

"It should be noted that, in all climates, the interior RH levels predicted by this method reach 90% even though cooling was assumed. Using these interior conditions, WUFI predicts that there is the potential for mold growth on the interior surface of the drywall in all climates. Realistically, we know that this is not true."

WHAT IS ASHRAE 160?

ASHRAE 160 is a published standard that provides moisture design loads for those who perform hygrothermal modeling. These design loads are similar in principle to design loads used by mechanical engineers. Among the design loads in the standard are a set of "design indoor conditions" that (for example) establish the amount of moisture that modelers should assume is generated by a building's occupants.

For some reason, the ASHRAE 160 values used by Arena and Mantha produced unlikely WUFI results. Arena and Mantha wrote, "Further research into the appropriateness of the ASHRAE 160-2009 interior conditions in moist climates is needed. Interior relative humidity levels generated with this method are higher than recorded in actual studies and result in overly pessimistic predictions for mold growth on the interior of the assembly. Considering that almost every wall in this study failed the ASHRAE 30-day criteria, it is recommended that this threshold be reevaluated by industry professionals."

Here's the translation: The modeling results don't pass the sniff test. Arena and Mantha clearly recognized that fact, and they accurately deduced that the anomalies stem from their use of the ASHRAE 160 values.

To find out how these unexpected WUFI results may have occurred, I spoke with Anton TenWolde, the building scientist who helped develop ASHRAE 160. TenWolde explained that the indoor moisture values first published in ASHRAE 160 needed to be tweaked. "We already fixed this," TenWolde told me. "We have passed and published three addenda to the standard since the original publication. The indoor relative humidity is now capped at 70%. The standard is under continuous maintenance. We felt it was the best possible standard at the time of publication, but it was by no means perfect."

TenWolde pointed out that the developers of the standard lack good data on indoor moisture levels. "When you look for the numbers on moisture generation in residences, you find that they are not there. All of the numbers floating around for the last 40 or 50 years are probably too high. It's also important to remember that this is a design standard, so conditions are not average conditions. They are extreme conditions, and they are supposed to be extreme. You can't use averages for design, because it's not the average house that fails."

Because the ASHRAE 160 conditions used in the WUFI modeling performed by Arena and Mantha were flawed, the WUFI results from that study shouldn't be used to make design decisions. Instead, it's worth looking at data from monitoring studies of real walls. Fortunately, we're beginning to get results from a few field studies of double-stud walls insulated with cellulose.

MONITORING RESULTS FROM FIELD STUDIES

From September 2007 to March 2009, Andy Shapiro, an energy consultant from Montpelier, VT, monitored the moisture content of the sheathing on a double-stud wall in Vermont. The walls were 12 in. thick and insulated with cellulose. The house had a single occupant and was equipped with an HRV.

One thing about the house was unusual: It had diagonal board sheathing rather than OSB or plywood sheathing. "The house was sheathed with rough-cut local lumber in random widths—a mix of hemlock, fir, and pine," Shapiro told me. "The siding was white cedar shiplap over Tyvek Drain Wrap™, which is very vapor-open. The interior was finished with painted gypsum wallboard with no interior vapor barrier."

The sheathing moisture content was higher during the winter months than Shapiro expected. In February and March of 2009, Shapiro recorded moisture content levels over 30% in two locations.

"The data aren't complete," Shapiro told me. "These measurements are really snapshots in time. But they are real moisture measurements. I chatted with John Straube about this, and given that this house has a moisture-open exterior, we're not worried. But if we had the same readings with OSB sheathing, we'd be worried."

MONITORING DATA COLLECTED BY LOIS ARENA

In addition to co-authoring a paper on the use of WUFI modeling on high-R walls, Lois Arena has been monitoring the performance of some double-stud walls at a residential project in Devens, MA. Some of Arena's data were reported in the September 2013 issue of *Energy Design Update*. Intrigued by the data, I called Arena and asked her to share up-to-date information from the monitoring study.

The monitored wall is an R-40 double-stud wall insulated with cellulose. The OSB-sheathed walls are clad with vinyl siding, and the interior finish is gypsum wallboard painted with a 0.5-perm vapor-retarder primer.

The research team installed temperature, RH, and moisture content sensors in a variety of locations in two stud bays—one on the south side of the house, and one on the north. "The OSB on the north wall is now down to a moisture content under 10%," Arena told me in October 2013. "In February, it was up to around 20%, but it came down to 10% in mid-April. The time at 20% was brief, and it doesn't sound too alarming to me. I like the fact that the walls are drying out."

According to Arena, one reason the sheathing dried quickly in the spring was the fact that the cladding (vinyl siding) is well ventilated. I asked her, "Would you agree that builders don't have to worry about the integrity of the OSB sheathing on a double-stud wall as long as the wall has a ventilated rain-screen gap?" She answered, "That's exactly right."

WHAT MOISTURE LEVELS ARE CONCERNING?

Before reviewing the field study data, it's worth discussing how wet sheathing can get before we should be concerned about the possibility of mold or rot.

Mold or fungi won't grow on wood unless its moisture content is above 20%—a level that corresponds to 80% to 90% RH—so that is the moisture content level that usually sets off alarm bells for researchers (especially if the 20% moisture content level occurs during summer, when temperatures are warm).

Decay won't set in unless the wood has a moisture content greater than 28% and unless temperatures are above 23°F. (Decay is quite slow when temperatures drop below 50°F.)

KOHTA UENO'S DATA

At a another house in the same residential development in Devens—at a house built by Carter Scott—a different research team is conducting a similar monitoring study. Kohta Ueno of the Building Science Corporation now has two years of data on several high-R walls, including a 12-in.-thick double-stud wall insulated with cellulose. Like Arena's research, Ueno's research is funded by the Building America program.

Some of Ueno's data were reported in a *Fine Homebuilding* article called "The Future of Housing in America." The article noted, "Twelve-in.-thick double-stud walls with cellulose insulation and [walls] with low-density foam were tested. In the stud bay insulated with cellulose, the moisture content of the sheathing on the north side of the house spiked to 28% in the winter. That's high enough to raise concerns about mold and rot. In the summer, though, it dried out to 8%, and given that cellulose is treated with borates, no one seems too concerned."

Ueno's data (like Arena's) show that south walls stay dryer than north walls. When I spoke to Ueno, he told me, "The first winter, the cellulose wall peaked at 20% to 25% moisture content. Those are the numbers for the north walls; the south walls were boring. For a few months over the winter the moisture content was high, then everything dried over the summer. Everything in all three monitored walls dropped over the summer to 10% to 12%."

The moisture content of the OSB sheathing monitored by Ueno is somewhat higher than the values measured by Arena. Ueno told me, "One of the key differences between the walls we're monitoring and the ones that Lois Arena is monitoring is that there is vapor retarder paint on her wall, while we're using straight-up latex paint."

I asked Ueno whether he thought the moisture spikes during winter were cause for concern. "I don't think it's an issue," he answered. "As Mark Bomberg says, 'We measure the moisture content of wood during the winter but it rots during the summer.' Everything was drying down by March. During the second winter of this study, the house was occupied by a family of four, and they didn't have the ventilation system running. The system was not hooked up correctly. So the interior RH was 40% to 50% during the first half of the winter. Later, after the exhaust fan was fixed, the RH came down to 30% for the second half of the winter. All of the walls on the north side had a high moisture content for a few months. But by the end of September, were back down to 10% to 12%."

JOHN STRAUBE'S DATA

To complete my roundup of monitoring data, I telephoned John Straube, a professor of building envelope science at the University of Waterloo in Ontario. Straube was happy to discuss his research.

"We're doing a study now," Straube told me. "We've got a test house here in Waterloo. The climate zone is similar to Burlington, Vermont. The interior humidity is kept between 30% and 40% in the wintertime. We're testing a variety of walls, all with OSB sheathing: a typical 2×6 wall, a 2×6 wall with 3 in. of exterior Roxul®, one with 2½ in. of exterior XPS, one with 2 in. of foil-faced polyiso, a 9½-in.-thick I-joist wall, and a 12-in.-thick double-stud wall insulated with cellulose. All the walls have Tyvek, furring strips, and fiber-cement siding. The study is entering its third winter."

Straube's measurements are similar to those made by other researchers. "The sheathing moisture content on the double-stud wall exceeds 20% in March, then hits a peak of 31% on the 26th of March," he told me. "It dips below 20% in the middle of April."

The walls with insulation on the exterior side of the sheathing are faring better than the double-stud wall. Straube posed a rhetorical question: "Maybe you're wondering, What is the moisture content of the sheathing on the walls with exterior XPS in February and March? Well, it's 8%."

One of Straube's colleagues, Trevor Trainor, provided further information on the researchers' protocol. "The peak moisture content levels occurred during a period of intentional, controlled air exfiltration," Trainor explained. "We intentionally injected interior air into the walls at a rate that we determined as a realistic natural air leakage rate for a building that meets Canadian Energy Star standards (0.2 cfm per square foot at 50 Pascals). We used a rate of 40 CFH per 4-ft. by 8-ft. wall panel (the equivalent of 0.2 L/sec/m^2). Depending on the geometry of the house, this roughly translates to 2.5 ACH50."

Trainor added, "Obviously a house that is significantly tighter than this should perform better—depending on the distribution of the leakage."

WHAT DO THESE MEASUREMENTS MEAN?

To understand whether the moisture spikes seen in double-stud wall sheathing are worrisome, it's useful to compare these measurements with the moisture content of OSB sheathing on ordinary 2×6 walls. "With an ordinary 2×6 wall, the moisture content of the OSB never gets as high as it does with these double-stud walls," Straube told me. "On a north wall in a humid climate, it might reach the high teens, but not the low 20s."

When researchers interpret data from double-stud wall studies, they often frame the conversation using a good news/bad news format. "We know that actually most of our wood products are surprisingly resilient," said Straube. "But these monitoring results show that we are right on the edge between risky and where we would be safe. These elevated moisture contents are lasting for several weeks to two months, depending on the study, into April. And in April, the sheathing may be at 50°. That is right in the zone where you might get a problem, though it might take years for the problem to manifest itself. It's in the gray zone."

Should builders worry? "The monitoring studies say that these double-stud walls are on the edge, not obvious failures," said Straube. "After all, where are the bodies? The failures happen only when we have a leaky window or an air leak or badly managed construction moisture."

The message for builders of double-stud walls is simple: Don't screw up the details. "These walls are on the edge," said Straube. "What that means is you don't have a lot of room to move when it comes to making mistakes. When I compare a double-stud wall to a wall with 3 in. of exterior rock wool or 2 in. of extruded polystyrene, I find more risk."

Straube advised, "Build a simple box with ventilated cladding, and do a good job with airtightness. Those are strategies to reduce the risk. Choose a sheathing that is more vapor-permeable than OSB—plywood, fiberboard, or DensGlass gold."

3

ENERGY MODELING

W hat's a good way for designers to get a ballpark estimate of future energy bills? One way is to look at the utility bills of a comparable nearby home. In most cases, though, energy use estimates are calculated using energy-modeling software.

Some energy-modeling programs can be downloaded for free, while others cost thousands of dollars. In general, you get what you pay for, but some free software programs are actually pretty good. However, no energy modeling program, whether free or expensive, will deliver meaningful information unless the user provides accurate inputs and understands the program's limitations.

Don't confuse energy and power—it's important to know the difference between Btu and Btu/hr, as well as kw and kwh

If you've ever been confused by the difference between 500 Btu and 500 Btu/hr, you probably could use a handy cheat sheet to explain energy units. As a guide through the thorny thickets of energy, power, and the units used to measure them, I've assembled some questions and attempted to answer them.

WHAT'S THE DIFFERENCE BETWEEN ENERGY AND POWER?

Energy is the amount of heat or work that can be obtained by burning a certain amount of fuel. Energy is measured in a variety of units, including kilowatt-hours (kwh), Btu, and joules. A quantity of energy can also be expressed in terms of barrels of oil, gallons of gasoline, or cords of firewood.

A unit of energy can be bought or sold. For example, electricity is usually sold by the kilowatt-hour. Your electric bill includes a monthly tally of the number of kilowatt-hours you used. If you are charged $80 for 800 kwh, then each unit costs you 10 cents.

A Btu (British thermal unit) is the amount of heat necessary to raise 1 pound of water by 1 F°. A joule is the work done by a force of 1 newton for a distance of 1 meter.

Power is different from energy. Power is the *rate* at which energy is burned or used (or, more precisely, the rate at which energy is converted from one form to another). In other words, power is a measure of how quickly work can be performed;

Power = Energy/Time, and Energy = Power × Time. Power is measured in watts, kilowatts, horsepower, Btu/hr, tons of cooling, and foot-pounds/minute.

Appliances are usually rated by their power consumption. When we talk about a 100-watt light bulb, we are describing it by its power rating. Furnaces also have power ratings—for example, a furnace can be rated at 40,000 Btu/hr. If the power rating is high, the appliance uses energy at a fast rate; if the power rating is low, it uses energy at a slow rate. So we can say that a 20-hp tractor is more powerful than a 12-hp tractor; we can also say that a 2,000-watt hairdryer is more powerful than a 1,000-watt hairdryer.

If you turn on a 1,000-watt hairdryer for 1 hour, you've used a kilowatt-hour. While it's possible to buy a kilowatt-hour, you can't buy a kilowatt.

When dealing with electricity, Power (in watts) = Current (in amperes) × Voltage. One watt is the power from a current of 1 amp flowing through 1 volt. (An ampere is the unit used to measure the flow of electricity, or current. Amperes measure the rate of electron flow.)

Can you provide some analogies to clarify these energy units?

Yes, I can provide an analogy. Here's one: Energy is a measurable quantity and can therefore be compared to distance. In this analogy, power (which is a rate) is like speed.

I especially like plumbing analogies, because I was a plumber before I was an electrician. If you are comparing electricity to piped water, here's how the analogy works:

- Kilowatt-hours (energy) are like gallons of water.
- Kilowatts (power) are like gallons per minute.
- Voltage is like water pressure.
- Wire gauge is like pipe diameter.

A tap that delivers a generous flow of water is like an appliance using a lot of watts. A tap delivering a trickle of water is like an appliance using few watts. So, if you need 10 gal. of water per minute, you can deliver it with a fat pipe operating at low pressure or with a skinny pipe operating at high pressure. Similarly, you can obtain 1,000 watts of electric heat from a low-voltage appliance with a large-gauge wire or from a high-voltage appliance with a small-gauge wire.

What's the difference between site energy and source energy?

Site energy is the amount of electricity and fuel consumed at a building. For ex-

---

How do I convert energy units?

Here are some handy conversion factors for energy units:

1 kwh = 3,413 Btu

1 kwh = 3,600,000 joules

1 joule = 1 watt-second

1 Btu = 1,055 joules

1 therm = 100,000 Btu = 29.3 kwh

1 calorie = 4.184 joules

1 Btu = 252 calories

Note: Try to avoid using the abbreviation MBtu because this unit has two definitions: 1 MBtu can mean either 1,000 Btu or 1,000,000 Btu; that's reason enough to stay away from MBtu.

How do I convert power units?

Here are some handy conversion factors for power units:

1 watt = 1 joule/second

1 watt = 3.413 Btu/hr

1 Btu/hr = 0.2931 watt

1 kw = 1,000 watts

1 megawatt (Mw) = 1,000,000 watts

1 kw = 3,413 Btu/hr

1 ton of cooling = 12,000 Btu/hr

1 hp (electric) = 746 watts

What's the energy content of common fuels?

A gallon of propane isn't equivalent to a gallon of fuel oil because fuel oil packs more Btu per gallon than propane. To compare different fuels, use this handy guide:

Natural gas: 1,000 Btu/cu. ft.

Propane: between 91,333 Btu/gal. and 93,000 Btu/gal.

Fuel oil: between 138,700 Btu/gal. and 140,000 Btu/gal.

Kerosene: between 120,000 Btu/gal. and 135,000 Btu/gal.

Gasoline: between 114,000 Btu/gal. and 125,000 Btu/gal.

Coal: 25,000,000 Btu/ton

Seasoned dense hardwood firewood: Between 21 and 26 million Btu/cord

Seasoned pine firewood: Between 14 and 16 million Btu/cord

Here are some useful conversion factors used for measuring natural gas:

1 centum cubic foot (ccf) = 100 cu. ft.

1 cu. ft. of natural gas = 1,000 Btu = 0.01 therm

1 therm = 1 ccf of natural gas = 100,000 Btu = 29.3 kwh

---

ample, in one year a house might require 12,000 kwh of electricity and 500 gal. of fuel oil. These quantities represent the amount of site energy consumed by the house; if we convert both types of energy to Btu, the house used 40,956,000 Btu + 69,500,000 Btu = 110,456,000 Btu of site energy.

Source energy is a calculation of the amount of fuel required to produce the energy consumed at a given site. Of all of the fuels, electricity has the biggest discrepancy between site energy and source energy—that is, the biggest "source-to-site ratio"—because most fuel-burning power plants require three or more units of fuel to produce one unit of electricity. (The energy that isn't converted to electricity is lost as waste heat.) Different power plants have different conversion efficiencies, so calculating source energy can be tricky; the source-to-site ratio for electricity varies by state and even by time of day.

When primary energy (for example, fuel oil or natural gas) is consumed at a house, the conversion to source energy must account for losses that occur during storage, transport, and delivery of the fuel to the building.

In the case of the house that uses 110,456,000 Btu of site energy each year (the example given earlier), it might require 40,080 kwh of coal (in other words, 136,793,000 Btu of coal) to generate 12,000 kwh of electricity for the house. Moreover, it might require 70,195,000 Btu of energy to deliver 69,500,000 Btu of fuel oil to the house. So the house in this example used 136,793,000 Btu + 70,195,000 Btu = 206,988,000 of source energy. That's considerably more source energy than site energy.

The Energy Star program assumes the following source-to-site ratios (based on national averages): grid electricity, 3.34; natural gas, 1.047; and fuel oil and propane, 1.01. In other words, it takes 1.047 units of source energy to deliver 1 unit of natural gas to a building.

Another source (Building Science Corporation) provides the following source-to-site ratios for the United States: grid electricity, 3.365; natural gas, 1.092; fuel oil, 1.158; propane, 1.151.

AVERAGE ENERGY USE PER PERSON

A nonprofit group in Switzerland, the 2,000-Watt Society, has calculated that the current level of worldwide energy use amounts to 2,000 watts per capita. This is the total amount of energy used continuously, on average, by one person, as long as the person is alive. The amount includes energy used for industry, commercial buildings, residential buildings, municipalities, and transportation— everything.

Per capita energy use in the United States is significantly above the world average, of course. The average American uses about 12,000 watts—six times the world average. In Bangladesh and sub-Saharan Africa, on the other hand, the figure is well under 500 watts per person.

It's hard to understand the quantity of the energy used by a typical U.S. family, but here's a mental exercise that helps: How big of a photovoltaic array (PV) would be needed to provide all of the energy used by the average American? Let's assume the American lives in Chicago. A person using 12,000 watts requires 288 kwh/day or 105,120 kwh/year. In Chicago, that much energy could be produced by a 90-kw PV array. The cost to install such a PV system would be about $315,000. A family of three would require an array costing $945,000. Of course, this PV array would produce enough energy to cover every aspect of one's life, including one's transportation and a personal share of the energy used for U.S. manufacturing.

Experts tell builders that HVAC equipment and ducts should be designed according to Manual J and Manual D; the problem is, no one wants to do the calculations

If you've been paying attention to energy-efficiency experts and green-building websites, you probably know that it's important to properly size your HVAC equipment. Most sources repeat the same advice: Oversize furnaces and air-conditioners cost too much, waste energy, and sometimes provide lower levels of comfort.

To avoid these problems, the first step is to insist that your HVAC contractor perform a Manual J calculation to determine the heat loss and heat gain for each room of your house under peak (worst-case) conditions. Then your contractor can specify equipment that meets Manual J requirements. If you're building a new home, your contractor should design your duct system using Manual D. (Manual D depends on the room-by-room heat loss and heat gain numbers supplied by the Manual J calculations.)

Sounds easy, right? Well, it isn't. In most areas of the country, it's very difficult to find a residential HVAC contractor who is willing to perform Manual J and Manual D calculations.

HELPFUL ADVICE FROM YOUR GOVERNMENT

According to the U.S. Department of Energy's Office of Energy Efficiency and Renewable Energy, "Homeowners should insist that contractors use a correct sizing calculation before signing a contract. This service is often offered at little or no cost to homeowners by . . . conscientious heating and air conditioning contractors." Yeah, right.

The government website goes on to advise, "When the contractors are finished, get a copy of their calculations, assumptions, and the computer printout or finished worksheet." Well, that's easy for *you* to say. But just see how easy it is to get that paperwork from Bob once his Do-It-Right HVAC Service has finished installing your new air-conditioner.

EASY ENOUGH FOR AN 8TH GRADER TO DO IT

Manual J and Manual D are calculation worksheets published by the Air Conditioning Contractors of America® (ACCA). For many years, these worksheets have been the standard methods for calculating residential heat loss, heat gain, and duct sizes.

Manual J and Manual D calculations are no longer performed with a pencil and paper; contractors now use software programs. Hank Rutkowski, the mechanical engineer who wrote (and continues to update) Manual J, explained to me how Manual J calculations are performed: "To bridge the gap between the complexity of the paper manual and the contractor you have to have software. It was never our intention that people do the calculations by hand. The manual serves as a guide to computer programmers. The key is the software, which takes the complexity and makes it simple enough for an eighth grader to use. . . . The contractor never has to deal with the equations."

The best-known Manual J software programs are Elite Rhvac, Wrightsoft® Right-J®, Adtek AccuLoad, and EnergyGauge®. Software programs for Manual D duct design include Elite Ductsize and Wrightsoft Right-D®.

A Manual J heat loss and heat gain calculation considers most of the factors that affect HVAC equipment sizing, including the climate; the size, shape and orientation of the house; the home's air leakage rate; the amount of insulation installed; the window areas, window orientations, and glazing specifications; the type of lighting and major home appliances; and the number and even the age of the occupants. For the calculations to be meaningful, information on all of these factors must be correctly entered into the software program.

MANUAL J AND MANUAL D CALCULATIONS ARE REQUIRED BY MOST BUILDING CODES

The 2006 IRC requires (in section M1401.2) that "Heating and cooling equipment shall be sized based on building loads calculated in accordance with ACCA Manual J or other approved heating and cooling calculation methodologies." (In the 2012 IRC, a similar requirement is found in section M1401.3.) Furthermore, IRC section M1601.1 requires that "Duct systems serving heating, cooling and ventilation equipment shall be fabricated in accordance with the provisions of this section and ACCA Manual D or other approved methods."

There's some wiggle room in the code, of course; individual inspectors can theoretically approve "heating and cooling calculation methodologies" other than Manual J. But the intent of the code is to outlaw

rule-of-thumb sizing—for example, "one ton of cooling per 400 square feet."

Where can I find a contractor to do it?

As with many code provisions, the requirement for Manual J and Manual D calculations is widely ignored and rarely enforced. Most residential furnaces, boilers, and air-conditioners are still sized by rules of thumb instead of careful calculations. As a result, almost all of the HVAC equipment installed in U.S. homes is oversize. Dozens of studies have confirmed that the degree of oversizing typically ranges from 30% to 200%.

Builders and homeowners who ask HVAC contractors about Manual J and Manual D calculations are usually met by a blank stare. On his GBA blog, Carl Seville reported that it "is difficult to obtain . . . an accurate HVAC Manual J calculation. It seems that few HVAC contractors understand how to prepare an accurate report, often oversizing systems out of habit rather than designing them for the actual house loads. Also, while the reports are supposed to be delivered before the equipment is installed, they rarely are, and mistakes are usually identified well past the time to make any corrections."

Michael Chandler, a builder and plumber who works in North Carolina, wrote on a GBA blog that his local planning board was "still not even enforcing the Manual J requirement which results in inefficient, oversized air conditioners and attendant humidity and mold problems. Even though reps of the local HBA pointed out the benefit of requiring Manual J, the county is still not requiring proof that a Manual J has been done to award a certificate of occupancy."

Energy consultant Allison Bailes, also writing for GBA, reported that "HVAC contractors, at least here in the Southeast, don't often do Manual J load calculations at all. They mostly use rules of thumb based on square footage (e.g., 500 sq. ft. per ton of AC capacity). When they take the time to enter data and run a Manual J, they usually do it incorrectly."

Even when they do the calculations, the results are usually wrong

Bailes raised an interesting point: the problem of "garbage in, garbage out" (GIGO) Manual J calculations. Rutkowski was interviewed for a profile posted on the Green Building Talk website. The report noted, "Rutkowski estimates that only 10% of heating and cooling equipment sizing decisions are based on some type of Manual J calculation and that less than 1% of the jobs are based on an aggressive implementation of the recommended design procedures."

Rutkowski explained the GIGO problem this way: "Manual J is a good tool if you use it aggressively. Follow the rules and it will give you a reasonable margin of safety. But the average contractor says, 'Better safe than sorry,' so he fudges here and there. He adds 5 to 10 degrees to the summer and winter design temperatures, calls the building 'average' instead of 'tight' and doesn't take credit for shading by interior blinds and drapes. Then when he finally comes up with a load number for sizing, he throws in an extra half-ton of AC just for the heck of it."

For a high-performance home, sizing by Manual J may still result in oversizing

Several years ago, I spoke with building scientist Joe Lstiburek about air conditioners installed in Building America homes in Las Vegas. "HVAC designers are committed to the institutional oversizing of air conditioning equipment," Lstiburek told me. "The average system is sized at 150% to 200% of the requirements of Manual J. They oversize because they don't know what they will get for a

building envelope, and to compensate for duct leakage and inappropriate refrigerant charge. If you size according to Manual J, there is already a fudge factor built in. But most designers then add another fudge factor."

According to Lstiburek, his experience proved that high-performance Building America homes in Las Vegas could have HVAC systems sized at about 60% of Manual J. To be conservative, his team recommended installing systems sized at 80% of Manual J.

Does oversizing matter?

There are strong arguments against routine oversizing of HVAC equipment. The best argument is simple: Oversize equipment usually costs more than right-size equipment. Oversize equipment suffers from short cycling. For example, an oversize furnace brings a home up to temperature quickly, and then shuts off. A few minutes later, it comes on again, only to shut off quickly. Many homeowners find the seesaw sound of a short-cycling furnace to be annoying.

When air-conditioners short cycle, the units don't run long enough to achieve much dehumidification—at least in theory. (During the first few minutes of operation, an air-conditioner cools a house. But not enough moisture has collected on the cold coil or on the pan below for any water to have actually gone down the drain. When the air-conditioner turns off, all of the moisture in the pan and on the coil just reevaporates.)

The conventional wisdom may be wrong

Increasing evidence shows that energy experts have exaggerated the negative effects of equipment oversizing, however. Studies have confirmed that oversize furnaces don't use any more energy than right-size furnaces. Moreover, newer modulating or two-speed furnaces operate efficiently under part-load conditions, solving any possible problems from furnace oversizing.

Although there are ample reasons to believe that oversize air-conditioners are less effective than right-size equipment at dehumidification, at least one field study ("Measured Impacts of Proper Air Conditioning Sizing in Four Florida Case Study Homes") was unable to measure any performance improvements or energy savings after replacing an existing oversize air-conditioner with a new right-size unit.

THE BOTTOM LINE

The main reason to choose right-size equipment is to avoid paying too much money for equipment you don't need. A Manual J calculation will ensure you don't spend more than necessary for your furnace, boiler, or air-conditioner. Moreover, a Manual J calculation will provide room-by-room heat loss and heat-gain information that is essential to good duct design. Without good duct design, you're running the risk of comfort complaints.

As explained in the previous chapter, the first step to designing a heating or cooling system is to perform a Manual J calculation to determine the heat loss and heat gain for each room of your house under peak (worst-case) conditions. Once this is done, your contractor can specify equipment that meets Manual J requirements and design a distribution system that delivers the right amount of heating or cooling to each room.

The unfortunate truth about heating and cooling load calculations is that fast methods aren't particularly accurate, and accurate methods require making measurements, checking specifications, and entering data into a computer program— in other words, a significant investment of time.

So how should builders go about making these calculations? There are several ways:

• You can use a rule of thumb (along with experience) to estimate your equipment needs.

• You can ask your HVAC contractor to make the calculations. (I don't recommend this method.)

• You can make the calculations yourself using a simple spreadsheet or an online calculator (like one available from the Build It Solar website).

• You can buy Manual J software and learn to use it.

• You can hire a consultant (usually an energy rater or an engineer) to perform the calculations for you.

WHY DO WE NEED TO PERFORM THESE CALCULATIONS?

There are at least two reasons we need to perform load calculations: to size heating and cooling equipment and to design heating and cooling distribution systems.

These are valid reasons, so a room-by-room Manual J load calculation makes a lot of sense. If you perform such a calculation, you may save money on your heating and cooling equipment (because it is less likely to be oversize), and there will be a lower chance that the homeowners will have comfort complaints arising from a poorly designed heat-distribution system.

In most areas of the country, a room-by-room Manual J load calculation is required by code. If you don't have the software yourself, you'll have to hire an energy rater or engineer to perform the calculations. Very few HVAC contractors are capable of performing an accurate load assessment, so I'd be wary of leaving this task to your furnace installer.

You don't always have to perform a Manual J

As long as there is no code requirement in your jurisdiction for a Manual J calculation for the type of work you are contemplating, you may not need a Manual J calculation. To understand why, we need to examine two myths that have long been promulgated by energy experts. The first myth is that rules of thumb are inappropriate; the second is that oversizing of equipment is disastrous.

SIZE IT RIGHT

Some houses need a big furnace, while other houses only need a tiny space heater. If you're not sure how big a heating system your home needs, you should definitely perform a load calculation.

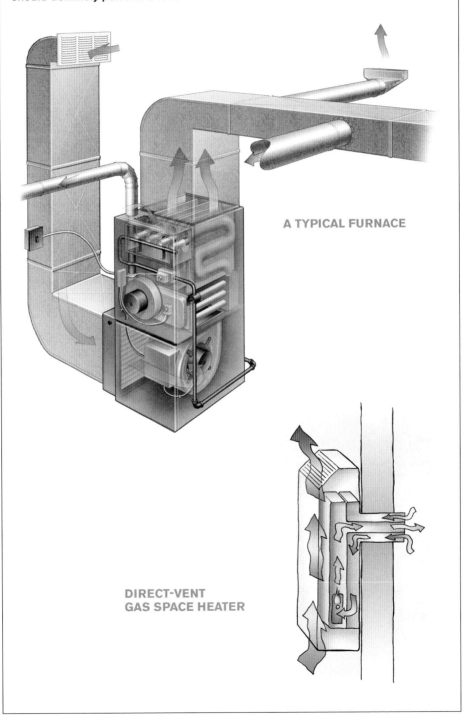

A TYPICAL FURNACE

DIRECT-VENT GAS SPACE HEATER

In fact, if you are an experienced builder who understands Manual J calculations, and if you have already built a few new homes, you probably already have a good rule-of-thumb understanding of how big a heating or a cooling system is needed in your climate. This rule-of-thumb method may be perfectly adequate for sizing heating and cooling systems for new homes. There are a few caveats, however:

• A rule of thumb is useful only if the homes fall into the same general category, with similar insulation levels, glazing specifications, and air leakage rates.

• A rule of thumb won't work for a house with unusual features (especially unusual glazing features).

• My advice applies only to people who have actually performed an accurate Manual J calculation or who have hired a knowledgeable professional to prepare one for them. If you're just guessing, you will almost certainly oversize your equipment.

Why am I comfortable with these seemingly risky recommendations?

• Even skilled users of Manual J software usually end up with slightly oversize equipment.

• Oversize equipment no longer really carries an energy or a comfort penalty. (Newer modulating or two-speed furnaces operate efficiently under part-load conditions, solving most problems from furnace oversizing; and oversize air-conditioners aren't as terrible at dehumidification as many energy experts claim.)

• As houses have become better insulated and tighter, heating and cooling distribution systems become less important because room-to-room variations in temperature are much smaller than in older homes.

Most comfort problems in existing homes are due to a poor building envelope (not enough insulation, low-performance windows, and a high rate of air leakage), stupid design details (like big unshaded west windows), and leaky ductwork. Once you control these factors, it's much easier to avoid comfort problems.

In an old, leaky house, it's not unusual for occupants to complain that one room is chronically cold or hot. A variety of factors are usually responsible, but it's a good bet that the walls and ceiling are leaking air, the windows have terrible glazing specifications, and the leaky ductwork is located in an unconditioned attic. The problem is almost never due to undersize heating and cooling equipment.

Passivhaus designers are now building homes with a single heat source (for example, a gas space heater with through-the-wall venting) in a central location. As these homes make clear, as building shells become tighter and better insulated, distribution system design is becoming less relevant.

Why is Manual J so complicated?

The better the envelope, the easier it is to perform load calculations. Moreover, if your envelope is good enough, errors in load calculations don't matter as much as they do when you have a leaky envelope.

It could be argued that current code requirements for Manual J calculations are necessary only because so many new homes have lousy thermal envelopes. If code enforcement officials were willing to insist on high-performance envelopes, full-scale Manual J calculations wouldn't be needed as often.

It's easy to imagine the development of a simplified version of Manual J for homes that exceed certain minimum airtightness, insulation, and window-performance specifications. After all, if we know that

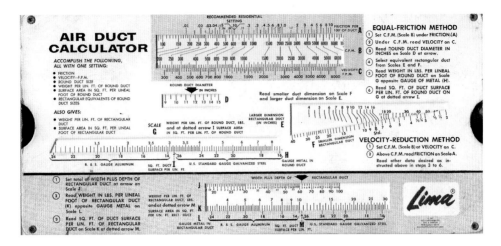

SIZE THE DUCTS. Once you've completed your room-by-room heat loss calculations, you can size your ducts. Back in the 1970s, I used this cardboard duct calculator (a type of slide rule) from Lima®. According to the calculator, a 6-in. round duct can supply 110 cfm (assuming 0.1 in. water column friction per 100 ft. of duct).

our envelope is well built, we should need fewer inputs when performing our load calculations.

The wild card is occupant behavior

Energy nerds can be fetishistic about their load calculations. The everyday variety of this species is the Manual J Fetishist—usually an engineer who warns homeowners that they will be uncomfortable and will face high energy bills unless they invest in more engineering.

The more exotic variety of this species is the PHPP Fetishist—usually a young architect who did a year of postgraduate study in Germany. This Passivhaus fetishist spends days at his or her computer, trying to reduce the U-factor of a troublesome thermal bridge in hopes of achieving the magical goal of 15 kwh per square meter per year.

Both types of fetishists are easily defeated by the Common American Homeowner, a casual oaf who buys several big TVs at the nearest big-box store, installs an extra refrigerator, leaves the bedroom window open, and never turns out the lights.

Be aggressive

If you do end up performing Manual J calculations, remember this motto: Be aggressive. This advice comes directly from ACCA Manual J, version 8: "Manual J calculations should be aggressive, which means that the designer should take full advantage of legitimate opportunities to minimize the size of estimated loads. In this regard, the practice of manipulating the outdoor design temperature, not taking full credit for efficient construction features, ignoring internal and external window shading devices and then applying an arbitrary 'safety factor' is indefensible."

Before spending time or money on energy modeling, it's important to know its limitations

Energy consultants and auditors use energy modeling software for a variety of purposes, including rating the performance of an existing house, calculating the effect of energy retrofit measures, estimating the energy use of a new home, and determining the size of new heating and cooling equipment. According to most experts, the time and expense spent on energy modeling is an excellent investment because it leads to better decisions than those made by contractors who use rules of thumb.

Yet Michael Blasnik, an energy consultant in Boston, has a surprisingly different take on energy modeling. According to Blasnik, most modeling programs aren't very accurate, especially for older buildings. Unfortunately, existing models usually aren't revised or improved, even when utility bills from existing houses reveal systematic errors in the models.

Most energy models require too many inputs, many of which don't improve the accuracy of the model, and energy modeling often takes up time that would be better spent on more worthwhile activities. Blasnik presented data to support these conclusions in 2012, at the Northeast Sustainable Energy Association (NESEA) sponsored BuildingEnergy 12 conference in Boston.

BLASNIK SEES MORE DATA IN A DAY THAN MOST RATERS DO IN A LIFETIME

Blasnik has worked as a consultant for utilities and energy-efficiency programs all over the country. "I bought one of the first blower doors on the market," Blasnik said. "I've been trying to find out how to save energy in houses for about 30 years. I've spent a lot of time looking at energy bills, and comparing bills before and after retrofit work is done. I've looked at a lot of data. Retrofit programs are instructive, because they show how the models perform."

According to Blasnik, most energy models do a poor job of predicting actual energy use, especially for older houses. And because large datasets show that the differences between the models and actual energy use are systematic, we can't really blame the occupants; we have to blame the models.

Blasnik isn't the only researcher to note that most energy models do a poor job with existing houses. Blasnik cited several other researchers who have reached the same conclusion, including Scott Pigg, whose 1999 Wisconsin HERS® study found that REM/*Rate*™ energy-use predictions are, on average, 22% higher than the energy use shown on actual energy bills.

Retrofit studies are consistent: projected savings are overestimated

Blasnik cited five studies that found that the measured savings from retrofit work equal 50% to 70% of projected savings. "The projected savings are always higher than the actual savings," said Blasnik, "whether you are talking about insulation retrofit work, air sealing, or lightbulb swaps."

MANY ASSUMPTIONS, INPUTS, SIMPLIFICATIONS, AND ALGORITHMS ARE BAD

The biggest errors in energy modeling occur in modeling estimates of energy use in older homes. "Post-retrofit energy use is pretty close to modeled estimates," said Michael Blasnik, "but pre-retrofit use is dramatically overestimated because of poor assumptions, biased inputs, and bad algorithms."

- **Poor assumptions.** "Models and auditors underestimate the efficiency of existing heating equipment," said Blasnik. "They often assume 60% efficiency for old furnaces."

- **Low R-value estimates for existing walls (R-3.5) and attics.** "They also use lots of biased defaults," said Blasnik. "They assume R-3.5 for an old wall, when many old walls actually perform at R-5 or R-6." Energy models often underestimate the effects of a high framing factor, thick sheathing, and multiple layers of old siding, all of which improve a wall's R-value.

- **Low R-value estimates for existing single-pane windows.** "They assume that old single-pane windows are R-1, when they are probably closer to R-1.35 or R-1.4. When calculating the outside surface film coefficient, they assume worst-case conditions—in other words, that the wind is always blowing away heat from the window. They do it that way because the design load is always calculated for the coldest, windiest day of the year (even though the coldest day usually isn't windy). If an auditor calculates single-pane windows at R-1, he's assuming that the wind is blowing continuously nonstop all winter long. But in a real house, the wind speed is often close to zero up against the window."

- **Low or absent estimates for thermal regain.** Blasnik explained that energy models underestimate thermal regain from basements and crawl spaces. "Most models get big things wrong, like how basements and crawl spaces work," he said. "Vented crawl spaces usually aren't at the outdoor temperature. When the outdoor temperature is 10°, a vented crawl space can be at 50°. Why is it that when you insulate a basement ceiling, you get very little savings—maybe zero savings, or maybe $20 a year? Well, if you have a furnace and ductwork in the basement, you are regaining a lot of the heat given off by the furnace and ducts, due to the directional nature of air leakage in the wintertime. The stack effect brings basement air upstairs. The basement is pretty warm, so the air leaking into the house is warmer than the models predict. A similar effect happens in attics: Because of the stack effect, most of the air leaving the house leaves through the attic. In a leaky house, you might have 200 cfm of air flow being dumped into the attic. That makes the attic warmer than the models predict. If the attic is 50°, the heat loss through the ceiling insulation is less than the model assumes."

- **Models also ignore interactions between air flow and conduction.** "Every single house acts like an HRV because outdoor air flowing through walls is picking up some of the heat that is leaving the house," said Blasnik. "The heat exchange is always going on, but it's not being quantified or accounted for. Complicated models use algorithms for air infiltration that aren't very good—the infiltration and conduction interactions aren't modeled."

So why do energy-efficiency programs almost always overestimate anticipated savings? The main culprit, Blasnik said, is not the takeback (or rebound) effect. Citing data from researchers who looked into the question, Blasnik noted, "People don't turn up the thermostat after weatherization work. References to the takeback effect are mostly attempts to scapegoat the occupants for the energy model deficiencies."

TOO MANY INPUTS

Anyone designing a computer model has to decide which inputs to require. "The trouble with the complicated models is that they ask for inputs that you can't measure well," said Blasnik. "After all, a lot of people don't even know which orientation is south. Unfortunately, many existing models ask for inputs that are difficult to assess—for example, window shading percentages, wind exposure ratings, and soil conditions. What's the water table height? What's the flow rate of the water? Who knows?" As Blasnik noted, "It's hard enough to get auditors to agree on the area of a house."

Many models ask for inputs that are open to interpretation. Blasnik asked, "How do you decide if a basement is conditioned or unconditioned? Perhaps it's semi-conditioned? Or unintentionally conditioned? Or maybe unintentionally semi-unconditioned?"

When making these types of assessments, it's hard for technicians to avoid unintentional bias. Technicians entering pre-retrofit information on an older home often come up with pessimistic R-value estimates for existing insulation levels, leading to overestimated savings projections.

Because of these problems with input accuracy, default assumptions are often more accurate than data collection. But even when using a model with the best possible default assumptions, there are limitations to accuracy. "Houses are complicated, and that's a problem," said Blasnik. "Lots of factors are difficult to model: foundation heat loss, infiltration, wall heat loss, attic heat loss, framing factors, edge effects, window heat loss, window heat gain, exterior shading, interior shading, the effect of insect screens, air films, HVAC equipment performance, duct efficiency and regain, A/C refrigerant charge, and air flows over HVAC coils. There are many unknowns: soil conductivity and ground temperatures are unknown. Wind speed is unknown. Leak locations are unknown."

THE GOOD NEWS: ENERGY MODELS DO A BETTER JOB WITH NEWER HOMES

Because newer homes tend to have lower rates of air leakage and higher R-values than older homes, energy models usually do a better job of predicting energy use in newer homes.

A study of 10,258 recently built Energy Star homes in Houston showed that the median discrepancy between the REM/*Rate* prediction and the actual energy use in the homes was 17%. In other words, in half of the homes the discrepancy between the modeled and actual energy use was 17% or less; in the rest of the homes, the discrepancy was greater.

IS ENERGY MODELING COST-EFFECTIVE?

Blasnik noted the irony that energy experts who analyze the cost-effectiveness of window replacement or refrigerator swaps haven't bothered to calculate the cost-effectiveness of energy modeling.

"How do the time, effort, and costs of collecting detailed data and using complicated models compare to the benefits?" Blasnik asked. "For most residential retrofits, it is hard to justify the cost of a detailed model that takes more than a few minutes to fill out. It makes more sense to just fix the obvious problems instead of doing a detailed modeling exercise. Data collection work distracts you from other tasks. Often raters spend so much time filling out the audit software that they never talk to the occupants—the homeowner is just sitting there. So here's an idea: Maybe you could talk to the homeowners."

Blasnik even questions the wisdom of modeling new homes. "If you are building super-efficient homes, the heating usage will be dominated by hard-to-model factors, including internal gains like light bulbs and plug loads," said Blasnik. "Small changes make a significant difference. Do the owners have a few big dogs? How long does the bathtub water sit before it drains down the pipes? Are the shading calculations accurate? What about internal shading by the occupants? How clean are the windows? How big a swing in indoor temperature will the occupants accept? Most models pay close attention to heating use, but in a super-efficient home, the hot water load and plug loads are bigger than the heating load—these other loads dominate. One large-screen plasma TV may matter more than the thickness of the foam insulation under the slab."

A STUDY COMPARES ENERGY MODELS

EnergyTrust of Oregon™ is an independent nonprofit organization that sponsors a variety of energy-efficiency programs; its work is funded by public benefit charges tacked onto ratepayers' electric bills. "In 2008, the EnergyTrust of Oregon was aiming to come up with a low-cost energy rating for homes," said Blasnik. "The question was, is there a low-cost alternative to paying $600 for a HERS rating of a house? Is there such a thing as a $100 energy rating—a 'light' energy rating?"

To help answer the question, the EnergyTrust hired Blasnik to give advice on which energy models to test. When the team couldn't identify a promising simplified model, Blasnik offered to develop a spreadsheet that would be easier to use than existing energy models. Dubbed the SIMPLE spreadsheet, Blasnik's creation required only 32 inputs and less operator knowledge than other energy models. Blasnik explained, "The spreadsheet was quickly designed to see if a simpler tool could work OK. The model asks for the conditioned floor area and number of stories, but it doesn't ask you the area of the windows, walls, or attic. The model doesn't want to know R-values for the walls or attic, or what kind of windows you have. No blower door or duct leakage numbers are necessary." Instead of requiring R-value inputs, the SIMPLE spreadsheet asks a technician to choose from a limited menu of options—for example, options like "some insulation," "standard insulation," or "average airtightness."

A research project called the Earth Advantage Energy Performance Score Pilot compared Blasnik's SIMPLE spreadsheet to three well-established energy models: REM/*Rate* and two versions of Home Energy Saver™, dubbed Home Energy Saver (full) and Home Energy Saver (mid). The Home Energy Saver models were developed by the Department of Energy and the Lawrence Berkeley National Laboratory. "The SIMPLE spreadsheet has 32 data inputs," said Blasnik. "This compares to 185 data inputs required for the full Home Energy Saver model."

The three energy models made energy use projections for 300 existing houses, and these projections were then compared to actual energy bills. The SIMPLE spreadsheet performed better in most situations; it had the smallest average error and far fewer cases with large errors. The mean absolute percentage error for the four energy models were:

- SIMPLE: 25.1%
- Home Energy Saver (full): 33.4%
- REM/*Rate*: 43.7%
- Home Energy Saver (mid): 96.6%

"My dumb spreadsheet does better than REM/*Rate* and the other models because the other models are horrible. For predicting gas use in older homes, REM/*Rate* had a median error of 85%. Two-thirds of the REM/*Rate* houses had huge errors. The mean actual use of gas was 617 therms a year, but REM/*Rate* predicted 1,089 therms. My SIMPLE spreadsheet overpredicted by only 27 therms."

Blasnik said, "The other models are very sophisticated, but they focus on the wrong areas. The moral is to get the big stuff right and don't waste your time with the other stuff. You can get worse answers if you collect more data than if you just make reasonable default assumptions. These detailed models are precise but not accurate—so they miss the target. The simplified models are accurate but not precise. It is better to be approximately right than precisely wrong."

Unfortunately, Blasnik's SIMPLE spreadsheet is not available for purchase.

REMEMBER, IT'S A HOUSE, NOT A SCIENCE PROJECT

Blasnik reminded energy nerds that not every house needs to be a science project. "For energy retrofits, don't waste your time doing simulations with dozens of inputs," he said. "Do the obvious stuff. Just fix the leaky uninsulated house— don't model it. If you need a computer to find out what work you need to do, then you don't know the answer—no matter what the computer says. There are more important issues that come up in a retrofit project, like: Do we have people who know how to do the work? Will they do the work well?"

Energy nerds can get distracted by modeling and testing. "Bruce Manclark, an energy consultant working with Puget Sound Energy, realized that their duct-sealing program would have been cost-effective if only they didn't have to do duct blaster testing before and after the sealing," said Blasnik. "So Bruce said, 'Let's not test them.' He called it the 'Duct Ninja' program. He recommended that workers just start sealing—seal the air handler and then seal every single duct connection you can access, without any testing. That way you don't need testing equipment or training in using testing equipment, and you don't need to spend hours testing. A lot of us are getting distracted by tests and computer software. What we really need are efficient processes to improve homes."

Experienced energy retrofit workers rarely rely on models. "When we make retrofit decisions, other factors like experience are more important than modeling," said Blasnik. "Even if you need modeling to make design decisions, you don't have to model every house. Model something well just once, and then apply the lesson to lots of buildings. If a house isn't unique, modeling is a waste of time."

WHAT ABOUT PHPP?

Blasnik's analysis raises important questions about the need for fine details in residential energy models. Passivhaus designers are on the opposite end of the spectrum from Blasnik; the software used by Passivhaus designers (Passive House Planning Package; PHPP) is so complicated that most energy consultants don't attempt to use it without first taking nine days of classroom training.

PHPP software requires users to enter a high number of inputs, many of which are obscure numbers that are hard to determine.

This level of detail raises several questions, including:

• Do most PHPP users supply accurate inputs?

• Is the PHPP model accurate?

• How much do the small differences that PHPP users sweat over really matter?

THE JA/NEIN FALLACY

At the BuildingEnergy 12 conference, Matthew O'Malia, an architect at GO Logic in Belfast, ME, explained how Passivhaus designers approach their work. "PHPP is a massive spreadsheet," said O'Malia. "It's the mother of all spreadsheets. Here's what I like about the Passivhaus approach: You either achieve the standard or you don't. At the end of the spreadsheet, your answer appears in this box. The answer is either Ja or Nein. There is no maybe in German."

Some Passivhaus designers go further than O'Malia, implying that a building that falls short of the magic 15 kwh per square meter is at risk of failure. To these designers, the Passivhaus standard represents an important threshold for performance and moisture control. The implication is that designers who aren't conversant with WUFI or THERM can end up designing buildings that encourage condensation and mold.

I propose a name for this mistake—the "Ja/Nein Fallacy."

In fact, there is no evidence that superinsulated buildings that fall on the Nein side of the Passivhaus divide are experiencing moisture or performance problems. Moreover, as Blasnik pointed out, once the homeowners move into their new Passivhaus abode, variations in plug loads can overwhelm the small envelope issues that Passivhaus designers lose hours of sleep over.

DON'T THROW YOUR ENERGY MODELS OUT THE WINDOW

Good energy models, including PHPP, can be very instructive for new-home designers. The best models clearly reveal the importance of choosing a compact shape, avoiding bump-outs, installing orientation-specific glazing, and addressing thermal bridges. Once learned, however, these valuable lessons do not need to be rediscovered for every new house.

Of course, designers of custom superinsulated homes are likely to continue using energy modeling programs, and their designs—resulting from an iterative process of continual refinement—help instruct designers and builders of simpler homes who may choose to avoid the expense of energy modeling.

PAYBACK CALCULATIONS FOR ENERGY-EFFICIENCY UPGRADES

How to perform a simple payback analysis and calculate net present value

If you are considering investing in an energy-efficiency improvement for your home—for example, additional attic insulation or a photovoltaic system—you probably expect that the investment will lower your energy bills. So it's only natural to ask, "Is this a good investment?"

For example, let's say that you are considering spending $5,000 on an improvement that will save you $350 a year on your energy bills. Does the investment make economic sense? The answer, of course, is "it depends." Among the factors affecting such a decision:

- How soon do you expect to move? Most people are more likely to invest in home energy improvements if they plan to stay in their house for a long time.

- Will the improvement increase the value of your home?

- Do you expect energy costs to rise in the future? If the cost of energy rises quickly, home energy improvements will prove to be a better investment than if energy costs stay flat.

- Can you finance the work with a low-interest loan? The lower your borrowing costs, the better the investment.

- What is the expected lifetime of the measure you are contemplating? A long-lived measure like attic insulation is likely to be a better investment than the purchase of short-lived equipment like a new water heater.

- Will there be any maintenance costs associated with the energy improvement?

- Do you value the environmental benefits associated with reduced energy use, even if the cost of achieving that goal is high?

- Do you value the peace of mind that comes from lower energy bills?

- Do you value the comfort improvements that may accompany some energy-efficiency improvements?

Some of the items on this list are quantifiable—for example, the interest rate on a loan. Others can only be estimated—for example, the rate of energy cost inflation. And some can't be quantified at all—for example, how much one values having a reduced carbon footprint.

SICK AND TIRED OF PAYBACK QUESTIONS

There are so many variables in this list, in fact, that some home performance contractors and solar equipment installers are sick and tired of hearing payback questions. The usual reaction from the sick-and-tired crowd is, "Nobody ever asks what the payback period is for a granite countertop or an SUV!" (Where would we be without granite countertops? They're such handy devices for making almost any argument!) However, I've noticed that the people who make this speech are usually people who sell home improvements with a very long payback. You never hear CFL manufacturers make the same speech.

Let's face it: Payback matters. It isn't the only factor in making home improvement decisions—other factors are important, including improved comfort and a smaller carbon footprint—but it's an important one. So now we come to the question: How should we calculate payback?

THERE ARE MANY WAYS TO PERFORM THESE CALCULATIONS

If you start diving into the world of payback calculations, you quickly learn that there are many ways to perform such an analysis. Among the terms you are likely to encounter are simple payback, cash flow analysis, net present value, internal rate of return, and return on investment.

If you're an accountant, all of these terms are familiar to you. If you're like me, however, you may need to study up a little before these terms become clear.

Simple payback analysis

Let's go back to our original example: You are considering a $5,000 improvement that will save $350 a year on your energy bills. To calculate the simple payback period, just divide the cost of the work by the annual savings to find the payback period in years. In this example, 5,000 ÷ 350 = 14.3, so the improvement has a simple payback period of 14.3 years. In a little over 14 years, you will break even. If the improvement lasts longer than 14.3 years, then all subsequent savings are gravy.

The main advantage of a simple payback calculation is that it is simple. It may not consider a variety of factors—for example, maintenance costs or energy cost inflation—but it's quick and easy to understand. And it's even arguable that, considering that many of the factors it ignores can't be determined precisely anyway, such a calculation may be accurate enough for many routine decisions we make.

Cash flow analysis

If you are borrowing the money to pay for the home improvements, a cash flow analysis probably makes more sense than a simple payback analysis. For example, let's say that the $5,000 measure is being rolled into a new home mortgage. Because you know your mortgage interest rate and term, it's fairly easy to calculate the annual cost to borrow $5,000. (One easy way to do this is with an online mortgage calculator.) If it's a 20-year mortgage at 6% interest, the cost to borrow $5,000 is $35.82 per month, or $430 per year. If the $5,000 improvement saves you only $350 per year on your energy bill, then borrowing money to pay for the improvement doesn't work out on a cash-flow basis.

But if the $5,000 improvement saves you at least $431 a year on your energy bills, then the improvement is cash flow positive from day one. If the cost of energy increases, your cash flow position improves.

Integrating inflation considerations into a cash flow analysis

The cash flow example I provided is fairly simple, but a cash flow analysis can account for more factors than I included. For example, if you are considering the purchase of a solar hot water system, it would be wise to budget for system maintenance. Maintenance costs are a negative cash flow, just like a mortgage payment.

It's also possible to include inflation assumptions in a cash flow analysis. Let's assume that a homeowner borrows $5,000 to install a solar hot water system that saves $350 on energy bills during the first year of operation. The homeowner wants to budget $50 per year for system maintenance and assumes that maintenance costs will rise at the rate of 3% per year.

Let's also assume that this homeowner wants to account for energy cost inflation. Of course, the future cost of energy is hard to predict. Building scientist John Straube has argued that the cost of energy has increased 8% per year in recent

Cash Flow Analysis Assuming 7% Energy Cost Inflation				
	Mortgage cost	Maintenance costs	Energy savings	Net cash flow
Year 1	430	50	350	−130
Year 2	430	52	375	−108
Year 3	430	53	401	−82
Year 4	430	55	429	−56
Year 5	430	56	459	−27
Year 6	430	58	491	3
Year 7	430	60	525	35
Year 8	430	61	562	71
Year 9	430	63	601	108
Year 10	430	65	643	148
Year 11	430	67	689	192
Year 12	430	69	737	238
Year 13	430	71	788	287
Year 14	430	73	843	340
Year 15	430	76	902	396
Year 16	430	78	966	458
Year 17	430	80	1,033	523
Year 18	430	83	1,106	593
Year 19	430	85	1,183	668
Year 20	430	88	1,266	748

decades—a rate that is higher than the underlying rate of inflation. However, this conclusion depends on your time frame; from 1981 to 2009, for example, energy cost inflation was actually lower than the general rate of inflation.

In this example, we'll assume that energy cost inflation is 7% per year. What would a cash flow analysis look like over the next 20 years? One way to answer this question is to create a table that breaks down cash expenses and savings by year. (If you create this table on a spreadsheet program, you'll save yourself a lot of data entry.)

This investment begins generating a positive cash flow in year 6 and continues to

generate a positive cash flow through the end of year 20. If we total all of the annual cash flow amounts, we discover that after 20 years, the homeowner has saved $4,405. So far, so good.

However, let's perform the same exercise with a different assumption. What if the cost of energy increases at a rate of only 3% a year instead of 7% a year? In this case, even though this investment is cash flow positive in year 14 and subsequent years, the outlays are greater than the credits. If we total all of the annual cash flow amounts, we discover that after 20 years, the homeowners have shelled out $539 more than they saved.

Cash Flow Analysis Assuming 3% Energy Cost Inflation				
	Mortgage cost	Maintenance costs	Energy savings	Net cash flow
Year 1	430	50	350	−130
Year 2	430	52	361	−121
Year 3	430	53	371	−112
Year 4	430	55	382	−102
Year 5	430	56	394	−92
Year 6	430	58	406	−82
Year 7	430	60	418	−72
Year 8	430	61	430	−61
Year 9	430	63	443	−50
Year 10	430	65	457	−39
Year 11	430	67	470	−27
Year 12	430	69	484	−15
Year 13	430	71	499	−2
Year 14	430	73	514	11
Year 15	430	76	529	24
Year 16	430	78	545	37
Year 17	430	80	562	51
Year 18	430	83	578	66
Year 19	430	85	596	81
Year 20	430	88	614	96

These two different results—one showing an investment that yields $4,405 in savings, and another showing an investment that results in a loss of $539—demonstrate how our conclusions about payback depend heavily on our assumptions. Or, as a cynic might say, all you have to do is tweak your assumptions, and you can prove any conclusion you want.

Net present value

Alert readers will note a problem with both methods of analysis introduced so far: They fail to account fully for the fact that the value of money changes with time. If we total all of the positive and negative cash flows in the last column of our table, the calculation assumes

that $100 in year 2 has the same value as $100 in year 19. Of course, it doesn't; because of inflation (or, to put it another way, to account for the opportunity cost incurred by spending money on an energy improvement instead of on a potentially more profitable investment), money held today is worth more than the same amount in the future.

If we go back to the table above, we see energy savings of $371 in year 3. For a homeowner who might earn 4% interest on a certificate of deposit, the present value of $371 received in three years is only $330 in today's dollars.

To compare cash flows that occur in different years, we need to discount the cash

DETERMINING THE REAL COST OF ENERGY

The exercises presented here show how different assumptions about the future cost of energy produce widely differing conclusions about payback. From the perspective of an environmentalist, however, trying to guess the future cost of energy is an irrelevant exercise.

Because the continued burning of fossil fuels at current rates is likely to lead to catastrophic environmental disruptions whose effects could linger for thousands of years, it's fundamentally impossible to choose an appropriate price for fossil fuel. Seen from this perspective, efforts to reduce our use of fossil fuels is a moral imperative, and the actual payback periods for energy efficiency measures are irrelevant.

We still need to make some simple calculations, however, so that we invest our money wisely. Efforts to reduce energy use should always start with the low-hanging fruit. To determine which fruit hangs lowest, it turns out that simple payback calculations are accurate enough for our purposes.

So, here's my advice: Sharpen your pencil if you want to, but in the long run, you really don't need a fine point. You can forget the exponents; fourth-grade long division is all you need.

three years from now must be discounted to determine its present value of $330.)

Once all of the anticipated cash flows over the life of an energy improvement measure have been discounted, we can add them all up and determine the net present value of the proposed improvement. (In other words, net present value is defined as the sum of the discounted net cash flows.)

If an energy-efficiency improvement is expected to last 20 years, we would calculate the net cash flow for each year; then we would discount each amount to determine its present value. Finally, the column of figures can be added up to determine the net present value of the proposed improvement. If the net present value is greater than zero, the proposed investment would be considered profitable. (These calculations are made easier if you use an online calculator.)

The formula to determine net present value (NPV), assuming that r is the discount rate and n is the number of years under consideration, is shown at the top of the facing page.

When the numbers from the table on p. 99 are entered into a net present value calculator, we learn that the net present value of the project is –$595, which is a lower value than the –$539 total that we obtained by simply adding up the cash flows without discounting them. The reason for the difference is that the present value of the positive cash flows in year 14 (and subsequent years) is less than the dollar value of the cash flow in year 14.

One problem with net present value calculations is that we don't really know what the discount rate should be over time because it's hard to anticipate future inflation or future interest rates. Like many other factors under consideration, including energy cost inflation, the discount rate is basically a guess.

flows in future years to calculate their present value. This is the first step in performing a net present value analysis. We use a discount rate to perform the calculation; a discount calculation is simply the reverse of an interest rate calculation. (In the previous paragraph, I assumed a discount rate of 4%. The cash flow of $371

$$NVP = \text{Year 0 cash flow} + \frac{\text{Year 1 cash flow}}{(1 + r)^1} + \frac{\text{Year 2 cash flow}}{(1 + r)^2} + \ldots \frac{\text{Year n cash flow}}{(1 + r)^n}$$

Internal rate of return and return on investment

If you love accounting, you can calculate the internal rate of return of a proposed energy improvement, using the net present value formula shown above. The internal rate of return is simply the discount rate (r in the formula) when the net present value is equal to zero.

It's also possible to calculate the return on investment for your proposed energy improvement. To do this you need to calculate your annual net cash flow, which is the sum of the present values of the anticipated cash flows divided by the number of years under consideration. The return on investment (ROI) formula is

$$ROI = \frac{\text{Annual net cash flow}}{\text{Capital cost}}$$

Once you know the internal rate of return or the return on investment for a proposed energy improvement, you could presumably compare the investment with a more conventional investment vehicle—for example, an investment in U.S. government bonds. However, note the following important distinction: If you invest $5,000 in a solar hot water system, the equipment will wear out in 20 years and be carted off to the dump. On the other hand, if your money is invested in a government bond, you might earn 2% interest per year—and you'll still have the $5,000 of capital at the end of 20 years.

THE BOTTOM LINE

I'm glad accountants have given us tools to perform a cash flow analysis and to calculate the net present value of a proposed investment. Because these calculations have been made, energy experts can advise homeowners that it always makes sense to swap their incandescent bulbs for CFLs, while window replacement doesn't make financial sense.

Every few years, it's important to take a fresh look at these calculations. For example, falling prices for photovoltaic modules mean that investing in a PV system now makes a lot of sense in areas with high electricity costs. Just a few years ago, however, it was hard to make the same statement.

Many energy-efficiency measures—for example, installing exterior rigid foam on an existing house—are hard to justify using any economic analysis. But that doesn't necessarily mean that they aren't worth considering. Remember, all of these cash flow and net present value calculations include a great many unknowns, most notably our assumptions about energy cost inflation. Whenever we're making a prediction about future prices, it makes sense to be humble.

On the other hand, many energy-efficiency advocates are overly optimistic in their cash flow predictions. For example, techno-nerds often underestimate maintenance costs and overestimate equipment lifetime—for example, in cash flow predictions for ground-source heat pumps or solar hot water systems. If you are hoping to save $350 a year on your energy bills, a single service call to repair a broken pump can wipe out one or two years of anticipated savings.

4

AIRTIGHTNESS

An essential tool for building energy-efficient homes, a blower door can also help you find leaks in old houses

eaky homes are hard to heat and hard to cool. The only way to know whether your home is leaky or tight is to measure its air leakage rate with a blower door test. A blower door is a tool that depressurizes a house; this depressurization exaggerates the home's air leaks, making the leaks easier to measure and locate.

An energy-efficient house must be as airtight as possible. Many older U.S. homes are so leaky that a third to a half of the home's heat loss comes from air leaks. There is no such thing as a house that is too tight. However, it's also true that there is no such a thing as an airtight house.

HOW LEAKY IS your house? The only way to know whether your home is leaky or tight is to measure its air leakage rate with a blower door test. By measuring the airflow of a fan that depressurizes a house to a standard pressure difference, a technician can determine just how leaky your home is.

Every house leaks, and that's why we perform blower door tests—to measure a building's leakage rate.

WHO NEEDS A BLOWER DOOR?

Blower door testing is useful for both new construction and existing homes. By testing a new home, a builder:

• Can determine whether a certain airtightness target has been met.

• Can document airtightness levels needed to qualify for certain home labeling programs, including Energy Star and Passivhaus.

• Can do a better job calculating heat loss and heat gain the next time he or she builds a similar house.

• Can brag about the home's airtightness to prospective homebuyers or drinking buddies.

If you're building a new home, the best time to conduct a blower door test is after the home is insulated but before the drywall is hung. If the test reveals major problems, the leaks will be easier to fix at that point than later on.

TESTING EXISTING HOMES

There are at least two reasons to conduct a blower door test on an existing house: to determine how leaky it is and to help locate and fix the leaks. When a blower door is used to help an air-sealing contractor locate and fix leaks in an existing house, the procedure is called "blower door directed air sealing."

During the 1960s, energy experts didn't realize the extent to which air leakage contributed to residential heat loss. During the early 1970s, however, a few researchers in Sweden, Saskatchewan, and New Jersey began studying air leakage in homes. In spite of these efforts, most early airtightness researchers still didn't understand how air was leaking out of most existing homes.

The Eureka moment came in 1977. A Princeton University researcher named Gautam Dutt was frustrated because he couldn't account for all of the heat escaping from a group of townhouses he was studying in Twin Rivers, NJ. According to a July 22, 1979, *New York Times* article, "Of 30 or so houses [Dutt] checked, all were losing three to seven times as much heat to the outside as the models predicted." After Dutt spent hours investigating the homes' nooks and crannies, he eventually pulled back some attic insulation and discovered a huge air leak through an unsealed utility chase. Dutt is now credited as the discoverer of the "thermal bypass."

The blower door was originally a research tool. It was simultaneously and independently invented in the early 1970s by two groups of North American researchers—the so-called Princeton House Doctors (David Harje, Ken Gadsby, Frank Sinden, and Dutt) in New Jersey and a group in Saskatchewan that included Harold Orr. The first commercially available unit, the Gadsco blower door, hit the market in 1980.

In 1981, Harry Sherman and his son Max—Max is now a senior researcher at the Lawrence Berkeley National Laboratory—started selling blower doors under the Harmax brand. A year later, Gary Nelson, the founder of the Energy Conservatory, started selling the Minneapolis Blower Door™. Of these three pioneer companies, only the Energy Conservatory is still in business.

WHAT'S A BLOWER DOOR LOOK LIKE?

A blower door kit includes several components:

• A frame and a flexible panel designed to temporarily fill a doorway;

• A powerful variable-speed fan that is attached to the blower door frame;

• At least two pressure gauges (mano-meters): one to measure the pressure difference between the home's interior and the outdoors, and another (the airflow manometer) to deduce the fan's airflow.

Three U.S. manufacturers sell residential blower door kits for prices ranging from $2,500 to $5,000.

BEFORE YOU TURN ON THE FAN, GO THROUGH THE CHECKLIST

Before a blower-door test can begin, the following preparation is necessary:

• Close all windows and storm windows.

• Close all exterior doors (except, of course, the door with the fan).

• Open all interior doors. In most tests, any doors between the basement and the first floor are left open.

• Disable heating equipment and non-electric water heaters by turning down their thermostats (and in some cases by shutting off electrical power to the equipment).

• If there are any wood stoves, verify that all fires are out. Cover the ashes in the wood stoves and fireplaces with damp newspaper.

- Shut all wood-stove dampers and fireplace dampers. Close glass fireplace doors.
- Turn off the clothes dryer and all bathroom and kitchen exhaust fans.
- If there is any reason to believe that plumbing traps are dry, fill all the plumbing traps with water.

In most cases, the openings for combustion flues and dryer vents are not sealed.

Ventilation system intake or exhaust vents (and passive air inlets) are usually (but not always) sealed, depending on the aims of the blower door test. If the test is being performed to comply with section N1102.4.2 of the 2009 IRC, the section requires that "exterior openings for continuous ventilation systems and heat recovery ventilators shall be closed and sealed." Moreover, in many cases a builder will seal passive air intake vents during a blower door test to determine the theoretical leakiness of the building's envelope without any passive inlets.

CRANK UP THE FAN

Once the house has been prepped, the blower door technician starts up the fan slowly to depressurize the house. Before cranking the fan all the way up, it's a good idea to walk through the house to make sure that nothing unexpected is happening—for example, to be sure that fireplace ashes aren't being pulled across the living room hearth.

The fan speed is then turned up until the pressure difference between the indoors and the outdoors reaches 50 Pascals. At that point the technician reads and records the fan's airflow as indicated on the airflow manometer. (Airflow is measured in cubic feet per minute, or cfm.)

The pressure difference at which blower door tests are conventionally performed

START SLOWLY. Gradually increase the fan speed with the controller until the manometer reaches about –25 Pascals. Walk around the house to look for any problems such as blowing fireplace ash. If everything's OK, increase the speed to –50 Pascals and record the results.

—50 Pascals—is arbitrary but useful. By establishing 50 Pascals as a standard pressure difference, a wide variety of houses can be usefully compared. Leaky houses require a high airflow to maintain this 50-Pascal pressure difference, whereas tight houses require a low airflow, so the airflow of the fan (in cfm) during 50-Pascal depressurization provides a number that correlates directly with a home's leakiness.

INTERPRETING THE RESULTS

There are two main ways that blower door tests are reported: airflow at a pressure difference of 50 Pascals (cfm50) or air changes per hour at a pressure difference of 50 Pascals (ACH50). The first number—cfm50—can be read directly off the airflow manometer at the time of the test. The second number—ACH50—can be calculated only once the building's volume has been determined. To calculate ACH50, multiply cfm50 by 60 minutes per hour and divide the product by the building volume, including the basement, measured in cubic feet.

Some blower door technicians estimate a home's "natural infiltration" or "natural air change rate" (ACHnat). This number shouldn't be taken too seriously because it is only an estimate. Natural infiltration rates (and rules of thumb for calculating ACHnat) vary by climate. In Minnesota, ACHnat approximately equals ACH50 divided by 17, whereas in Florida, ACHnat approximately equals ACH50 divided by 30. According to Gary Nelson, the president of the Energy Conservatory in Minneapolis, "ACHnat is probably only accurate plus or minus a factor of two."

BLOWER DOOR DIRECTED AIR SEALING

Any competent energy audit of an existing home must include a blower door test. Once you know your air leakage rate, you can formulate a plan for improving your home's performance. The leakier a home, the more economic sense it makes to hire an air-sealing contractor. "Homes with more than 6,000 cfm50 may merit days of labor and hundreds of dollars of materials," wrote energy experts John Krigger and Chris Dorsi in their book, *Residential Energy*. "Homes with 1,500 cfm50 are difficult to improve."

If your house is leaky enough to justify air-sealing work, you'll need a blower door test to efficiently locate and fix the leaks. Blower door directed air sealing is done while the house is depressurized to about 30 Pascals. Once the blower door has been set up, it usually makes sense to leave the fan running for several hours. By walking from room to room, many leaks can be found by feeling around with your bare hands. Subtler leaks can often be found using a smoke pencil or smoke bottle. In cold weather, an infrared camera can also be used to find air leaks.

The most important areas to seal air leaks are down low—in the home's basement or crawl space—and up high—at the attic floor. Because of the stack effect, leaks in these areas matter much more than leaks in the middle of the house, where there isn't as much of a difference in air pressure between the indoors and outdoors.

Many homeowners assume that gaps around windows and doors are responsible for most of a home's air leaks. In fact, air leaks in the areas listed in "Potential Air Leaks" on p. 125 are usually much more significant.

With the blower door running, air-sealing work begins, using a variety of materials, including spray foam, caulk, and rigid foam board. Workers first attack the largest and most obvious leaks. As they proceed, they periodically check the blower door fan's air flow rate to determine whether the air-sealing work is effective.

DON'T FORGET A COMBUSTION SAFETY CHECK

After air-sealing work in an existing house is complete, it's vitally important to conduct a combustion safety test. This usually involves a worst-case depressurization test: All of the home's exhaust fans, including the clothes dryer, are turned on at once, and every combustion appliance is checked to be sure there is no spillage of flue gas into the home. Sealed-combustion appliances are immune to spillage and therefore preferred for tight homes.

Air-sealing contractors need to have a good understanding of "house as a system" principles to be sure their work doesn't cause or exacerbate indoor humidity problems, radon exposure, or a variety of other potentially hazardous conditions.

DO YOU NEED MECHANICAL VENTILATION?

Many air-sealing contractors aim to lower the air-leakage rate in an existing home to somewhere in the range of 1,000 cfm50 to 2,000 cfm50. If air-sealing work continues until the house is tightened below

ALTERNATIVES TO BLOWER DOOR TESTING

For those who can't afford to buy a blower door, there are other ways to locate air leaks. In his excellent book, *Insulate and Weatherize*, energy consultant Bruce Harley advised, "You can make your own blower door if you can obtain a powerful fan (a regular box fan won't work). You won't be able to measure the air leakage, but you can use it to feel the air leaks."

Another method requires a theatrical fog machine. For more information on this technique, see "Pinpointing Leaks with a Fog Machine" on p. 113.

1,000 cfm50, it's advisable to install a whole-house mechanical ventilation system.

So why would anyone want to first tighten a house and then turn around and ventilate it with a fan? For several reasons:

• Leaky homes don't provide dependable volumes of fresh air. In a leaky house, air infiltration rates are very high in some conditions (when it's cold outdoors and when it's windy) and very low in other conditions (when outdoor temperatures are mild and there is little wind).

• Leaky houses tend to be overventilated in zones that are leaky and underventilated in zones that are relatively tight.

• Air leakage through wall and ceiling assemblies can lead to condensation, mold, and rot.

• Leaky homes are uncomfortable.

• Tight homes use less energy than leaky homes—even taking into account the energy penalties associated with mechanical ventilation.

QUESTIONS AND ANSWERS ABOUT AIR BARRIERS

Every home needs an air barrier that limits infiltration and exfiltration

Builders of a certain age—say, those older than 55 or 60—started their careers at a time when no one talked about air leakage or air barriers. Back in the early 1970s, even engineers were ignorant about air leakage in buildings, because the basic research hadn't been done yet. Times have changed, and most residential building codes now require builders to include details designed to reduce air leakage. Today's young carpenters are working on job sites where air barriers matter.

Q. What materials make good air barriers?

A. A wide variety of materials make good air barriers, including poured concrete, glass, drywall, rigid foam insulation, plywood, and peel-and-stick rubber membrane. (Note that evidence is increasing that OSB may not be an air barrier.)

Although air can't leak through these materials, it can definitely leak at the edges or seams of these materials. When these materials are used to form an air barrier for your home, additional materials such as tape, gaskets, or caulk may be required to be sure seams and edges don't leak.

To make a good air barrier, a material not only needs to stop air flow but also needs to be relatively rigid and durable. If you want to determine whether a material is an air barrier, hold a piece of the material up to your mouth and blow. If you can blow air through it, it's not an air barrier.

Engineers distinguish between air barrier materials (drywall, for example), air barrier assemblies (such as plywood with taped seams attached to wall framing), and air barrier systems (all of the materials and assemblies that make up a building's air barrier).

Q. My builder installed Tyvek under my siding, so I already have an air barrier—right?

A. Not necessarily. Although Tyvek and other brands of plastic housewrap are sometimes marketed as air barrier materials, the primary function of housewrap is to act as a water-resistive barrier. In other words, the Tyvek is there to protect the wall sheathing from any wind-driven rain that gets past the siding.

Some builders have experimented with using Tyvek as part of an air-barrier system. If the seams of the Tyvek are taped, and if the gaps between the Tyvek and window openings are carefully sealed, and if the transitions between the Tyvek and other materials at the bottom of the wall and the top of the wall are detailed in an airtight manner, then Tyvek can work as part of an air-barrier assembly. But siding contractors often rip holes in the housewrap with their ladders; they also penetrate the housewrap with hundreds of nails and staples. Builders interested in achieving a tight air barrier have found that other air-sealing methods are more effective than an approach that depends on housewrap to be a wall's primary air barrier material.

Q. If a wall has polyethylene under the drywall, is the polyethylene layer acting as an air barrier?

A. Probably not. During the 1980s, interior polyethylene was widely promoted as an interior vapor barrier. Its use in new homes is now relatively rare, except in very cold locations (for example, Minnesota, Canada, and Alaska).

Most polyethylene installations leak a lot of air, especially at the seams between adjacent sheets of poly, at penetrations, and around electrical boxes. That's not usually a problem because polyethylene is an effective vapor barrier even when it is not installed in an airtight manner.

Some cold-climate builders have successfully used polyethylene as part of an air-barrier system. To act as an effective air barrier, however, polyethylene needs to be installed with careful attention to a long list of fussy details, including the use of acoustical sealant (nonhardening caulk) at all seams and the use of airtight electrical boxes. This type of polyethylene installation is relatively rare.

Q. Where are the most common air barrier defects located?

A. Most air leaks happen at the seams or cracks between different materials: for example, where the mudsill framing meets the foundation, where floors meet walls, and where walls meet ceilings. Although gaps around windows and doors—the first areas of concern for many homeowners—occasionally contribute to air leakage problems, the most significant air leaks are usually in hidden

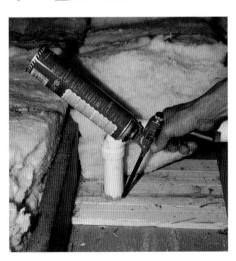

ATTENTION TO DETAILS. An air barrier can't be considered complete until air leakage is addressed at seams, electrical boxes, and any place a wire or pipe penetrates the surface.

areas. Because such hidden leaks (called "thermal bypasses" by weatherization contractors) usually don't cause obvious drafts, homeowners are often unaware of their existence.

POTENTIAL AIR LEAKS

Here's a list of some of areas that are often poorly sealed, and therefore responsible for significant air leakage:

- Basement rim joist areas.
- Holes cut for plumbing traps under tubs and showers.
- Cracks between finish flooring and baseboards.
- Utility chases that hide pipes or ducts.
- Plumbing vent pipe penetrations.
- Kitchen soffits above wall cabinets.
- Fireplace surrounds.
- Recessed can light penetrations.
- Cracks between ceiling-mounted duct boots and ceiling drywall.
- Poorly weatherstripped attic access hatches.
- Cracks between partition top plates and drywall.

Q. What's the best way to test whether my house has a good air barrier?

A. Tracking down air leaks can be tricky, especially for builders who are unfamiliar with the devious paths that air can take. For example, builders are often surprised to learn that significant air leakage paths can occur through interior partitions located far from exterior walls. The best way to test the integrity of a home's air barrier is to perform a blower door test. To learn more about blower door testing, see "Blower Door Basics" on p. 103.

Q. During the winter, I've seen water dripping from the can lights in my cathedral ceiling. An energy consultant told me that the problem is that my ceiling doesn't have an air barrier. Can you explain what's going on?

A. If you have punctuated your insulated cathedral ceiling with recessed can lights, it's very difficult to keep the ceiling airtight. (Unfortunately, even so-called airtight can lights are actually fairly leaky.) Warm humid air can enter insulated rafter bays through cracks around the can-light trim. The air is drawn into the rafter bays by the stack effect; the air usually exits the rafter bays through cracks near the ridge.

Because fiberglass batts are air permeable, they do little to slow air movement. Regardless of whether the rafter bays are vented or unvented, there are usually plenty of cracks that allow humid indoor air to find its way to the underside of cold roof sheathing, where the moisture condenses. On cold nights, a layer of frost can build up on the underside of the roof sheathing. When the weather warms up, the frost melts, leading to dripping can lights.

The solution is to create a tight air barrier at the ceiling plane. The best way to achieve this goal is to remove the can lights, patch the drywall, and substitute surface-mounted light fixtures like track lighting.

Q. How do I create an air barrier for a basement?

A. An air-barrier system is a three-dimensional balloon surrounding the conditioned area of a home. Assuming that your basement is part of your conditioned area—and I think it makes sense to include it—then there are several areas of concern.

First, it's important to note that the stack effect depressurizes basements during winter. In fact, stack-effect depressurization is strong enough to pull air through soil under the basement slab. (Believe it or not, most soils are porous enough to allow a connection between the air in the soil—even 7 ft. below grade—and exterior air above grade.)

A basement slab is an effective air barrier. However, the perimeter crack where the basement slab meets the footing or foundation wall is a source of air leakage and should therefore be caulked.

Basement sumps can allow significant volumes of air to enter a house. The solution is to install a sump with an airtight lid; these are available from Jackel, Inc. in Mishawaka, IN (jackelinc.com).

Most builders know the importance of installing sill seal between the top of the foundation wall and the mudsill. If the sill seal is ineffective, this joint may need to be caulked or sealed from the inside with spray foam.

If the rim joist in the basement isn't insulated, it should be. Closed-cell spray polyurethane foam is the best insulation for this location; fortunately, spray foam also helps seal air leaks in the rim-joist area. To limit the stack effect, you may want to consider weatherstripping the door at the top of the basement stairs.

Q. What's the "neutral pressure plane"?

A. Several different driving forces affect air leakage rates. Some of these driving forces—including wind, exhaust appliances like bathroom fans, and unbalanced or leaky ductwork used for forced-air heating or cooling systems—are intermittent. However, one driving force, the stack effect, acts continuously on a house, as long as the exterior air temperature is significantly below the interior air temperature.

Because of the stack effect, it's fairly easy to predict infiltration and exfiltration routes during winter. Warm air usually exits the house through cracks near the top-floor ceiling. The stream of departing air pulls air into the house through cracks in its lowest level—

for example, through the crack between the basement wall and the mudsill. In other words, the air at the top of the house is pressurized with respect to the outdoors, while the air in the basement is depressurized.

In the center of a house, maybe somewhere in the vicinity of the living room windows, the indoor air is neither pressurized nor depressurized. It's at about the same pressure as the air outdoors. This is called a home's "neutral pressure plane." Even if a living room window has all kinds of cracks, not much air will leak through, as long as the wind isn't blowing. That's because there is no driving force. The outdoor air and the indoor air are at the same pressure.

What happens to a home's neutral pressure plane when you turn on an exhaust fan in an upstairs bathroom? It moves upward a few feet, that's what. More air is now leaving your house, so more air needs to enter the house to replace it. As more air enters—perhaps through those cracks around the living room window—the neutral pressure plane moves a few feet higher, up near the ceiling.

Understanding these pressure dynamics helps guide the efforts of weatherization contractors when they perform air-sealing work. The most important cracks to seal are those under negative pressure (that is, cracks in a basement or crawl space) and those under positive pressure (that is, cracks in the attic floor). Air leaks in the center of the house, in the vicinity of the neutral pressure plane, are less important.

Q. Can I tell where my home's air barrier is supposed to be located by looking at the house plans?

A. Probably not. Unfortunately, most house plans don't indicate the location of the air barrier. As a result, a home's air barrier details—if such details even exist—are usually made up by the builders on the job site.

A wall's air barrier can be located at the exterior sheathing (by taping the sheathing seams), at the interior drywall (by following the airtight drywall approach, an installation

method that reduces air leaks to a minimum), or in the middle of the wall (by using spray polyurethane foam). If the details are done correctly, any of these methods can result in a very tight air barrier.

Q. My designer brags that his house plans include air-barrier information and that the air barrier can be traced "without lifting your pen from the paper." What's that mean?

A. It means you have chosen a good designer. Although it's rarely done, a good section drawing of a house design should indicate the location of the air barrier. Because this air barrier must be continuous, without any interruptions where the walls meet the ceiling or at other transitions, it should be possible to trace the air barrier on the section drawing— from the basement slab, up the walls, over the ceiling, and down the other side—without lifting your pen from the paper.

Q. I live in a hot climate where heating bills are low and air-conditioning bills are high. Do homes in a hot climate need a decent air barrier?

A. Yes. If your home lacks a decent air barrier, lots of cool indoor air can escape through cracks in the walls and ceiling. That departing cool air is replaced by hot outdoor air that sneaks in other cracks, forcing your air-conditioner to work overtime.

If your summers are humid, these air leaks carry a double penalty. When outdoor air enters your home, the air-conditioner struggles not only to cool the air but also to wring the moisture out of the air. In states with humid summers, a significant portion of air-conditioner run time is actually devoted to dehumidification. The tighter your home, the easier it is to keep the indoor air cool and dry.

Q. I want to make my house as airtight as possible. Is there any way to do that without spray foam?

A. Absolutely. Many builders have achieved very low levels of air leakage without any spray foam at all. Moreover, many homes that have been insulated with spray foam still have high levels of air leakage.

How is this possible? The reason is simple: Most walls and ceilings don't leak in the middle of the wall or ceiling. They leak at edges, penetrations, and transitions. So even when a wall is insulated with spray foam, you still need to worry about the details.

The lowest levels of air leakage are achieved by builders who have studied airtight construction techniques, who think through potential air leakage paths during each phase of construction, who are conscientious and methodical, and who have already built a few homes that were tested by a blower door.

Most air-sealing details don't require fancy materials. In many cases, a few rolls of gasketing material, some tubes of high-quality caulk, and a few rolls of high-quality tape are all that's necessary. Attention to detail usually matters more than high-tech tools or equipment. When it comes to air sealing, the proof is in the pudding—in other words, the blower door results.

THREE LINES OF DEFENSE IN THE BATTLE AGAINST AIR LEAKS

If the roof deck isn't insulated with spray foam, do the following:
• Seal the tops of light fixtures that penetrate the envelope.
• Seal at all wire, pipe, and duct penetrations that go from the top floor to the unconditioned attic spaces.
• Seal attic hatches or stairs with air-sealing products or weatherstripping.

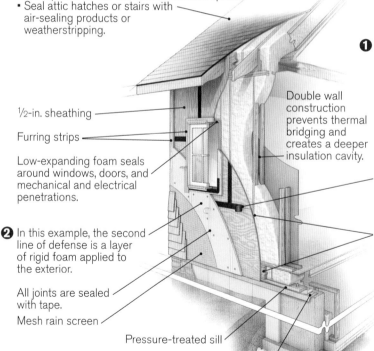

½-in. sheathing

Furring strips

Low-expanding foam seals around windows, doors, and mechanical and electrical penetrations.

❷ In this example, the second line of defense is a layer of rigid foam applied to the exterior.

All joints are sealed with tape.

Mesh rain screen

Pressure-treated sill

Double wall construction prevents thermal bridging and creates a deeper insulation cavity.

❶ The first line of defense is to tape all exterior sheathing joints. When using OSB or plywood, use 3M® sheathing tape or Siga Wigluv tape.

Apply construction adhesive between the rim joist and the exterior sheathing, and between the sheathing and the frame, especially around all openings.

Use two layers of sill sealer between the top of the foundation and the bottom of the sill plate.

In the last few years, energy consultants have developed a quick and easy way to pinpoint air leaks in a building envelope. The technique uses a theatrical fog machine—a small, inexpensive device that creates smoke-like fog for dances, Halloween parties, or theatrical events. Fog machines have heating elements that vaporize "fog juice," a solution of water and glycol or water and glycerin. With the help of a blower door or a window fan, a fog machine can dramatically reveal holes in a building envelope.

WITH AIR LEAKS, IT'S ALL ABOUT LOCATION, LOCATION, LOCATION

Since the 1980s, energy raters have been using blower doors to determine a building's leakiness. The results of a blower door test—reported as infiltration airflow (in cfm) at a pressure difference of 50 Pascals—usually reveal how tight a building is, but not the location of any leaks.

The fog-machine technique adds a whole new dimension to leak discovery. It's leak detection for dummies. Instead of crawling around on your hands and knees with a smoke pencil, you look for leaks by standing around in the front yard. The leaks don't reveal themselves as subtle whiffs of moving air; they shout, "Over here! I'm leaking!"

THE FAN BLOWS INWARD

During a conventional blower door test, the fan is set up to blow outward, depressurizing the house. A fog test, on the other hand, requires the house to be pressurized, with the fan blowing inward. Fog tests are usually scheduled after a house has been insulated but before the drywall has been hung.

The fog machine is set up indoors. Before beginning the test, it's important to open two or three windows in rooms distant from the fog machine. (The windows need to be opened only a crack.) The fog machine is then turned on, and all the workers on the job site assemble outdoors for the show. Once fog can be seen escaping from the deliberately cracked windows, the windows are shut and the test begins. The observers then look for escaping fog, which can show up almost anywhere: at the mudsill, at the eaves, or around windows.

TELL-TALE FOG. Once a theatrical fog machine has clouded the interior of a pressurized building, builders can find envelope leaks by looking outdoors for the escaping fog.

Small buildings are easier to test than large ones. "For a residential test, we can fill the whole building with fog," explained Vermont-based building envelope consultant Henri Fennell. "But with a large commercial building we can't do that. So we 'bag' an area with polyethylene—for example, after the first window is installed—and test a smaller area. If we aren't getting any fog flow, we poke a hole in the bag with a knife. When we see the fog come out, we patch the hole with duct tape."

OH, NOW I GET IT

Fog tests are so dramatic that they quickly convince skeptics of the value of air sealing. "Anyone who sees the fog coming out gets it right away," said Fennell. "The test doesn't require a college degree to interpret it."

According to Marc Rosenbaum, a Massachusetts energy consultant, most contractors are humbled and cooperative when fog reveals a building's holes. "My experience is that if you have a blower door specification for new construction—so many cfm at 50 Pascals—and the test comes in 10% more than the specification, the builder will usually ask, 'Why isn't that good enough?'—especially if you are fairly far along in the construction process," said Rosenbaum. "But when you use a fog machine, and you have fog blowing out of a hole in the building, I've never had anyone point to it and say, 'Why isn't that good enough?'"

All you need is a window fan

You don't necessarily need a blower door to perform a fog test. "All it takes is a window fan," said Fennell. "Just be sure you have a positive pressure, and go out into the front yard and look at the house. The big holes show up very easily."

If the building is large or particularly leaky, however, a window fan may prove ineffective. "If you need to create a pressure difference across a boundary, it's easier to do when the envelope is tight," explained Fennell.

FOG HELPS SEAL DUCTS, TOO

Gary Nelson—the president of the Energy Conservatory, which manufactures the Minneapolis Blower Door and the Duct Blaster®—pointed out that fog machines can also be used to test for duct leaks.

"You tape up all the registers and you pressurize the ducts," explained Nelson. "Then you introduce fog into the Duct Blaster—you aim the fog nozzle at the fan blades, without letting the fog get drawn into the vent holes in the motor, and you watch where the fog pours out. Sometimes you may be working with an HVAC contractor who says, 'This is a good duct system. This is the way we have always done it. This is normal.' Well, when you show them the fog coming out of the leaks, they shut up really fast."

LEAK TESTING ON THE CHEAP

One of the virtues of the fog test is that the necessary equipment is inexpensive. A recent Internet search showed that a fog machine can be purchased for as little as $37. As with any tool, however, you get what you pay for. Both Fennell and Rosenbaum use Rosco® fog machines that retail for about $400. "The most common problem with most fog machines is that they gum up," said Fennell. "You have to follow the manufacturer's instructions for maintenance. As long as you flush them out between uses with distilled water, they will last a long time."

A fog test quickly answers an important question, Where are the leaks? But according to Rosenbaum, there's another reason to conduct a fog test: "It's a lot of fun."

ALL ABOUT ATTICS

Answers to frequently asked questions about the space under your roof

Most six-year-olds can draw a house. The typical child's depiction of a house shows a rectangular building with a door and a few windows, topped by a gable roof. This type of house is fairly common in most areas of the United States. If the house was built 100 years or more ago, it usually had a cellar or basement underneath the first floor and an attic above the top floor.

In the middle of the 20th century, modern architects attempted to do away with basements and attics. They designed flat-roofed homes on slab foundations. While many Americans are happy to live in this type of home, others feel that basements and attics are useful spaces and have no desire to see them go away.

As originally conceived, attics were supposed to be outside a home's conditioned envelope. Because of their location, however, attics (along with basements and unheated mudrooms) actually represent a type of in-between area that isn't quite outdoors and isn't quite indoors.

Q. What are the advantages of a traditional attic?

A. A house with a traditional attic has several benefits compared to a house without one:

- Ceiling air leaks are easier to fix when a builder has access to an attic above the ceiling.
- It's usually easier and cheaper to install deep insulation on an attic floor than it is to try to insulate a sloped roof assembly.
- Roof sheathing facing an attic is less likely to have moisture problems and is far easier to inspect than roof sheathing facing insulated rafter bays.

TYPES OF ATTICS

There are several kinds of attics.

- The classic attic is located above a flat ceiling and has the same footprint as the house below.
- Some attics are smaller than the footprint of the house, like the attic above the second-floor ceiling of a Cape.
- Some attics have a triangular cross section, like the attics behind the kneewalls on the second-floor of a Cape.
- Some attics are low spaces without enough room to stand up, like the attics under a flat or low-slope roof.

Traditional attics under steep-sloped roofs are easy for builders and insulation contractors to work in, while cramped attics with difficult access are not builder-friendly.

Q. Are attics usually dry or damp?

A. A well-built attic shouldn't have any moisture sources like dripping plumbing pipes or roof leaks. Because most roofs get good solar exposure, attics tend to be dry spaces. If an attic has signs of moisture problems—for example, sheathing rot or mold on the underside of the roof sheathing—something is clearly wrong. It's usually fairly easy to identify a roof or flashing leak; telltale signs are soaked sheathing, especially after rainy weather.

If you're seeing mold on the underside of the roof sheathing, however, a roof leak probably isn't responsible. Attic mold is almost always caused by air leaks from the house below.

If the leaking air holds enough moisture to contribute to attic mold, the usual explanation is a direct air path from a damp basement or damp crawl space to the attic—for example, a poorly sealed chimney chase or plumbing chase. The solution is simple: Find the air leaks and seal them.

Q. What about venting?

A. While most building codes require attics to be vented, the usefulness of attic venting is overrated. In the old days, code officials recommended attic venting to handle all the moisture entering the attic though leaky ceilings. These days, however, building scientists note that it makes more sense to build an airtight ceiling than it does to try to remove the moisture after it's escaped through ceiling holes.

Q. Is there a way to take advantage of the fact that attics are hot?

A. If you have ever climbed into an attic on a summer afternoon, you know that attics can get hot. This fact has led many tinkerers to experiment with ways to put the hot air in an attic to good use. For example, inventors have installed coils of tubing in their attic, hoping to invent an inexpensive solar water heater without any glazing. Others have installed ducts that pull hot attic air down to their mechanical room, hoping to use the heat for one purpose or another.

These experiments have all reached the same conclusion: The heat collected in this manner isn't valuable enough to justify the cost of the hardware needed to gather it.

Q. How should an attic floor be insulated?

A. Before installing insulation on an attic floor, it's important to seal all of the air leaks in the ceiling. For more information on this work, see "Air Sealing an Attic" on p. 119.

In many areas of the country, the most common type of insulation installed on attic floors is fiberglass batts. This is a poor choice. Fiberglass batts don't conform well to

oddly shaped spaces and most installations of batts are sloppy. If you inspect your attic insulation, you'll probably find voids and areas where batts are compressed or overlapping. Fiberglass batts also do a very poor job of reducing air leakage.

By far the best type of insulation for attic floors is cellulose. If you live in an area where cellulose isn't sold, the next-best choice is probably blown-in fiberglass. (However, blown-in fiberglass is subject to more problems with wind-washing and convective loops than cellulose.)

BLOWN-IN FIBERGLASS.

Requirements for attic insulation vary by climate zone. The 2012 IRC requires the following minimum levels of insulation for attic floors:

- R-30 in climate Zone 1.
- R-38 in Zones 2 and 3.
- R-49 in Zones 4, 5, 6, 7, and 8.

If you are using cellulose insulation, that means that you need at least:

- 8.5 in. of insulation in Zone 1.
- 10.5 in. of insulation in Zones 2 and 3.
- 14 in. in Zones 4, 5, 6, 7, and 8.

If your attic has fiberglass batts on the floor, don't despair. Here's the good news: It's perfectly acceptable to blow cellulose insulation on top of a layer of poorly installed fiberglass batts. The added cellulose insulation will fill the nooks and crannies that are presently uninsulated; will reduce convective loops that degrade the performance of the fiberglass insulation; and will improve the R-value of the insulation layer.

If you hire a contractor to do this work, don't skimp on insulation depth. Much of the cost of the work is the cost of getting the crew and equipment on site; once they are there, the difference in cost between 8 in. of cellulose and 16 in. of cellulose isn't very much.

Q. Can I use my attic for storage?

A. In general, it's a bad idea to use an attic for storage. In many homes, the joists or roof trusses aren't designed to handle the extra loads from heavy objects stored in attics. Every time a homeowner visits an attic, there's a good chance that insulation will be disturbed, or that the gasket on the access hatch will be damaged. That's why builders usually advise homeowners to stay out of their attics.

If you insist on using your attic for storage, and if you think that the existing framing can handle the expected loads, you'll need to add new floor framing on top of your existing joists (at 90° to the joists) so that the top of the floor framing is at least as deep as your insulation. Then install a sturdy plywood or OSB subfloor in the area of the attic that you intend to use for storage. (You may have to cut the plywood into small pieces to get it through your attic access hatch.)

Q. What do I need to know about access hatches?

A. Attics are usually accessed through hatches. In general, a well-designed attic hatch is preferable to pull-down attic stairs. (Most pull-down attic stairs are poorly insulated and extremely leaky.) While some energy-conscious builders argue against attic

hatches—they prefer to install an exterior access door in a gable wall, to prevent homeowners from entering their attic without an extension ladder—most homeowners would rather have a convenient hatch than one that is deliberately hard to use.

Interior hatches should be large enough to allow a person to get into the attic without difficulty. It's better to locate the hatch above a hallway than above a closet. (Closet hatches are notoriously hard to use.)

Unless the hatch is carefully built and installed, it can be responsible for significant air leakage and heat loss. A good attic hatch has the same R-value as the insulation on the attic floor; this is best achieved by gluing several layers of rigid foam to the attic side of the hatch. The hatch needs weatherstripping at its perimeter, and it needs latches that pull the hatch tightly to the weatherstripping when closed.

ATTIC ACCESS: A big leak that can be fixed quickly. Build or buy an insulated cover for the access bulkhead. The key is to provide a rim to connect to the sealing cover. This access hatch has a low R-value; it needs much thicker foam.

Note that the IRC requires attic access hatches to "be weatherstripped and insulated to a level equivalent to the insulation on the surrounding surfaces." In other words, if you have R-49 insulation on your attic floor, you need an R-49 attic access hatch.

Q. Should I install a radiant barrier in my attic?

A. The short answer is: probably not. Here's a more nuanced answer: If your attic includes ductwork and HVAC equipment, and you live in a hot climate, you may want to staple a radiant barrier to the underside of your rafters. However, the energy savings from this work may not justify the cost of the radiant barrier. This type of retrofit has a very long payback period, especially if you have to pay a contractor to do the work. Other retrofit measures usually make more sense.

Q. What should I do about the ducts in my attic?

A. If the builders of your house installed ducts in an unconditioned attic, they made a big mistake. I have no idea why our building codes allow builders to make this mistake. Ducts in unconditioned attics waste huge amounts of energy. Correcting this building flaw is expensive.

The best way to solve the problem is to install insulation along the roofline of your house, converting the vented unconditioned attic into an unvented conditioned attic. While there are many ways to insulate sloped roofs, the most common method is to install spray foam insulation on the underside of the roof sheathing.

If you don't want to create a conditioned attic—either because the work is too expensive or because you think that spray foam is environmentally irresponsible and risky—you can try to improve the thermal performance of your ducts by carefully sealing duct seams and by adding additional duct insulation. For more information on this topic, see "Keeping Ducts Indoors" on p. 206.

Q. I want to convert my attic into living space. Are there any problems with this idea?

A. In some cases, converting your attic into a spare bedroom or home office may make sense. However, bad (or even dangerous) attic conversions are more common than attic conversions that are graceful and energy-efficient.

Some points to bear in mind:

- Some building codes require third-floor bedrooms to include two modes of egress—a requirement that is often interpreted to mean two separate stairways.

- Older homes often have 2×6 or 2×8 rafters that don't provide enough depth for adequate roof insulation. Skimping on insulation to gain an inch or two of headroom is a flawed strategy; better approaches include popping a dormer or adding rigid foam insulation above the existing roof sheathing.

Your unfinished attic may appear spacious. Once it becomes clear that the space can't be finished unless an adequate thickness of insulation is installed, however, ceilings usually end up lower than homeowners expect. When a conflict arises between a homeowner's desire for adequate headroom and an energy consultant's advice on minimum R-values, the energy consultant usually loses. Unfortunately, the result is often a space that is both cramped and inefficient.

That said, it's possible to convert an attic into usable space and still maintain the integrity of your home's thermal envelope. Before you commit to an attic conversion, however, consult a reputable architect.

If you haven't done it yet, it's time to climb into your attic and plug as many holes as you can find

If you want to improve the energy performance of an older house, one of the first steps is to plug your attic air leaks. Here, I'll try to explain how you can seal air leaks in a conventional vented, unconditioned attic. (If your house has cathedral ceilings—that is, insulated sloped roof assemblies—the air sealing tips in this article don't apply to your house.)

There are four basic steps to sealing attic air leaks:

- Inspecting your attic;
- Patching the big holes;
- Sealing the cracks and small holes;
- Weatherstripping the access hatch.

Once this air sealing work is done, you may want to add more insulation to your attic floor. If you want to add insulation, remember that air leaks have to be sealed first.

INSPECTING YOUR ATTIC

The easiest way to find air leaks is with a blower door test. In some cases, a theatrical fog machine is also very useful. (For more information on these two pieces of equipment, see "Blower Door Basics" on p. 103 and "Pinpointing Leaks with a Fog Machine" on p. 113.)

If you don't have a blower door, you'll have to find your attic air leaks using your eyes and your powers of deduction. You'll also need a powerful flashlight. If you don't like balancing on joists, bring a couple of 2 ft. by 3 ft. pieces of plywood to step on while inspecting your attic.

Needless to say, you don't want to step between the floor joists and punch a hole in the ceiling.

Warning: If your attic floor is insulated with vermiculite, a type of insulation that may contain asbestos, don't touch the insulation. Don't attempt any air-sealing work in an attic insulated with vermiculite. Removal of vermiculite insulation should be performed only by a certified asbestos abatement contractor.

If your attic has no vermiculite, the first step is to get your bearings and look around the entire attic. You may be surprised at what you discover. For example, it isn't too unusual to find gross insulation or ventilation system defects in the attic, including joist bays with no insulation and bathroom fans that direct exhaust air into the attic. Needless to say, these defects will need to be remedied. The first order of business, however, is to seal the air leaks.

If the attic floor is insulated with fiberglass batts, look for stained or dirty insulation. The most common cause of dirty fiberglass batts is air leakage; if the batts are very dirty, it means that dusty indoor air has been rushing through the batts for years. The batts strain out the dust from the flowing air, just like a furnace filter. If you lift the dirty batts, you'll probably find a crack or a gaping hole.

Look for sunken batts. These are often a clue that there is a soffit or suspended (dropped) ceiling under the insulation. In most cases, these soffits and dropped ceilings lack any drywall—and therefore lack an air barrier.

Look for plumbing vent pipes, ducts, and exhaust fans. Areas near these items are frequent leak locations.

Think about the layout of the floor directly under the attic. If you know of any dropped ceilings or soffits, try to locate those areas in your attic. You'll probably want to lift the existing batts (or redistribute the blown-in insulation) to find out what's underneath.

If you take your time and you're thorough, you should be able to find all of the big holes in your attic using these techniques.

PATCHING THE BIG HOLES

Big holes in your attic floor—holes above soffits, dropped ceilings, and utility chases —can be patched with drywall, plywood, or OSB. Perhaps the easiest material to use, however, is foil-faced polyisocyanu-rate because it's easy to cut and easy to tape.

Whatever type of sheet material you use to seal your large holes, cut a piece of material so that it covers the hole, and secure it in place with nails or screws. The perimeter of each piece of material can be sealed with caulk, nonhardening acousti-cal sealant, or canned spray foam.

Gaps around brick chimneys are dealt with differently from holes above soffits. Because chimneys can be hot, these gaps should be covered with sheet metal, not rigid foam. After nailing four pieces of sheet metal in place—one on each side of the chimney—the seams where the metal pieces overlap and the gaps between the metal and the chimney can be sealed with high-temperature silicone caulk.

Gaps around metal chimneys are sealed with techniques that are similar to those used for brick chimneys. The easiest way

CLOSING GAPS AROUND brick chimneys. Nail or screw down wide strips of sheet metal (recycled drip edge here) along the perimeter. Seal the gaps between the metal and the chimney with high-temperature silicone caulk.

to seal around a metal chimney is with two overlapping pieces of sheet metal; of course, you'll need to cut each piece with a half moon hole that corresponds to the chimney diameter. Manufacturers of metal chimneys and most building codes require a 2-in. air space between the chimney and any framing lumber. Respect this air space; avoid the temptation to fill the air space with insulation.

Finally, it's worth checking whether chimneys are in use before you begin your air sealing work. Unused chimneys represent a thermal bridge as well as an air leakage path, so all unused chimneys—both brick chimneys and metal chimneys—should be removed. At the very least, the top section of an unused chimney should be demolished down to a level that is lower than the ceiling air barrier, so the penetration through the attic floor can be patched.

SEALING CRACKS AND SMALL HOLES

Here are some of the cracks and small holes that need to be sealed in a typical attic:

- Cracks near recessed can lights;
- Cracks around ceiling-mounted duct boots;
- Cracks around bath exhaust fans;
- Cracks around plumbing vent pipes;

COMMON AIR LEAKAGE LOCATIONS

Before any attic insulation is installed, or any existing insulation is improved, air leaks must be sealed. These leaks can range in size from a pinhole to the 3-ft. by 4-ft. access hatch. For the contractor or homeowners who wants to create a tighter building envelope, the hardest part of the task is finding the leaks; sealing them is relatively easy.

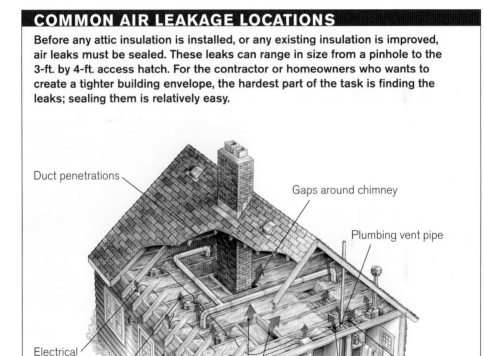

Duct penetrations

Gaps around chimney

Plumbing vent pipe

Electrical cable penetrations

Unsealed soffit

Recessed can lights

Access hatch

Drywall joints between ceiling and wall plates

- Leaks at ceiling electrical boxes;
- Holes drilled in top plates for electrical cable;
- Cracks between partition top plates and partition drywall.

Cracks near recessed can lights

Recessed can lights are bad news; most are responsible for very significant air leaks. The best solution to the can light problem is to permanently remove them and replace them with surface-mounted fixtures. If you aren't willing to do that, you may be able to install airtight covers on the attic side of the recessed cans to reduce air leakage, as long as the fixtures are IC-rated.

Cracks around ceiling-mounted duct boots

If your house has ceiling-mounted HVAC diffusers or grilles, you'll need to seal the crack between the galvanized duct boots and the ceiling drywall. It's usually easier to seal these cracks from below than from above.

Cracks around bath exhaust fans

Most ceiling-mounted bath fans have a removable plastic grille. Remove the grille from below and caulk the crack between the fan housing and the drywall.

Cracks around plumbing vent pipes

These cracks around plumbing vent pipes need to be sealed with caulk or acoustical sealant. Some builders prefer to use European air-sealing tapes.

Leaks at ceiling electrical boxes

Leaks around electrical boxes are fairly straightforward to seal. Using caulk, seal the crack between the electrical box and the ceiling drywall. Then seal around the knockouts at the sides and back of the box as well as any location where electrical cables enter the box. Don't make the mis-take of filling the box with canned spray foam—that would be a code violation and would create a fire hazard.

Holes drilled in top plates for electrical cable

Leaks caused by holes for electrical cable are fairly straightforward to fix. Seal them with caulk or canned spray foam.

Cracks between partition top plates and partition drywall

A surprising volume of indoor air can escape through cracks at the top plates. Usually, the conditioned air enters the partition stud bays through electrical outlets and cracks at the bottom of the wall. Unless the drywall contractor installed a bead of adhesive along the top plate—

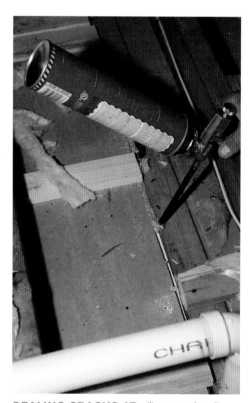

SEALING CRACKS AT ceiling-corner drywall seams. A surprising amount of air can leak at the seam between partition top plates and partition drywall; seal with spray foam or caulk.

most don't—air will continually escape along this crack.

To seal these cracks, peel back the insulation above each partition top plate. The cracks can be sealed with caulk. If the top plates have lots of wiring penetrations, it's often easiest to seal the entire top plate with spray foam from a two-component spray foam kit.

ACCESS HATCHES AND PULL-DOWN STAIRS

There are two problems with attic access hatches and pull-down attic stairs: They usually aren't properly insulated, and they are rarely weatherstripped. It's easier to deal with an attic hatch than pull-down stairs. As long as the existing hatch is sturdy, the usual solution is to fasten or glue multiple layers of rigid foam on the attic side of the hatch. (Make sure any adhesive you use is compatible with rigid foam.) Then install weatherstripping on the lip where the hatch rests as well as at least two latches that pull the hatch tightly against the weatherstripping. To stop air leaks at pull-down attic stairs, you'll need to install an elaborate cap—either a site-built cap or a commercial product like the Energy Guardian cap.

KNEEWALLS

So far, we've mostly been talking about ceiling leaks. But air leakage routes get more complicated if your attic includes kneewalls. A typical Cape-style home has several different attics. There are usually two cramped attics behind the second-floor kneewalls; there is also a low attic above the second-floor ceiling. Kneewalls are also common in some new homes built in the 1980s and 1990s, especially large homes with chopped-up roofs, dormers, and multiple ceiling planes.

There are at least two problems with most kneewalls:

• Kneewalls often lack an attic-side air barrier, even though they are insulated with air-permeable insulation (usually fiberglass batts) that require such a barrier.

• When builders install kneewalls, they often forget to install solid blocking between the floor joists under the kneewall bottom plate as well as solid blocking between the rafters above the kneewall top plate. If the kneewall is insulated, such blocking is essential; moreover, each piece of blocking needs to be carefully air sealed. Without the blocking, cold outdoor air can migrate horizontally between the floor joists, robbing heat from the house.

If you discover that your kneewalls are uninsulated, don't despair. It's possible that your builder decided to insulate the sloped roof assembly above the attic instead of the kneewall. If that's the case, you're in luck. As long as the work was done conscientiously, the best way to insulate attics behind kneewalls is at the sloping roof.

VENTILATION BAFFLES, INSULATION DAMS, AND DUCT LEAKS

Once you have completed your air sealing work, there are a few more details that you may need to address before you add more insulation to your attic: ensuring that the ventilation channels that connect your soffit vents to the attic aren't blocked by insulation, making sure that all of your insulation dams are high enough, and checking any attic ducts for problems.

If your attic has soffit vents and ridge vents, you'll need a ventilation gap under the roof sheathing at the perimeter of your attic—a clear channel that allows air to flow from your soffit vents to your attic. In some attics, this area is blocked by insulation. The solution is to install ventilation baffles—either commercially available baffles or site-built baffles. If you need to install these baffles, you'll also need to install insulation dams from the top plates of your exterior walls to the underside of the ventilation baffles.

If you plan to add more insulation to your attic floor, you'll probably need to extend the insulation dam around your attic hatch. This dam needs to be at least as high as your anticipated insulation depth. You can use either 2× lumber or plywood to build this insulation dam.

Remember that installing insulation on top of live knob-and-tube wiring is a code violation and a possible fire hazard. If you have knob-and-tube wiring in your attic, you can insulate on top of the knob-and-tube only if you are sure that it has been permanently disconnected. When in doubt, call an electrician to have your wiring evaluated before proceeding.

Finally, if there are any ducts in your attic, you'll want to inspect them. Make sure that there are no disconnected ducts, that all duct seams are sealed with mastic or high-quality HVAC tape, and that the ducts are adequately insulated.

It's usually a bad idea to locate ducts in an unconditioned attic—but just because it's a bad idea, doesn't mean that attic ducts don't exist. If you've got them, you'll have to do your best to deal with them. For more information on attic ducts, see "Sealing Ducts: What's Better, Tape or Mastic?" on p. 201 and "Keeping Ducts Indoors" on p. 206.

If you don't have time to seal every last crack, which cracks should you seal first?

Most new homes are leaky. In the typical new home, significant volumes of air enter through cracks near the basement rim joists and exit through ceiling holes on the building's top floor. These air leaks waste tremendous amount of energy. In recent years, after years of prodding by building scientists, code officials have finally taken a few stabs at addressing air leakage.

Of course, some builders have focused on energy efficiency for years, and many of these builders own a blower door. If you have your own blower door, you have probably learned by trial and error which cracks matter most. However, the vast majority of contractors build homes without any feedback from a blower door. If these builders want to improve the airtightness of the homes they build, they probably don't know where to start.

GET THE BIG HOLES FIRST

The first step is to make sure that there aren't any really big holes in your homes. (Joe Lstiburek calls these "the Joe-size holes"; they're the holes that are big enough for Joe to crawl through.) You may be thinking, "Can a house really have holes that big?" The answer, sadly, is "Yes, it really can."

Let's raise the bar just a little, and make a list of holes that are big enough for a cat to walk through. These include

- Holes in the air barrier behind zero-clearance metal fireplaces.
- Unsealed holes above kitchen soffits.

- Unsealed holes above dropped ceilings.
- Attic access hatches or pull-down attic stairs without any weatherstripping.
- Unsealed utility chases that connect basements with attics.
- Holes behind bathtubs installed on exterior walls.

Once these holes are patched—in most cases, using OSB, plywood, rigid foam, or Thermo-ply®—what's next? If you are a Passivhaus builder aiming to achieve 0.6 ACH50, the answer is simple: every conceivable crack in the home's thermal barrier needs to be sealed. In some cases, Passivhaus builders use a redundant approach—for example, using both caulk and a gasket.

If you are a production builder, you probably don't have the time or inclination to approach air sealing with a fastidious attention to detail that Passivhaus builders employ. So perhaps you buy a case of caulk and begin by sealing the cracks between double studs and the cracks between double top plates. Or maybe you focus on sealing the cracks around windows. When you run out of caulk, you might call it a day.

Does this approach make sense? Not really.

QUANTIFYING THE RESULTS OF SEALING MEASURES

Dave Wolf, a senior research and development project leader at Owens Corning®, completed a study to determine which cracks and holes result in the "biggest bang for your air-sealing buck" ("Characterization of Air Leakage in Residential Structures," 2012). Wolf's research had two components: laboratory measurements of air leakage through several 8-ft. by 8-ft. mockups of building assemblies, and field research at a 1,400-sq.-ft. Owens Corning test house. (To measure the results of different air-sealing measures, the researchers used a blower door: "All joints were selectively sealed and/or unsealed for measuring their contribution to the overall air leakage of the house.")

Wolf concluded that the five most important areas for builders to focus their air-sealing efforts are:

- Cracks at recessed can lights in the top-floor ceiling.

RIM JOIST. The rim joist is prone to air leaks from the multiple gaps: mudsill to rim joist, rim joist to subfloor, and butt joints in the rim joist itself. Install rigid foam insulation in each joist bay and seal its perimeter with spray foam.

- Cracks between duct boots in the top-floor ceiling and the ceiling drywall.

- Cracks between the top plates of top-floor partitions and the partition drywall.

- Leakage through walls separating a house from an attached garage.

- Cracks in the rim-joist area.

A few comments on Wolf's findings

The researchers did not test leaks around floor-mounted duct boots. Nor did they test leaks at cracks between ceiling drywall and bath exhaust fan housings. Wolf speculated that these leaks might be worse than the leaks around ceiling-mounted duct boots, because with most bath fans, "There isn't necessarily a flange. Unlike with a duct boot, it is a flangeless opening."

Because leakage was measured by a blower door, the reported results exaggerated the importance of leaks near the neutral pressure plane and didn't properly evaluate the way the stack effect disproportionately depressurizes the lowest areas of a house and pressurizes the highest areas of a house. In spite of this fact, four out of five of the highlighted areas are either down low (the basement rim joist) or up high (recessed cans, ceiling duct boots, and top-plate cracks). My conclusion: These leakage areas are even more important than Wolf's research indicates. So be sure to seal these areas!

Walls between a house and an attached garage made the list due to the fact that these walls leak more than other walls—not because of any concerns over indoor air quality or to the fact that air in a garage is often contaminated. Why are these walls leaky? "These are the only exterior walls where you have drywall on both sides," Wolf told me. "Drywall is a flimsy material compared to OSB sheathing or plywood. When you mechanically fasten drywall on the

CEILING-MOUNTED DUCT BOOTS.
Ceiling-mounted duct boots are one of the five most important areas for air sealing in the home. Seal to the ceiling with foam or an acoustical sealant.

outside of the studs, the crack where it mates with the framing is not as tight as what you get with OSB or plywood." These walls are good candidates for the airtight drywall approach (see p. 111).

At the opposite end of the spectrum are the cracks that take a lot of sealant and a lot of time to seal, without reducing total air leakage by very much. This group—let's call it the "why bother?" list—includes vertical sheathing joints, the cracks between double top plates, and the cracks between the wall sheathing and the framing of window rough openings.

A few caveats

Wolf provided a helpful list of caveats:

- The study provided a "blower-door-centric point of view. All of the... results are prioritized based on the effect on whole-house leakage, not thermal comfort, IAQ, etc."

- It best to try to "seal all the joints, if you can. The sealing of all joints/openings is important, although some are more important than others."

- It makes sense to "get the big holes first. This study focuses on small joints/openings only (i.e., the big holes are presumed to be blocked & sealed)."

- "Sometimes the cladding matters. The wall cladding is assumed to be air permeable (e.g., vinyl, fiber-cement, wood siding, or brick, not stucco or stone veneer)."

- "These results are for general guidance. These results should be considered directional, not absolute, since construction quality varies from house to house."

- "Don't abandon common sense. If you can see daylight through a joint, it should be sealed, regardless of what this study may indicate."

DRYWALL IS THE UNSUNG HERO OF AIR-SEALING EFFORTS

When weatherization contractors try to seal leaks in an existing home, the work is known as "blower door directed air sealing." Veterans of this type of work know that some time-consuming measures have little effect on a home's air leakage rate, while other simple measures produce good results. Here are two lessons that weatherization contractors have learned:

- It always makes sense to seal the big holes first.

- Holes near the bottom of the house (in a crawl space or basement) and holes near the top of the house (in the ceiling of the top floor) matter much more than holes near the center of the house (an area that is also known as the "neutral pressure plane").

Wolf's research looks at these issues from the perspective of a new home builder rather than of a weatherization contractor. His results give important guidance to builders who are just beginning to think about air sealing.

The research results correlate well with long-standing advice on air sealing. "When you stack up these results with typical air-sealing advice, the list passes the gut check for what has been said for a long time," Wolf told me. "That might be deflating since we just found out what the industry already knew. But what is novel about this is that we have quantified the amount of leakage per unit length for all of these joints. We know for a top-plate-to-drywall crack how many cfm50 per foot that the crack leaks. And we can take those parameters to do calculations: 'Is it worth it to me to seal this particular joint?' With the information we have, you can calculate that if you have 100 ft. of this type of joint, the sealing ought to be worth about so much to me from a blower door standpoint. We can use the information to help make strategic decisions."

Wolf's research demonstrated the contribution that drywall makes to the airtightness of wall assemblies. "When we tested naked walls without drywall in place, they leaked a lot," Wolf told me. "Sometimes you could even see daylight through the cracks. But when you put the drywall on, the leakage went down dramatically. The drywall is providing a secondary air barrier. There might be five different locations in the wall cavity where air is leaking in, but the air is having a hard time getting past the drywall. The pressure in the wall cavity builds up, and you don't have a 50-Pascal pressure difference across your sheathing; you do across the drywall, but not across the sheathing. It took making the measurements for me to see the effect of this traffic jam in the wall cavity."

If you care about airtightness, it's probably time for you to bring your painter a box of donuts. "When the painter comes along, the builder holds the painter accountable," said Wolf. "The painter has to make sure that finishes look magnificent, and the work includes caulking the trim pieces to the drywall. What the painter is inadvertently doing is improving the airtightness of the drywall layer. We would never advocate using painter's caulk as part of your air barrier. It is not the right approach. But it is interesting that it does have an impact. The painter is playing a role in improving the airtightness of the wall."

Which materials, substances, and practices are important to keep your indoor air fresh and healthy?

Many owners of green homes are concerned about indoor air quality, worrying that some building materials emit dangerous chemicals. For example, I've been asked these questions:

• Will the glue in my plywood or OSB subfloor emit dangerous fumes?

• Will borate-treated cellulose insulation off-gas enough to affect the health of my children?

• What type of clothes dryer is best from the perspective of indoor air quality?

If there is a theme running through these questions—and I think there is—it would be this: Homeowners are worrying about the wrong materials and substances.

OCCUPANT BEHAVIOR MATTERS MORE THAN CONSTRUCTION SPECIFICATIONS

Indoor air quality (IAQ) is a big topic. To get a handle on it, we need to break it down into small bites. Here's how I'd like to proceed:

First, provide an overview of the issue. Then present three lists of substances that are worrisome. The first list includes worrisome substances that are found only in older houses. The second list includes worrisome substances arising from construction methods sometimes used in new homes. The third list includes worrisome substances that homeowners are exposed to because of occupant behavior.

Next, share a list of new home specifications that are important for anyone concerned about indoor air quality (see "New Home Specifications and Advice" on p. 133). Finally, summarize researchers' findings about which chemicals are most concerning.

INDOOR AIR IS LOW-QUALITY AIR

In most U.S. locations, indoor air is more polluted than outdoor air. According to the ASHRAE, "Studies from the Environmental Protection Agency on human exposure to air pollutants show that indoor levels of pollutants may be two to five times, sometimes more than 100 times, higher than outdoor levels."

There are exceptions to this rule, of course. If your house is located near a busy intersection or a location where buses or trucks often idle their engines, the outdoor air near you house may be more polluted than your indoor air. If you live in such a location, increased ventilation may not improve the quality of your indoor air. For the rest of us, however, ventilating a house with outdoor air usually improves the situation.

If you're worried about IAQ, the most important test you should perform is a radon test. If you've tested for radon, you're done. In most cases, further testing isn't justified.

WORRISOME SUBSTANCES THAT ARE FOUND ONLY IN OLDER HOMES

Asbestos fibers. Most building products containing asbestos were removed from the U.S. market by the mid-1980s. If you live in a house built before 1985, however, it may include building materials (for example, pipe insulation or vermiculite) that contain asbestos. If your house was built in 1985 or later, you don't have to worry about asbestos. Friable (crumbly) asbestos insulation on pipes or ducts can be dangerous; so can vermiculite. If you suspect that your home includes hazardous asbestos, consult a certified asbestos abatement contractor.

Lead. Lead-containing paint is very common in houses built before 1950. According to the Centers for Disease Control and Prevention, more than 250,000 American children under the age of six have elevated blood lead levels. Lead-containing dust can originate from lead paint or lead-contaminated soil; the dust can be ingested through the lungs or the stomach (by hand-to-mouth contact). Lead-containing dust can be generated by scraping, sanding, or demolition activities; it can also be generated by opening and closing an old window sash. (Intact and undisturbed painted surfaces are usually not a health hazard.)

Although it's possible for adults or children above the age of six to be poisoned by lead, young children and pregnant women are the most vulnerable. In the United States, lead paint for residential use continued to be sold until 1978. If your house was built after 1979, you don't have to worry about lead paint.

For more information on avoiding lead paint hazards, see www.epa.gov/lead.

WORRISOME SUBSTANCES RELATED TO CONSTRUCTION METHODS

Radon. Radon is a naturally occurring radioactive gas that is present in many soils. It can enter a house through cracks in the foundation. If exposure levels are high enough, radon can eventually cause cancer. Fortunately, construction details have been developed to reduce or eliminate dangerous levels of radon. Unfortunately, some builders still build homes without these necessary details.

For more information on avoiding radon hazards, see www.epa.gov/radon.

Formaldehyde. In the past, products made of particleboard (especially inexpensive kitchen cabinets and inexpensive furniture) and some other composite wood materials contained worrisome levels of formaldehyde. Formaldehyde is a gas; at high concentrations, formaldehyde can cause health problems, including cancer.

The good news is that federal legislation enacted in 2010 established new lower limits for permissible formaldehyde emissions from composite wood products (including hardwood plywood, medium-density fiberboard, and particleboard). Since this legislation (the Formaldehyde Standards for Composite Wood Products Act) was passed, health risks associated with cabinets and furniture made from these composite wood products have been greatly reduced. That said, concerned homeowners may want to specify formaldehyde-free cabinets and furniture.

In the past, manufacturers of fiberglass batts used a formaldehyde-containing binder (glue) to help hold the fibers together. In 2015, however, the last fiberglass manufacturer in the United States using a formaldehyde-based binder switched over to an acrylic-based binder—so we can scratch that worry off our list.

Manufacturers of mineral wool still use formaldehyde-based binders. Where this fact is worrisome depends on your appetite for risk; the level of formaldehyde that remains in the product after the glue has cured is low, and in most homes, there is an air barrier between the insulation and the indoor air.

Formaldehyde is also a component of tobacco smoke and the fumes given off by a gas range. Smoking tobacco indoors (or anywhere, frankly) is a very bad idea. And anyone concerned about the formaldehyde emissions produced by a gas range should choose an electric range (either one with electric-resistance burners or an induction range).

For more information on avoiding formaldehyde hazards, see www.epa.gov/formaldehyde.

Volatile organic compounds. Volatile organic compounds (VOCs) are found in many liquid products, including solvents, household cleaning products, paints, varnishes, and fuels like gasoline. Reducing the levels of VOCs in your home is mostly a matter of occupant behavior: To the best of your ability, choose paints and cleaning products that are low-VOC or zero-VOC.

That said, there is one aspect of VOC exposure that depends on construction specifications—namely, whether your home has an attached garage. Homeowners often store products that emit VOCs—including gasoline, solvents, and old cans of paint—in their garage. If you have an attached garage, air from the garage can enter your house through leaks in the common wall. There are two ways to avoid this problem: Either specify a detached garage or make sure your builder pays extremely close attention to the air barrier between your garage and your house.

Water vapor. At high levels, water vapor lowers your indoor air quality.

While water vapor doesn't directly cause health problems, at high concentrations it can encourage the growth of mold and dust mites. If anyone in your family has asthma, indoor relative humidity levels matter, because mold and dust mites can aggravate asthma symptoms.

Sloppy construction details—especially bad basement details or crawl space details—can contribute to high indoor humidity levels.

WORRISOME SUBSTANCES RELATED TO OCCUPANT BEHAVIOR

Smoking tobacco. Smoking threatens the health of smokers, and indoor smoking threatens the health of everyone who lives in the house. Smoking tobacco belongs near the top of any list of habits to avoid. Do it outdoors or don't do it at all.

Using insecticides or pesticides indoors. If you have ants in your kitchen, research safe ways to discourage them without the use of insecticides.

Using solvents or industrial cleaning products indoors. Some Q&A columns advise homeowners to clean their bathtub with paint thinner or acetone. Sure, it works—but you don't want to try this at home.

Hobbies that require using chemicals or solvents. If you refinish furniture indoors, you may be using varnishes that emit VOCs. Do this type of work in a detached garage, or get a powerful exhaust fan.

Plug-in air fresheners. Plug-in air fresheners release volatile chemicals into your indoor air. If your bedroom smells like dirty socks, you should collect the dirty socks and wash them. Don't use a plug-in air freshener.

Forgetting to operate an exhaust fan. Your bathroom and range hood have exhaust fans for a reason: to exhaust humidity, particulates, and aerosols from your house. Use your fans.

Using an unvented gas heater. Gas space heaters and gas fireplaces emit lots of water vapor and, if the burners are not adjusted properly, can emit carbon monoxide. If you want a gas space heater in your house, make sure it is vented.

Wood smoke. If you have a wood stove, you know that smoke sometimes enters your house when you open the stove to load fuel. Wood smoke contains acrolein, formaldehyde, and small particulates that aren't good for your lungs. Some homeowners accept this level of risk; but for others, this type of indoor pollution is unacceptable.

Pets. People who keep pets usually love them, but cats and dogs can add lots of pet hair and dander to your home. Is this a problem? You decide.

Flame retardants in furniture cushions. The foam used in furniture cushions usually contains brominated flame retardants, and some experts worry that these flame retardants may have negative health effects. If you're worried about flame retardants, you may want to seek out furniture that is flame-retardant-free.

Emissions from new carpeting. In the 1990s, many magazine articles proposed a link between "new carpet smell" and health problems. Since then, carpet manufacturers have made a concerted effort to identify chemicals of concern and to reduce emissions. Research sponsored by the U.S. Consumer Product Safety Commission (CPSC) determined that none of the chemicals found in new carpeting are emitted at levels known to be hazardous. That said, if you are worried about emissions from carpeting, you can certainly specify hardwood flooring or tile.

Meth labs. If you are reading this book, you probably don't have a meth lab in your kitchen. If you're thinking of setting one up—don't.

Aerosols and particulates from cooking. Cooking releases acrolein and tiny particulates that can harm human health. Cooking over a gas flame releases nitrogen dioxide, formaldehyde, and carbon monoxide. From an IAQ perspective, cooking with an electric appliance is far preferable to cooking with a gas appliance. No matter what type of fuel you use, it's important to operate an exhaust fan that vents outdoors when you are cooking.

Burning candles. Burning candles releases small particulates into the air. Unless it's someone's birthday, don't light candles indoors.

WHAT DO THE RESEARCHERS SAY?

Max Sherman, a senior researcher at Lawrence Berkeley National Laboratory (and a recipient of ASHRAE's Louise and Bill Holladay Distinguished Fellow Award, named after my grandparents), helped develop a list of the top nine contaminants that lower the quality of indoor air. These contaminants are both relatively common and relatively concerning (due to their known deleterious health effects).

Most of the chemicals that show up in questions posted by concerned homeowners on web forums don't make the list. What matters most? It turns out that fine particulates—PM2.5—cause the most health damage. In fact, these fine particulates are three times more concerning (from a health perspective) than the next most worrisome contaminant on the list. Some of these particulates come from outdoor air, due (for example) to diesel exhaust or wood smoke. The rest come from indoor activities like cooking and burning candles.

Just because I have included an item in one of the lists in this chapter, doesn't mean that the items on these lists have equal weight. If you smoke a pack of cigarettes a day indoors, you are endangering the health of your family. On the other hand, there isn't much evidence that you have to worry about carpeting (as long as you keep your house clean).

Here are a few key points for anyone concerned about IAQ:

- Every bathroom should have either an exhaust fan or an exhaust grille connected to an HRV or ERV.

- Your kitchen range should have a range hood equipped with an exhaust fan that is ducted to the outdoors.

- If your home has a furnace, boiler, or water heater that burns propane, natural gas, or oil, make sure that these appliances have sealed-combustion burners that resist backdrafting.

- Your house should have a ventilation system capable of meeting ASHRAE 62.2 requirements. In some cases, a bathroom exhaust fan, properly controlled, can perform this function. To limit the entry of small particulates into your home, supply ventilation systems and balanced ventilation systems should include a MERV 13 filter. If you choose to install an exhaust-only ventilation system, most of the particulates in the outdoor air that enters your home through building cracks are likely to be filtered out as the air passes through building assemblies on the way to your home's interior.

- If your house has a basement or crawl space, make sure that it is detailed to limit the entry of moisture and radon.

- A detached garage is preferable to an attached garage. If you have an attached garage, make sure that the common wall has an impeccable air barrier, and that the door to your garage has excellent weatherstripping.

- Never install an unvented gas space heater or an unvented gas fireplace in your home.

- Remember that most IAQ problems are related to occupant behavior. If you want clean indoor air, you will need to police your family.

If your home has a supply ventilation system (for example, a central-fan-integrated supply ventilation system), it's a good idea to include a MERV 13 filter. This filter should be installed at your air handler or furnace. If your home has a balanced ventilation system (an HRV or ERV), choose a ventilating appliance that offers a MERV 13 option. A MERV 13 filter will eliminate most of the PM2.5 particles entering your home.

According to Terry Brennan, a building scientist who serves on the ASHRAE 62.2 committee, "The kitchen range is the biggest stationary source of fine particulates in a residential setting. It's the pyrolizing and burning of food that makes most of the particulates and contaminants." So install a good range hood fan, and use it.

After fine particulates, the next two most worrisome contaminants are acrolein and formaldehyde. Acrolein comes from cooking, wood smoke, and tobacco smoke. Formaldehyde is a component of tobacco smoke and is emitted by many types of particleboard.

Radon may or may not be a contaminant of concern. Anyone worried about indoor radon should certainly test their air for radon. If concerning levels of radon are detected, it's important to install a radon mitigation system.

There's a lot that researchers still don't know

Every tight home needs a mechanical ventilation system. Research has shown that operating a ventilation system helps reduce indoor levels of most air-borne contaminants that can injure human health. That said, researchers haven't been able to determine the ideal residential ventilation rate needed to optimize occupant health. (According to Terry Brennan, most studies seem to support a ventilation rate in the range of 10cfm to 20 cfm per occupant.) In fact, researchers haven't yet been able to show any correlation between residential ventilation and occupant health.

That doesn't mean that we should be skeptical of the need for mechanical ventilation; it only means that we need to be aware of the many uncertainties surrounding advice on optimizing indoor air quality.

Assessing the risk

Researchers have noted that there are serious health problems associated with inhaling fumes given off by food that is being cooked and inhaling wood smoke. These are some of the most worrisome contaminants found in indoor air. Yet we all know that people have been breathing fumes given off by food that is being cooked, and have been inhaling wood smoke, for thousands of years. My mother doesn't know what a range hood is, and would never think of operating an exhaust fan. Moreover, she has spent countless hours—weeks and months, actually— sitting around smoky camp fires. She is 88 years old. Most families include elderly people who have breathed a lot of cooking fumes and wood smoke.

While these contaminants are dangerous, humans have a lot of experience with them—so it's important to keep these risks in proper perspective.

Whenever there is a temperature difference between the interior of a house and the outdoors, heat flows through ceilings, walls, and floors. We can slow down this heat flow, but we can't stop it. The thicker the insulation we install, the slower the rate of heat flow. That's why thick insulation is always better than thin insulation.

5

INSULATION

For decades, designers and builders of wood-framed homes didn't spend much time thinking about insulation. The usual approach, still followed in much of the United States, was to fill the stud bays with fiberglass batts and, once the ceiling drywall was installed, to unroll some fiberglass insulation in the attic.

Because of this decades-long legacy, it's not unusual for a designer, builder, or homeowner to post the following question on GBA: "We just finished framing, installing windows, and roofing. Now we have a few questions about the best way to insulate."

My usual reaction is, "Really? You're asking *now*?"

THESE DECISIONS NEED TO BE MADE EARLY

In many cases, these insulation questions are posted a few weeks too late. Why?

Once the windows have been installed, it's usually too late to install any rigid foam on the exterior side of the wall sheathing.

Once the roof trusses have been installed, it's too late to order raised-heel trusses (which are needed to make sure there's room at the perimeter of the attic to install enough insulation between the top plates of the exterior walls and the roof sheathing).

Assuming the house has some cathedral ceilings—and these days, many designs do—it's too late to install any rigid foam on the exterior side of the roof sheathing once the roofing has been installed.

PLAN AHEAD. Insulation decisions should be finalized before construction begins.

Why would builders leave these decisions to the last minute? Well, some builders think, "We'll either fill the stud bays with fiberglass batts—or, if the homeowner wants to pay for an upgrade, we'll just use spray foam." The trouble with that approach is that a wall with insulation between the studs has a lot of thermal bridging through the framing. If you care about this thermal bridging, you really need to include exterior rigid foam insulation or exterior mineral wool insulation—or frame a double-stud wall.

So this important decision—about how to address thermal bridging—has to be made at the design stage, before the walls are framed.

Other examples of not planning ahead

Plenty of projects have gone off the rails due to the failure to plan ahead. Delays in figuring out where the insulation will go is just one example. Another example: failing to make the mechanical room big enough.

Mechanical equipment for a typical house may include some or all of the following:

- A furnace, air handler, or boiler.
- A water heater.
- A water pump and a pressure tank.
- A water softener.
- An HRV or ERV, along with associated ductwork.

Some of these appliances have access panels, so the designer of a mechanical room has to provide enough room for service personnel to get to those panels. The manufacturers of these appliances all specify how much access is needed for proper servicing of the equipment. Failure to follow manufacturers' installation instructions is a code violation. Finally, the designer of a mechanical room has to consider where all the ducts are going and has to leave plenty of room to install these ducts.

How often do residential designers do a good job of designing a mechanical room? In my experience, less than half the time. What happens when these issues are left to the last minute? The builder posts a question on GBA: "We've decided to install an HRV, but we're not sure where to put it. Can we install an HRV in the garage or the attic?"

Where do the ducts go?

Sometimes a designer or owner-builder does a good job of designing the mechanical room. There's plenty of room for the furnace, the HRV, the water heater, and all the rest of the equipment. But no one has thought about how to run the ducts, and everyone now realizes that there is a major beam in the way. Or maybe the designer thought about the supply air system, but forgot about the need to install return air ducts. Suddenly, everyone on the team

YOU HAVE TO PLAN AHEAD FOR ROOF INSULATION, TOO

In most climates, cathedral ceilings are best insulated with exterior rigid foam. But the decision to install rigid foam has to be made before the roofing is installed. True, it's possible to thoroughly insulate a cathedral ceiling without installing any exterior rigid foam. But if you install enough insulation to meet minimum code requirements, you may have to lower the ceiling—and a lot of homeowners don't want to do that.

GBA regularly receives questions from readers with poorly performing cathedral ceilings. Problems include high energy bills, temperature stratification problems, and ice dams. In almost all cases, the best solution includes the installation of exterior rigid foam. On an existing house—especially one with skylights—this is very expensive work. On a new house, the work is much simpler and cheaper, but you have to plan ahead for this work.

And why would anyone who is planning a vented unconditioned attic forget to order raised-heel trusses? I don't know. But it happens all the time.

is discussing trade-offs: What's worse, a duct soffit or an imperfect duct system?

HIRE AN ARCHITECT

If you are an owner-builder, you will probably make some mistakes, even if you've read this chapter. (They'll just be different mistakes from the ones mentioned here.) If you hire an architect or a residential designer, ideally one with gray hair, you won't regret the decision.

R-value measures heat transfer by conduction, convection, and radiation

R-value measurements are subject to a fair amount of ridicule, especially by marketers of radiant barriers. As it turns out, however, the ridicule is mostly unwarranted.

R-value is a measure of a material's resistance to heat transfer. Before 1945, resistance to heat flow was measured by referring to a material's U-factor. The lower a material's U-factor, the better the material is at resisting the flow of heat. Because many people assume that high numbers on a scale are "better" than low numbers, insulation manufacturers found it hard to market insulation by bragging about a low U-factor. So the R-value—which is simply the inverse of U-factor—was proposed by Everett Shuman, the director of Penn State's Building Research Institute. Since R = 1/U, the higher the R-value, the better the insulation.

DOES R-VALUE MEASURE ONLY CONDUCTION?

Some manufacturers of radiant barriers falsely claim that R-value measures only conductive heat flow while ignoring the other two heat-flow mechanisms, convection and radiation. In fact, R-value calculations include all three heat-transfer mechanisms.

The usual procedure for testing a material's R-value is ASTM C518, *Standard Test Method for Steady-State Thermal Transmission Properties by Means of the Heat Flow Meter Apparatus*. The test method requires a technician to measure the ther-

mal resistance of a specimen placed between a cold plate and a hot plate.

When a fiberglass batt is tested, heat flows from the hot side of the batt to the cold side. Wherever individual fibers of insulation touch each other, heat is transferred from fiber to fiber by conduction. Where fibers are separated by air, the heat is transferred from a hot fiber to a cooler fiber by radiation and by conduction through the air. Finally, the effects of any convective loops within the insulation are also captured by the test procedure. Because a material's R-value is the measurement of its resistance to all three heat-flow mechanisms—conduction, radiation, and convection—it is a useful way to compare insulation products.

R-VALUE MATTERS, BUT SO DOES AIR LEAKAGE

Of course, an insulated wall is affected by many factors not addressed by R-value testing. Although the R-value test captures the effects, if any, of convective loops within the insulation, it obviously cannot be expected to measure the amount of air leakage through a wall assembly once the insulation is installed. The rate of air leakage is affected by the density of the insulation, the presence or absence of an air barrier in the wall assembly, wind speed, and the stack effect.

Because of these factors, a leaky wall assembly insulated with fiberglass batts will usually perform worse than a wall assembly insulated with spray foam having the same R-value as the batts. The performance differences are due to spray foam's ability to reduce air leakage, not to any difference in R-value between the two materials. It doesn't make any sense to blame the R-value test for differences in air leakage between the two wall assemblies.

To obtain the best performance from fiberglass insulation, the Energy Star Homes program requires most fiberglass-insulated framing cavities to be enclosed by air barriers on all six sides. While the recommendation is sensible, it's hard to achieve in the field. If such a six-sided air barrier can be created, however, fiberglass insulation will meet the performance expectation promised on the product's R-value label.

Some marketers of radiant barriers or spray foam insulation imply that R-value measurements are meaningless. On the contrary, R-value is a useful measurement. But just because you know a product's R-value doesn't mean you know everything necessary to predict heat flow through a wall or ceiling. R-value is just one factor among many to be considered when deciding which insulation to use. Builders must also understand many other topics, including air leakage and moisture movement. No one has yet invented a "magic number" that replaces the requirement for builders to study and understand building science principles.

DOES RADIANT HEAT PASS THROUGH INSULATION LIKE RADIO WAVES?

Another scare tactic employed by some marketers of radiant barriers is the idea that conventional insulation materials— sometimes called "mass insulation"— allow radiant heat to pass right through them. Scam artists have been known to warn builders that mass insulation is

transparent to radiant heat. The implication is that a layer of aluminum foil is necessary to prevent radiant heat from traveling like radio waves right through a deep layer of cellulose.

In fact, most mass insulation products do a good job of stopping radiant heat flow. Radiant heat easily travels through air (for example, from a wood stove to nearby skin) or a vacuum (for example, from the sun to the earth). But radiant energy can't travel through a solid material. If the sun is shining on a concrete patio, for example, the heat travels to the soil below by conduction, not radiation. Here's what happens: The concrete is first warmed by the sun (by radiation), and then the warm concrete gives off some of its heat to the ground below (by conduction). There is no radiant heat transfer from the sun to the soil.

When radiant heat hits one side of a deep layer of insulation, only a tiny percentage of that heat is "shine-through" radiation that manages to miss all of the fibers in the insulation blanket and emerge unscathed on the other side.

The fact that heat flows through a layer of insulation doesn't mean that the insulation isn't working. By definition, insulation slows down heat flow; it doesn't stop it. Heat will always flow from hot to cold. The more insulation, however, the slower the rate of heat flow.

It's hard to do a perfect job

Of all of the commonly used types of insulation—including cellulose, rigid foam, and spray polyurethane foam—fiberglass batts perform the worst. As typically installed, fiberglass batts do little to reduce airflow through a wall or ceiling assembly; rarely fill the entire cavity in which they are installed; and sometimes permit the development of convective loops that degrade insulation performance. Knowing this, why would any builder choose to install fiberglass batts? The answer is simple: because fiberglass batts cost less than any other type of insulation.

Before we totally dismiss all fiberglass batt installations, however, it's important to note that there is a big difference between the typical fiberglass batt installation and a best-practice installation. If a conscientious builder installs fiberglass batts carefully, it's possible—although not easy—to get the best of both worlds: adequate thermal performance at a relatively low price.

LOTS OF SLOPPY INSTALLATIONS

Study after study has shown that most fiberglass batt jobs are sloppy. In 2002, the California Energy Commission contracted with researchers Marc Hoeschele, Rick Chitwood, and Bill Pennington to conduct a study of new California homes. In its March 2003 issue, *Energy Design Update* reported, "The performance problems uncovered by the study were particularly disappointing in light of the fact that all 30 houses [studied by the researchers] were enrolled in programs promoting building-envelope improvements and duct tightness."

PROPER INSTALLATION takes time. Few fiberglass contractors take the time to install batts carefully.

The article went on to note that "the California Energy Commission's 'envelope protocols,' which include standards for air sealing and insulation installation, were widely ignored . . . . Not a single builder managed to implement any of the following standards:

- Insulation batts cut to fit around wiring, plumbing, and electrical boxes;
- Skylight shaft batts installed in contact with the drywall;
- Installation of a facing to limit air intrusion on the attic side of kneewall and skylight well batts."

Even builders enrolled in the EPA's Energy Star Homes program have struggled to achieve good thermal performance in fiberglass-insulated homes. An article in the April 2005 issue of *Energy Design Update*, "Fiberglass-Insulated Homes Are the Leakiest," discussed the findings of Bruce Harley, the Conservation Services Group's technical director for residen-

Many builders don't realize that sloppy fiberglass installation is a code violation. For example, section 303.2 of the 2009 and 2012 IECC requires that "All materials, systems and equipment shall be installed in accordance with the manufacturer's installation instructions and the International Building Code."

This provision is relevant because the installation instructions provided by fiberglass batt manufacturers are widely ignored. Harley wrote, "Most installation instructions require fluffing insulation to the proper thickness, covering continuously, filling cavities completely, and fitting products around all obstructions, such as wiring, plumbing, and framing."

CertainTeed® instructs installers of its fiberglass batts to follow these recommendations of the North American Insulation Manufacturers Association (NAIMA):

- "When insulating side walls, place the insulation in the cavity and check to be sure it completely fills the cavity, top to bottom."

- "It is important that insulation be correctly sized for the cavity and fit snugly at the sides and ends."

- "Even the smallest openings between framing members should be insulated."

- "Junction boxes for wall switches and convenience outlets at outside walls should be insulated between the rear of the box and the sheathing. Place insulation behind the junction box and if necessary, cut insulation to fit snugly around it."

---

tial energy services. "Harley assembled airtightness data on Energy Star homes (including single-family and multifamily homes) completed in 2004 in Massachusetts and Rhode Island. All of the homes were blower-door tested after completion," the article reported. "Harley found that houses with walls insulated with spray polyurethane foam were significantly tighter than those houses with walls insulated with cellulose, and that houses with walls insulated with cellulose were significantly tighter than those insulated with fiberglass."

DOING IT RIGHT

We've all seen sloppy fiberglass jobs—installations with a wavy surface that include sections of insulation recessed from the studs. Typical fiberglass jobs often have gaps at the edges of batts. The insulation is often pinched by wiring, and batts are rarely trimmed neatly around electrical boxes. Moreover, many installation problems—for example, gaps behind electrical boxes—can't be seen unless batts are lifted for inspection.

In a good installation job:

- Insulation should be installed without gaps, including at cavity corners.

- Batts should be trimmed about 1 in. oversize so they fit the cavity snugly.

- The entire framing cavity should be filled, without any air gaps between the insulation and the drywall.

- Batts should not be folded or compressed.

- Batts should be delaminated where necessary to fit around wiring. There

FIT THE BATT. With the batt tight to the top plate, an installer cuts the batts to length and width in place using a batt knife. When the cavity is longer than the batt, a piece is added to the bottom.

FILL THE CAVITY. Once the batt is sized, it is inserted carefully into the cavity. The installer uses the batt knife to push the sides, tip, and bottom flush to the sheathing. If you're careful, you can do this without compressing the batt.

FLUFF THE EDGES. Once the batt is in place, any compressed areas are fluffed out with the batt knife. For out-of-reach sections, a long pole with a spike in the end places and fluffs the insulation.

should be no gaps behind wiring, electrical boxes, or pipes.

• Attic insulation should be installed over the top plates of exterior walls.

• Batts installed in kneewalls and skylight shafts should be protected on all sides by a rigid air-barrier material like drywall, OSB, Thermo-ply, or rigid foam.

• If the roof assembly includes ventilation channels, insulation must not block air flow.

Defining sloppy installation

Gaps in fiberglass insulation have a disproportionate effect on thermal envelope performance; in other words, a 5% insulation gap in a wall lowers the wall's R-value by much more than 5%.

The Residential Energy Services Network (RESNET®), a national association of home energy raters, has long struggled with the question of how to estimate the R-value of walls that vary widely in performance depending on the skill of the insulation installer. Eventually, RESNET developed a rating system for insulation installation quality. The system was described in an article published in the January/February 2005 issue of *Home Energy* magazine, "Insulation Inspections for Home Energy Ratings," by Bruce Harley.

The RESNET rating system recognizes three levels of insulation installation quality: Grade I, Grade II, and Grade III. "In order to qualify for a Grade I rating, insulation must . . . fill each cavity side to side and top to bottom, with no substantial gaps or voids around obstructions (that is, blocking or bridging), and it must be split, or fitted tightly, around wiring and other services in the cavity. In general, no exterior sheathing should be visible through gaps in the material," Harley wrote. "Compression or incomplete fill amounting to 2% or less of the surface area of insulation is acceptable for Grade 1, if the

Inspectors from RESNET give batt-insulation installations a rating of Grade I, II, or III. The grades describe the quality of the installation and the completeness of the air barrier. Grades I and II assume a durable and continuous air barrier. Installations without an adequate air barrier are automatically downgraded to Grade III or "uninsulated."

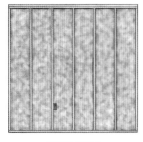
GRADE I

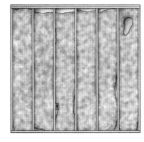
GRADE II

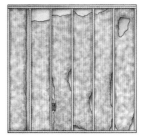
GRADE III

compression or missing fill spaces are less than 30% of the intended fill thickness (that is, 70% or more of the intended insulation thickness is present)."

The standard for a Grade II installation is lower. "A Grade II rating represents moderate to frequent defects: gaps around wiring, electrical outlets, plumbing, other intrusions; rounded edges or 'shoulders,' larger gaps, or more significant compression. No more than 2% of the surface area of insulation missing is acceptable for Grade II."

Grade III installations are the worst: "A Grade III rating applies to any installation that is worse than Grade II."

IT'S HARD TO DO IT RIGHT

Although the steps required to install fiberglass batts well are easy to describe, they are fairly difficult to achieve. It is the nature of a fiberglass batt to want to be installed sloppily. Unlike cellulose or spray polyurethane foam, a fiberglass batt doesn't volunteer to fill a cavity com-

pletely; on the contrary, it tends to fight an installer's attempt to make it fit snugly.

It's interesting to compare the structural performance of a commonly used construction technique—stick-frame construction—with the thermal performance of a typical fiberglass batt job. Stick-frame construction is redundant and forgiving. Even done sloppily—with a few missed nails or split plates—wood framing rarely experiences structural failure.

By contrast, almost every fiberglass insulation job fails to live up to the R-value promised on its label. Unlike stick framing, the system is unforgiving and totally lacking in redundancy. To achieve the R-value shown on its label, a fiberglass batt must be installed perfectly in a wall or ceiling cavity enclosed by a six-sided air barrier.

Knowing this, builders who want their installed insulation to achieve decent thermal performance have two choices: they can either learn how to install fiberglass batts perfectly or choose a more forgiving insulation system.

HOW TO INSTALL CELLULOSE INSULATION

Insulation expert Bill Hulstrunk provides detailed instructions for blowing loose-fill cellulose on attic floors and for dense-packing walls

In some parts of the United States—notably northern New England—cellulose insulation has been widely used for more than 30 years. In other parts of the country, however, cellulose insulation is just beginning to gain traction.

Of course, cellulose insulation is installed with different techniques from those used to install fiberglass batts or spray foam. To help explain these techniques to builders who are unfamiliar with cellulose, I interviewed Bill Hulstrunk, the technical manager at National Fiber®, a manufacturer of cellulose insulation in Belchertown, MA. Hulstrunk has worked as an insulation installer, an energy auditor, a weatherization program director, and a trainer. The following answers are his.

Q. What type of equipment is used to blow cellulose?

A. If you are going to be an installer, you need to own your own blowing equip-

ment, which typically costs from $5,000 to $10,000. We don't recommend that our installers use rental machines.

These machines will be reasonably sized. Typically an installer will show up in a box truck or pulling a trailer. The equipment draws from 15 amps to 30 amps, depending on the machine. The 15-amp machines can be plugged in, but the 30-amp machines need their own generators.

Q. What is the most important thing to remember when installing loose-fill cellulose on an attic floor?

A. Because you are installing the insulation at a lower density, be sure you do all of the necessary air sealing work beforehand. Air sealing is critical. When homeowners say, "I don't have enough money to do both air sealing and insulation," I tell them, "Then it's better to wait until you have enough money

THE FASTEST WAY to move cellulose to an attic floor is through a big 3-in. hose.

to do the air sealing—otherwise the insulation doesn't make any sense."

Many of our cellulose installers, especially the ones who are BPI-certified, will do both air sealing and insulation work. With some of the utility efficiency programs, though, there will be a separate air-sealing crew that comes in first.

Q. What diameter of hose is used for installing loose-fill?

A. Usually a 3-in.-dia. hose, the same size that comes off the machine. We find that when you get over 200 ft. of hose you have a harder time pushing the material, but it depends on the equipment. If you're installing loose-fill on an attic floor, that's one application where you could run a machine rented from a local hardware store—it's a less critical application than dense pack.

Q. How much settling should an installer expect?

A. Approximately 13% settling. That occurs weeks or months after the installation. I always recommend that owners specify the settled thickness or R-value they want, and leave it up to the installer to do the calculations to determine how much material to put up there.

The installed thickness is somewhat dependent on how you hold the hose. The settling chart on the bag assumes that you hold the hose at a 45° angle and shoot it upward. But if you don't have the room to do that, and you shoot it straight out or downward, you increase the installed density—and in some cases it won't settle at all. The coverage per bag goes down, but you don't have any settling.

Most installers, if they are looking for 12 in., will put in 14 in. just to be sure they don't have any issues with settling. I always tell installers to be careful with these calculations, because you don't want a customer to call you back to install more insulation. Once you have to go back a second time, you've lost money on the job.

Q. Is it possible to cover recessed can lights with cellulose?

A. It depends on the rating on the can. If it is an IC-rated can, you can cover it—depending on a couple of factors. The National Electrical Code® seems to indicate that you can't put any insulation above can lights, but in fact we do it all the time. The code addresses worries that you can trip the thermal switch with some high-wattage bulbs. In all areas except Massachusetts, we just cover the can lights, and we don't have problems. But in Massachusetts, many of the utility programs don't allow coverage of the can lights.

There are really two kinds of IC-rated cans: ordinary IC and IC airtight. The regular IC lights are really leaky, so if that's what we're dealing with, we need an airtight enclosure around the light anyway. Instead of building a box, a lot of installers are using a large Sonotube®. You cut a length of the Sonotube and foam it to the ceiling below. Then you make a top out of Sheetrock® and foam the top in place. Once you've done that, you can cover the whole thing with cellulose. That stops the air leakage and ensures that the thermal switch won't blink on and off.

Q. Is it possible to cover bath fans with cellulose?

A. Yes. That's routine. However, if it is an older combination fan/light that takes a standard screw-in incandescent bulb, it's better to treat as if it were a non-IC recessed light fixture and enclose it in a box before insulating.

Q. Can you blow cellulose against a chimney?

A. No, you need to keep cellulose away from chimneys and metal flues. A masonry chimney requires 2 in. of clearance. We advise installers to air-seal the crack where the chimney penetrates into the attic, using metal flashing and high-temperature caulk. Then the installer should take a 3½-in.-thick Roxul batt—a mineral-wool batt—and wrap it around the chimney, securing it with a wire so it doesn't fall off. Then you can blow cellulose right up against the mineral wool batt.

We do the same thing with metal chimneys, although with B-vents the clearances get a little higher. National Fiber has published a technical bulletin listing the clearances.

Q. Is there a maximum depth of cellulose insulation that can be installed above a drywall ceiling before you have to start worrying about the weight of the insulation causing the drywall to sag?

A. We have never seen a sagging issue due to the weight of the cellulose installed above a ceiling. That may be because some of the weight of the cellulose is being redistributed onto the ceiling joists. We have blown very high R-values, up to R-100, and never had any issues with the ceiling sagging.

Q. How should air-permeable netting—for example, Insulweb®—be attached to the studs?

A. The best technique is to staple it with a pneumatic stapler right to the face of the stud. By *face*, I mean the 1½-in.-thick edge of the stud facing the room. The staples have to be less than 1 in. apart, so you'll go through a good number of staples.

Some installers prefer inset stapling or "lip stitching"—they put the staples at the corner of the studs, wrapping the Insulweb a little bit around the corner as they staple. But that really isn't necessary. I don't like the lip-stitch method, because I want the insulation to be close to the Sheetrock. Installers who use lip-stitching are usually worried about bulges, but we've found that an aluminum roller works well to eliminate any bulges.

There's another method of installing the Insulweb: using glue. First, you tack the Insulweb up quickly. Then you apply watered-down Elmer's® glue to the studs through the Insulweb, using a trim roller— you roll through the Insulweb to push in the glue. It gets the Insulweb really tight and

nice. By the time you get to the last wall in the house, the first wall you glued is usually dry enough to start blowing cellulose. It's best to wait at least 6 hours for the glue to dry.

Q. What do you do about bulges?

A. After you're done blowing the walls, the material will be bulged out a little bit between the studs—maybe out 1 in. or so in the middle. So you take an aluminum roller— it's about 1 ft. long, maybe 3 in. in dia., and sold specifically for this purpose—and you roll the bulge really quickly. If you do it right, it will leave the cellulose flat, and a long metal straightedge will touch the studs. We recommend that owners or builders include this language in their wall insulation specs: "The material will be rolled flat, ready for drywall."

Q. Is it really possible to achieve a density of 3½ lb. per cubic foot behind netting?

A. Yes, if you use the right technique. We recommend using a rigid tube—a 4-ft. aluminum tube, 2 in. in dia. The tube should have a 45° bevel at the end—the bevel lets you pop the tube through the Insulweb without cutting a hole first. It also allows you to aim the cellulose with good directionality.

With experience, the installer can determine the density by the way it feels. Between 3 lb. and 4 lb. per cubic foot, the feel of the installed material goes from soft (at 3 lb.) to actually hard at 4 lb. At 3½ lb. per cubic foot, it will feel like a firm mattress. It really changes dramatically between 3 lb. and 4 lb.

When I first heard people claim that they could determine density by the feel, I thought there would be no way to tell. But it does change in a dramatic way, and you can feel the difference. The density is important—partly for increased resistance to air leakage but also because you want the material to be self-supporting. If it is dense enough, there is no downward force, and it can't settle.

In each stud bay, you need a single hole about halfway up from the floor. The trick is to move the pipe around and back and forth. You start at the bottom, and you move the tube back and forth. The corners are the areas where you might end up with a soft spot, so you should start at the corners and then work your way up through the hole. Then when you reach the hole, you flip the tube upward and work from the top down.

You can always feel the material through the Insulweb, and if you find a soft spot, you can move the tube to that area and inject a little more. Then you move on to the next stud bay.

Q. Do you have to patch the holes in the Insulweb once you're done insulating a wall?

A. No. The cellulose won't fall out, so there is no need to patch the holes.

Q. What about holes in the Insulweb near penetrations and electrical boxes—will a lot of cellulose blow out of these holes and cracks when the stud bay is being filled?

A. No. You don't have to worry about holes or cracks—even cracks up to 1 in. wide. If you have a really big hole, you can staple up a new strip of Insulweb, from stud to stud, before you start insulating. The stud bay is filled from the bottom up to the middle, and from the top down to the middle. When the hose nozzle gets close to a big hole or crack in the Insulweb, the installer might temporarily put his hand over the hole to minimize the amount of cellulose that blows out. But not much will blow out. Once the bay is full and dense-packed, the cellulose won't fall out. In any case, it all gets covered with drywall soon enough.

Q. Is damp-spray cellulose installed at a lower density than an Insulweb installation?

A. No. With a damp-spray installation, we are looking for the same density—3½ lb. per cubic foot.

Q. Why do some installers prefer the damp-spray method?

A. Some installers choose to spray because it takes less time for the installer to get in and out. For some jobs, a spray installation could cost a little less. One limitation: when you spray, the floor has to be clean because the installer is recycling the material. If there is a lot of lumber or other construction material in the way, it can interfere with the installer's ability to recycle the material that falls to the floor.

Q. How is water added to damp-spray cellulose?

A. The spray truck contains a water tank. When the installer is spraying, there are usually three nozzles close together—a flattened nozzle with cellulose blowing through, and two water-misting nozzles. The water is added to the dry cellulose as the material exits the nozzle.

Q. Can the installer adjust the water application if there are signs that the insulation is too wet?

A. Yes. They have a couple of adjustments. Usually the easiest way to adjust the amount of water is to change the tip size at the end of the water nozzles. There are very small orifices that atomize the water—the water-pump pressure is usually at 500 psi to 1,000 psi. If you see that the material is going on too damp or too dry, you can swap to a different orifice size.

Q. Do damp-spray cellulose applications ever include glue?

A. It's possible, but we feel that if you have a well thought-out system you don't need to add glue. I haven't had much experience with the glue method. We can spray very dry without adding any glue. Glue can make it easier to spray cellulose at a lower density, but I am not an advocate of dropping the density down very much. I'd rather have a density of 3½ lb. per cubic foot.

Q. Can you describe the steps of a damp-spray installation?

A. You start at the bottom of the wall and build the materially up vertically. After the stud bays are filled, there will be some high spots and low spots. To make the high spots even with the studs, we use a "scrubber" to scrape the wall and even it out.

The scrubber is like an elongated paint roller with a rubber face. When you scrub the wall, the scrubber removes anything beyond the face of the studs. The material falls to the ground, where it is collected by a vacuum recovery system hooked up to the truck. The truck has two hoppers—one for the dry material, and one for the recycled material. By keeping them separate, you make sure you end up with a consistent moisture level when the material is sprayed.

Q. Can you determine whether a wall is dry enough to hang drywall just by looking at it?

A. Visually, we can get a really good idea of the moisture content of the material once it is scrubbed. After scrubbing, if the cellulose looks mottled, with some darker areas and some lighter areas, that means that the moisture content is how we like it.

But if it is consistently dark, we know the material is wetter than we like. That's not good, because when it is that wet, it can sag. If that happens, you can see a gap at the top of the stud bay. In the industry, these gaps are referred to as "smiles."

If you have a stud bay that looks dark in the entire bay, you probably want to pull the material out so there is no chance of it settling, and then respray with less water.

Q. Are moisture meters useful?

A. Most moisture meters are set up for the density of lumber or drywall. If you talk to the manufacturers, they'll tell you that the meters are not calibrated for the density of insulation, which is a low-density material. That's why moisture meters tend to be misleading when used on cellulose. And you tend to get into questions about how deep you should poke it in. You'll find that the numbers vary quite a bit depending on how deep you insert the probes.

So we just say, if you cover the walls after 24 hours, we guarantee there will be no damage to the wall or finishes as the moisture migrates out. People don't realize that the longer you leave the insulation exposed, the chances are good that it can actually get wetter. It's because we have tight buildings with lots of construction moisture. It is counterintuitive. It often helps to crack a window or two.

Q. Is it possible to install damp-spray cellulose overhead, in an open ceiling?

A. No, cellulose insulation cannot be sprayed overhead—except for specific cellulose-based fire-retardant products with a high glue content that are used as thermal barriers over steel or foam insulation.

Q. Some builders install drywall with a 4-in. horizontal gap in the middle of the wall, 4 ft. off the floor, and then blow cellulose behind the drywall. Does this system work well?

A. I'm not a fan of that method. I prefer to dense-pack behind Insulweb, because you can feel the cellulose through the Insulweb, and you can see what is going on. Another problem: You are injecting the cellulose pneumatically, so the wall needs air relief. If the wall is too tight, the installer can mistakenly think he has reached the proper insulation density when there is really a problem with air relief.

Q. Does the same problem with air relief occur when you install cellulose behind polyiso foam on a ceiling?

A. Usually we don't see a problem with air relief when the installer is blowing into a ceiling. I think that installing polyiso foam on the ceiling and injecting cellulose behind it is a good application method.

Q. When you are blowing behind rigid foam into rafter bays, how far apart do you space the holes?

A. Usually one hole per rafter bay is enough—one hole in the center of the span.

But it depends on the diameter of the hose. The bigger the diameter, the lower the velocity of the cellulose leaving the end of the hose, and the shorter the distance that we can dense pack. Smaller diameter hoses give you better density and better consistency.

If you're dense-packing a ceiling, we recommend that you prefill the assembly using a big hose—the 3-in.-dia. hose. You insert the big hose and prefill the cavity. That will result in a lower density than what we're aiming for, so then you want to go back with a smaller tube—a 1½-in. or 2-in. tube. You want an aluminum or Tigerflex® tube that you can insert through the prefilled material.

If you have a 12-ft. ceiling span, you'll be accessing the ceiling from one 3-in.-dia. hole in the center of the room, so you can blow 6 ft. in either direction. Once you reach the desired density, 3½ lb. per cubic foot, you can't push a tube back through the material anymore, because it's too dense. That's one way to tell if you've reached the density you're aiming for. But if there is a weaker area, you will be able to move the tube toward that low-density area.

If the rafters are 16 in. on center, you can usually blow down the center of the cavity and get good consistent density. But if the rafters are 24 in. on center, you want to move the tube first to the right and then to the left and then back to the center as you pull the tube through.

The installer should also know how many bags they need to fill the bay to the right density, and they should double-check the bag count. If it's not dense enough, you can always put the tube back in and blow some more.

Q. Does the same technique work with 12-in.-thick double-stud walls?

A. Yes. With very thick walls, we also use the prefill method. First you prefill the wall loosely, using the 3-in. hose right off the machine, with the feed gate opened right up and the air all the way up. You poke a hole through the Insulweb near the top of the wall, every 24 in., and using a 3-in.-dia. hose, you just dump the material into the wall and fill it up.

Once you've done that, you go back with the 2-in.-dia. dense-pack hose—the hose attached to the 4-ft. aluminum tube. You come back and pop a hole near the center of the cavity, about 4 ft. off the floor, and you aim the aluminum tube downward. Beginning at the bottom of the wall and working your way all around the cavity, feeling for soft spots, you dense-pack the wall and then draw the tube back up. Then you aim the hose up, and you do the same thing, working from the top of the cavity downward toward the hole. You do this all around the wall, every 24 in., until you're sure you've got the density you need.

When it comes to thick walls, it's all about density. One thing I have learned over the years is that when we get to thicker walls, we have to increase the density a little more—to just over 4 lb. per cubic foot for a 12-in.-thick wall, and to as much as 5.1 lb. per cubic foot for a 27-in.-thick R-100 wall.

These recommended densities are based on a study performed by the Danish government. The Danish researchers built cavities of different thicknesses and installed cellulose with different densities. They put the wall assemblies on a vibrator. Based on that research, I modified the information on our expanded bag coverage chart to reflect the need for greater densities for wider walls.

Q. When dense-packing cellulose in the walls of an existing old house from the outside, how many holes are drilled per stud bay?

A. One hole per stud bay. The best technique is to remove a section of the siding—my preference is to pull the siding nails and drop the siding, and then to put the siding back on at the end of the job. I'm against drilling through siding, and I don't like siding plugs.

If you pull off some of the siding and it starts disintegrating, it's best to stop the job and talk to the homeowner. You don't want to wait until the end of the job to tell the homeowner that the siding can't be reinstalled. There are some siding types that are very difficult—old clapboard that is ready to fall off the building, or blind-nailed asbestos siding. In some cases we can blow the walls from the inside, but that's not a great way to proceed because of all the plaster dust or drywall dust.

If you can get some of the siding off, you drill a $2^9/_{16}$-in. hole in each stud bay. If you can, it's a good idea to bevel the hole a little on the inside by tilting the drill as you finish the hole.

For ergonomic reasons, I want the holes to be between waist and chest high. That means the holes will be toward the bottom of the bay. You'll be using a $1^1/_4$-in.- or $1^1/_2$-in.-dia. hose, a 10-ft. tube made out of Tigerflex—a helix-reinforced rubber hose with plastic braid that runs around it.

You start at the bottom of the stud bay. You push the hose to the bottom plate, then pull it up 6 in. You turn the machine on, and you wait until the material stops flowing, then you quickly pull up the hose until the material starts flowing again. You do that until you reach the hole. Then you do the same thing starting from the top, working down. If the hose doesn't go up to the top of the stud bay—if you can't twist the hose past the obstruction because of fire blocking or something else, you have to drill another hole.

Q. What about the rim joist area?

A. You climb up the ladder and remove the siding at the rim joist. You drill a 3-in. hole and look in the hole. If you are looking down a joist bay, you take a feed bag—we used to use one of the 100-lb. grain bags from Blue Seal® feeds, the plastic ones, but now that most grain is sold in 50-lb. bags, they're harder to get. But we've found a source for the big bags—we can still get them.

You pull the bag over the end of your tube, so the tube is ready to fill the inside of the bag, and you insert the tube with the bag over the end into the 3-in. hole. You want to keep holding on to the bag so the bag doesn't go flying when you start to fill it. The bag is mostly in the joist bay when you do this. You fill the bag with cellulose—you literally fill the bag.

Now the key to this technique is getting around the edges of the filled bag. The bag doesn't always completely fill the joist bay that it is in. So after you have filled the bag, you pull the hose out. You stuff the end of the bag into the hole. You push it back 6 in. or 1 ft., and then you dense-pack the gap between the bag and the hole. You aim the hose to seal off any gaps.

Q. Is there a good way to patch holes in stucco when retrofitting cellulose in an existing stucco home?

A. Typically stucco homes are done from the inside, because stucco is hard to patch. You can drill through stucco with a carbide-tipped hole saw, but patching the stucco is difficult.

Q. What type of ventilation chutes can resist the pressures of dense-packed cellulose?

A. The baffles need to be rigid enough, so the Styrofoam® ones are completely out. We have had good luck with AccuVent baffles. They will withstand the pressure of the dense-pack without collapsing.

Q. Do you have any comments about the controversy surrounding dense-packing unvented cathedral ceilings?

A. We feel comfortable enough to warrant the material in that assembly for the life of the building. We will stand behind these installations. The installations that have had issues have always been related to density problems. We tell our installers, "If you aren't

sure of the density of your installations, you shouldn't be using this technique." The material has to be at the right density, and in full contact with the exterior sheathing.

The argument we make is that when you consider the combination of the dense-packed cellulose and the drywall, the assembly is air impermeable. The intent of the code is to prevent moist air from having contact with the sheathing, and all we need to do is convince the code official that that won't happen.

Q. What about vapor retarders?

A. We have been injecting cellulose into buildings without vapor retarders since the mid-1970s, and there have been no moisture issues with these buildings. We know from experience that cellulose can be installed without an interior vapor retarder.

We recently had a professional engineer run some WUFI models for us. According to the models, a cellulose wall without a vapor barrier in Massachusetts will remain dryer than a wall with a vapor barrier because of summer vapor transmission into the wall assembly from the exterior—walls with a vapor barrier have accumulation behind the barrier in the summer. Vapor barriers shouldn't be used in buildings that have both heating and cooling because vapor flow reverses during the summer.

However, even if you decided to install a vapor barrier, I have never seen a problem when a vapor barrier is used with cellulose. If somebody really wants a vapor retarder, we recommend installing a vapor retarder paint.

The only type of building where a vapor barrier might make sense would be in something like a swimming pool facility.

What you need to know to install exterior polyisocyanurate, XPS, or EPS

One of the best ways to reduce thermal bridging through studs is to install rigid foam on the exterior side of your walls. But which type of rigid foam should you choose? There are three major types of rigid foam: expanded polystyrene (EPS), extruded polystyrene (XPS), and polyisocyanurate. All brands of EPS and XPS sold in the United States include a brominated flame retardant—hexabromocyclododecane (HBCD)—that many environmentalists find worrisome.

Moreover, most green builders avoid using XPS because it is manufactured with a blowing agent with a very high global warming potential. That leaves polyiso, which enjoys a reputation as the most environmentally friendly type of rigid foam insulation. However, polyiso doesn't perform very well at cold temperatures. The bottom line: Green builders in hot climates tend to prefer polyiso, while green builders in cold climates tend to prefer EPS.

If you prefer not to use rigid foam, you can use mineral wool panels instead.

USING RIGID FOAM ON THE WALLS OF A NEW HOME

If you are building a new home, there are two basic ways to install rigid foam on the exterior of a wall: Either the foam can be attached directly to the studs or the walls can be conventionally sheathed with OSB or plywood before the foam is installed.

If you decide to omit some or all of the OSB or plywood sheathing, you'll need to

EXTERIOR RIGID FOAM improves airtightness, adds R-value, reduces the chance of condensation in wall cavities, and greatly reduces thermal bridging through studs.

come up with a plan to brace your walls. There are at least four ways to brace a foam-sheathed wall:

- Include a few sheets of plywood or OSB at critical areas like corners;
- Install 1×4 let-in bracing;
- Install diagonal metal strapping;
- Install inset shear panels.

In most cases, alternative bracing plans need to be approved by an engineer.

If you decide to install rigid foam insulation after your walls are conventionally sheathed with OSB or plywood, you don't have to worry about special bracing details. However, the foam needs to be thick enough to keep the OSB or plywood above the dew point during the winter. To determine the minimum R-value of the rigid foam, see "Calculating the Minimum

Thickness of Rigid Foam Sheathing" on p. 155.

FASTENING FOAM TO YOUR WALL

Rigid foam is usually attached to studs or wall sheathing with cap nails, which can be purchased in a variety of lengths up to 8 in. If you intend to install vertical 1×4 furring strips on top of the foam to create a rain-screen drainage gap, then you need to install only a few fasteners—just enough to hold the foam in place until the strapping is screwed to the wall.

If you are installing more than one layer of rigid foam—for example, two layers of 2-in.-thick polyiso—remember to stagger the seams of the second layer to improve airtightness and to reduce the chance of thermal bridging. On at least one layer of the rigid foam, seams should be sealed with caulk, canned foam, or a compatible tape.

Most foam-sheathed walls include vertical furring strips to create a rain-screen gap. It's better to use 1×4s than 1×3s because 1×4s are less likely to split. Vertical furring strips should be installed directly over the studs, which means they will usually be 16 in. or 24 in. on center. The furring

ROLL OUT THE HOUSEWRAP. Each roll of housewrap should be installed in as continuous a sheet as possible. Fewer taped seams mean fewer air or water intrusions. Fasten the housewrap with cap nails.

INSTALLING RIGID FOAM ON THE EXTERIOR OF AN EXISTING HOUSE

If a house needs new siding, the homeowner has a rare opportunity to improve the thermal performance of the walls. Once the old siding has been removed, the wall sheathing can be inspected for rot or other problems, and these problems can be corrected. If necessary, dense-packed cellulose insulation can be installed in the wall cavities from the exterior.

The next steps would usually be to install a layer of housewrap followed by one or two layers of rigid foam and vertical furring strips. Of course, these new materials will add thickness to your walls. If you are installing new windows at the same time, you may want to install them as "outies" to simplify water management details.

If you keep your existing windows, they will end up being "innies," and you'll need to spend a lot of time detailing the flashing, the exterior jamb extensions, and the new windowsill required for such an approach.

strips are attached to the studs with long screws through the foam; the strips usually require one long screw every 24 in. Some suppliers of long screws include

- Best Materials® (a source of Dekfast 6-in. roofing screws and Dekfast 9-in. roofing screws);
- Wind-Lock™ (a source of long screws and plastic hold-down buttons);
- FastenMaster® (a source of screws up to 10 in. long).

WHAT DO I USE FOR A WRB?

The most popular material to use as a water-resistive barrier for a foam-sheathed

FLASHING A WINDOW in a foam-sheathed wall. To make the window's perimeter watertight, seal the flange with overlapping layers of self-adhering flashing applied against the housewrap. The bottom flange of a window should never be sealed.

wall is plastic housewrap. However, it's also possible to use the foam itself as a WRB. If you want to use rigid foam as a WRB, you need to understand the code implications of your decision and you need to have a good flashing plan. Not all brands of rigid foam have been approved for use as a WRB. Moreover, when the rigid foam is used as the WRB, it's much harder to integrate the WRB with flashing. Before deciding to use rigid foam as a WRB, consult with the foam manufacturer.

If you are using housewrap as a WRB, you have to decide where to install it. The housewrap can either be installed under or over the foam; in either case, remember that the WRB has to be integrated with window flashing and door flashing. (For more information on this issue, see "Where Does the Housewrap Go?" on p. 178.)

WHAT ABOUT WINDOWS?

There are several ways to install windows in a foam-sheathed wall. If your foam is relatively thin, it's possible to nail or screw the window flanges through the foam to the rough framing. If the foam is thick, you'll probably want to install a "picture frame" around the rough opening

to provide secure nailing or to install a cantilevered window buck (usually made out of plywood) to hold your window. If you go the window-buck route, you have two options: the windows can be installed as "innies" or "outies."

To learn more about installing windows in a foam-sheathed wall, see "'Innie' Windows or 'Outie' Windows?" on p. 176.

How do I flash the windows?

There are almost as many ways to flash windows in a foam-sheathed wall as there are window brands. The most important point: Window flashings need to be integrated with your WRB. (If you aren't sure whether your rigid foam or your housewrap is your WRB, that's a sign of trouble.) Flashings should direct water to drain toward the exterior, usually to the rain-screen gap between the siding and the foam.

As a conceptual framework for your flashing plan, it's a good idea to remember this motto: "Flash the rough opening, not the window." If the rough opening is waterproof, and if the rough sill directs rain to the exterior face of your WRB, you've done a good job.

CALCULATING THE MINIMUM THICKNESS OF RIGID FOAM SHEATHING

In this case, the code is your friend—just follow the IRC's foam thickness table

If you plan to install exterior rigid foam on the walls of your house, how thick should the foam be? Thick foam is almost always better than thin foam. Thin foam is dangerous, because it reduces the ability of the wall to dry to the exterior without warming the sheathing enough to prevent moisture accumulation (a phenomenon that is usually but incorrectly called "condensation").

Fortunately, building scientists have calculated the minimum foam thickness required for different wall thicknesses and different climates. By following their

THICK FOAM IS BETTER than thin foam. If you're installing rigid foam on the outside of your walls, make sure the foam is thick enough to prevent moisture accumulation and make sure that your wall is able to dry inward.

recommendations, your wall sheathing (or the interior face of the rigid foam) will stay warm enough to prevent moisture accumulation during the winter.

Because foam sheathing reduces the ability of a wall to dry to the exterior, all foam-sheathed walls must be able to dry to the interior. That means you don't want any materials with a very low permeance on the interior of a foam-sheathed wall or between the studs. If you are building this type of wall, you should not include interior polyethylene or vinyl wallpaper, nor should you install any closed-cell spray foam between the studs. It's perfectly acceptable to fill the stud bays with open-cell spray foam, however, because open-cell foam is vapor permeable.

INSTALL THICK FOAM AND NO INTERIOR POLY

Of course, foam-sheathed walls must comply with existing building codes. Until recently, that was difficult because some building inspectors insisted on the need for interior polyethylene—even on foam-sheathed walls, where poly definitely does not belong. Fortunately, the 2007 Supplement to the IRC came to the rescue. Since that Supplement was adopted, the IRC has allowed certain cold-climate walls to dry to the interior. The code now includes Table N1102.5.1, listing which types of wall assemblies have minimal requirements for an interior vapor retarder.

(In the 2009 IRC, these provisions can be found in section R601.3, Table R601.3.1. In the 2012 IRC, the relevant provisions can be found in section R702.7, Table R702.7.1.)

The relevant table serves two purposes:

- It gives permission to builders of foam-sheathed walls to use a minimal interior vapor retarder—one with the highest permeance values, known as a Class III vapor retarder. (Ordinary latex paint is all you need.)

- It spells out the minimum R-values for exterior foam to be sure that moisture won't accumulate in a wall.

ALL YOU NEED TO KNOW

The essential information from Table N1102.5.1 that applies to foam-sheathed walls is shown in the chart below.

Once you know the minimum required R-value for your foam sheathing, you can determine your foam thickness. To do that, you need to know the R-value per inch of your foam. The most common type of EPS has an R-value of about R-3.6 per inch, while XPS has an R-value of R-5 per inch.

The R-value shown on polyisocyanurate labels is usually equivalent to R-6 or R-6.5 per inch. However, the actual performance of polyiso decreases in cold temperatures. Concerns about the cold-temperature performance of polyiso

are real, so cold-climate builders should use caution when choosing a rigid foam designed to keep wall sheathing above the dew point during the winter. Either EPS or XPS is probably a safer choice for this purpose than polyiso, unless you derate the performance of the outermost layer of polyiso to about R-4 per inch.

What if I live in one of the warmer climate zones?

If you are building a house in one of the warmer climate zones—zone 1, 2, 3, or 4 (except for Marine Zone 4)—you don't have to worry about the thickness of your foam. Any foam thickness will work, because your sheathing will never get cold enough for moisture accumulation to be a problem.

What about flash-and-batt jobs?

Builders following the flash-and-batt method—that is, a hybrid insulation system using a thin layer of closed-cell spray polyurethane foam against the interior side of the wall sheathing, with the balance of the stud bay filled with fiberglass or cellulose insulation—can follow the recommendations in the chart below for the minimum thickness of the spray foam. Closed-cell spray polyurethane foam has an R-value of about R-6.5 per inch.

The 2012 IRC specifically endorses this approach to flash-and-batt calculations in footnote a to Table R702.7.1. The relevant footnote reads, "Spray foam with

Minimum Required R-Value for Foam-Sheathed Walls	
Climate Zone	Minimum R-Value of Foam Sheathing
Marine Zone 4	R-2.5 for 2×4 walls; R-3.75 for 2×6 walls
Zone 5	R-5 for 2×4 walls; R-7.5 for 2×6 walls
Zone 6	R-7.5 for 2×4 walls; R-11.25 for 2×6 walls
Zones 7 and 8	R-10 for 2×4 walls; R-15 for 2×6 walls

FLASH AND BATT. The flash coat of spray foam is the air seal; the batt layer of unfaced fiberglass is the money saver.

a minimum density of 2 lb/ft³ applied to the interior cavity side of wood structural panels, fiberboard, insulating sheathing or gypsum is deemed to meet the insulating sheathing requirement where the spray foam R-value meets or exceeds the specified insulating sheathing R-value."

The table can also be used as a minimum foam thickness guide when following the cut-and-cobble method (insulating between studs by combining a layer of rigid foam installed against the interior side of the wall sheathing with fiberglass batts in the rest of the stud cavity).

Although the fiberglass batts in a flash-and-batt stud bay will be thinner than the fiberglass batts in a wall with exterior foam sheathing, thinner batts move the wall in the direction of more safety rather than more risk because thinner fiberglass keeps the interior surface of the cured foam warmer (and therefore less likely to collect condensation).

If you want to sharpen your pencil, you can get away with thinner foam for a flash-and-batt job than an exterior-foam job. As long as you retain the ratio of foam R-value to fluffy-insulation R-value shown in the table, you should be OK. For example, the table recommends R-5 foam

for a 2×4 wall filled with R-13 fiberglass insulation in climate Zone 5 (38% foam and 62% fiberglass). For a flash and batt job, you could get away with R-3.6 foam and R-9.5 fiberglass insulation. However, in most cases you don't really have to sharpen your pencil quite this much.

Why doesn't every cold-climate wall have rotten sheathing?

Because most homes don't have foam sheathing, what keeps the cold sheathing on a typical home from developing moisture problems? Good question; the answer can be found in "How Risky Is Cold OSB Wall Sheathing?" on p. 69.

Unless you're careful, your low-slope roof can end up with damp sheathing

There are lots of ways to insulate a low-slope roof, and most of them are wrong. In older buildings, the usual method is to install fiberglass batts or cellulose on top of the leaky ceiling, with a gap of a few inches (or sometimes a few feet) between the top of the insulation and the roof sheathing. In some cases, but not all, there is an attempt to vent the air space above the insulation to the exterior.

It's rare for anyone to inspect the roof sheathing—unless, of course, the boards gets spongy enough to be noticed when the building is reroofed. If there were any way you could squeeze into the tiny attic under the flat roof, however, you would probably see evidence of mold or rot.

VENTING THE ATTIC UNDER A LOW-SLOPE ROOF IS POSSIBLE BUT DIFFICULT

So what's wrong with insulating a flat roof the traditional way? Nothing, really—as long as the job is done correctly—that is, with an airtight ceiling and adequate attic ventilation.

The problem is that most of these roofs aren't built correctly. The ceilings leak air, and the attic ventilation is inadequate. There's just enough ventilation to pull warm, moist interior air through ceiling cracks; once the moist air is in the tiny attic, the moisture accumulates in the cold roof sheathing. The result is rot and mold.

Here's some advice from Joe Lstiburek, a principal at the Building Science Corporation: "If you have an airtight ceiling, and you have an air gap of at least 6 in. between the top of the insulation and the roof deck, and if you have perimeter air coming in at vents at the soffit or fascia above the insulation, and if you also have ventilation openings near the center of the roof through some kind of cupola or doghouse—not just a whirlybird turbine vent—there is nothing wrong with your roof assembly," Lstiburek told me. "You can build a 2-ft. by 2-ft. doghouse that sticks up a few feet, and put in some rectangular vents. If the ceiling is airtight, then the makeup air comes from the outside. That's the least expensive way to do things."

Lstiburek continued, "The problem with this type of roof is that it is rarely executed correctly. Usually, architects don't want to provide any ventilation around the perimeter. Or the architect won't provide a deep enough truss to get enough insulation. If you just have a few whirlybird vents and a leaky ceiling, the whirlybirds will suck moisture-laden air out of the building and the roof will rot."

Bruce Harley, the technical director for residential energy services at the Conservation Services Group, shared Lstiburek's contempt for turbine vents. "I dislike turbine vents," Harley told me. "I'd prefer a big mushroom vent or two over a turbine vent."

THE RIGHT WAY TO VENT A LOW-SLOPE ROOF

If you want to build a low-slope roof that is insulated with fluffy insulation, here are the details you need to include

- Specify very deep roof trusses. The trusses should be deep enough for 12 in. to 16 in. of insulation (depending on your climate), plus room for an air gap of at least 6 in. between the top of the insulation and the roof sheathing. Even better: frame the roof separately from the ceiling, so that there is an attic that is deep enough for human access.

- Provide vents at the perimeter of the shallow attic. These can be soffit vents, fascia vents, or wall-mounted vents, as long as the vents allow exterior air to connect with the air gap between the top of the insulation and the underside of the roof sheathing.

- Provide one or more vented cupolas ("doghouses") in the center of the roof. Most building codes require 1 sq. ft. of net free ventilation area for every 300 sq. ft. of attic floor area; half the ventilation area should be located at the perimeter of the building, and half of the area should be located at the cupolas near the center of the roof.

- Perform air-sealing work at the ceiling before the insulation is installed. Pay close attention to electrical penetrations, plumbing vent penetrations, the top plates of partition walls, and access hatches. The ceiling should be airtight as you can make it.

Harley emphasized the importance of air sealing. He said, "Besides the standard bypasses—the partition walls and plumbing penetrations—remember that these older masonry buildings often have furring strips at the perimeter walls, and the cavities created by the furring strips may reach into the attic and need to be air sealed."

DEFINING OUR TERMS

What's a low-slope roof? It's a roof that is flat or almost flat. This type of roof is common in urban areas (for example, on triple-deckers in Boston and row houses in Philadelphia) as well as in the Southwest. Some of these roofs have parapets—perhaps on just one side of the roof, or perhaps on three or four—while others have no parapets at all.

These roofs are either framed with deep roof trusses, or are framed with roof rafters that are separate from the lower ceiling joists (creating a cramped attic between the flat roof and the ceiling). In some of these buildings, the attic is high enough to allow a person to climb into the attic through a hatch; in others, the attic is too cramped for human access.

If you forget to vent the attic, lots of things can go wrong

Builders in Arizona often use open-web trusses to frame low-slope residential roofs. Some of these builders cut corners: They omit the air space above the insulation and don't bother to install any ventilation openings. They just jam the fiberglass batts up against the underside of the roof sheathing, wire the insulation in place, and cross their fingers.

Oops. About 10 years ago, this insulation method was implicated in a cluster of wet-roof failures in Arizona. The first signs of problems were drywall cracks at the intersections between ceilings and partition walls—classic signs of truss uplift. (Truss uplift occurs when the top chord of a roof truss experiences different humidity conditions from the bottom chord; the humidity difference causes the trusses to deform.)

Uncertain of the cause of the drywall cracks, one of the builders called in William Rose, the well-known building scientist from the University of Illinois, to investigate. Rose discovered that the homes had wet roof sheathing—due in part to the type of roofing installed on the affected homes (white membrane roofing). "In December, January, and February, the fiberglass was wringing wet," Rose told me. "In this climate, radiant effects become really important. There is nothing standing in the way of the roof radiating out to space. You have a whole lot of heat loss from the roof surface, day and night. With this white roofing, 80% of the heat that hits the roof is reflected. The sun can't keep up with the heat losses to the sky. What you've created is a sky-powered cooling coil, and the fiberglass insulation is like a dirty condensate pan. The roof sheathing gets so cold that it is sucking wetness out of dry air."

John Tooley, a senior building science consultant at Advanced Energy Corporation in Raleigh, NC, was also called in to help investigate the case. "At one roof I investigated—it was a flat-top roof assembly with a hot tar membrane roof coated with an off-white elastomeric coating—we pulled the roof off to take a look," said Tooley. "The roof deck was totally saturated, and there was mold growth all over the bottom of the sheathing. The moisture content was greater than 30%. The fiberglass insulation was totally wet. This was in a house that was less than a year old."

Tooley told me that this type of failure was common. "If you busted open roofs all over the Southwest, you'd find that the lower the pitch of the roof, the more you would see the evidence of moisture," he said. "All of these roofs get wetting and drying cycles. If the wetting cycle is long enough, mold will grow and the insulation will get wet. I think if you cut roofs open, you will often find out that they are wet."

The recommended solution to the problem of these wet Arizona roofs was to add a layer of rigid foam insulation above the roof sheathing.

INSULATING A VENTED LOW-SLOPE ROOF

A vented roof needs intake vents at the attic perimeter and cupolas at the center of the roof to maintain airflow between the sheathing and the top of the insulation. The ceiling must be airtight to prevent condensation on the underside of the sheathing.

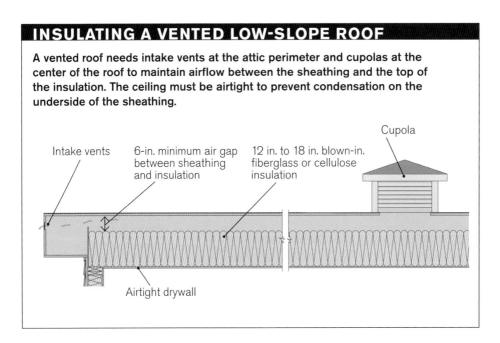

Intake vents

6-in. minimum air gap between sheathing and insulation

12 in. to 18 in. blown-in. fiberglass or cellulose insulation

Cupola

Airtight drywall

RIGID FOAM for low-slope roofs. The most common types of rigid foam insulation installed under low-slope roofing are EPS (left) and polyisocyanurate (right). Both types of foam are available in tapered configurations to create a slope on an existing flat roof.

WHAT IF YOU DON'T WANT TO DEPEND ON ROOF VENTING?

Let's face it—it's hard to vent a flat roof. That's why most commercial low-slope roofs, including the roof on your local Walmart®, are unvented.

In many ways, it's easier to build an unvented low-slope roof than a vented low-slope roof. If you go this route, there are several possible ways to proceed:

- You can install a thick layer of rigid foam insulation (6 in. or more) above the roof sheathing.
- You can install a more moderate layer of rigid foam insulation (2 in. to 4 in.) above the roof sheathing, supplemented by a layer of air-permeable insulation below the roof sheathing.
- You can install a layer of closed-cell spray polyurethane foam roofing on top of the roof sheathing, supplemented by layer of air-permeable insulation under the roof sheathing.
- You can install a thick layer of closed-cell spray polyurethane foam on the underside of the roof sheathing.
- You can install a more moderate thickness of closed-cell spray polyurethane foam on the underside of the roof sheathing, supplemented by a layer of air-permeable insulation below that.

Of course, the total R-value of your roof insulation must at least meet minimum code requirements. Moreover, if you install a combination of foam insulation and air-permeable insulation, you need to be sure that the foam insulation is thick enough to keep the roof sheathing (or the lower surface of the foam insulation) above the dew point during the winter. The minimum R-values needed for the rigid foam insulation needed for this type of roof assembly are shown in the table on p. 162.

THESE ROOF ASSEMBLIES DRY INWARD

The insulation methods described here—those used for unvented low-slope roofs—are similar to those used to build an unvented cathedral ceiling. To read about the methods in greater detail, see "How to Build an Insulated Cathedral Ceiling" on p. 24.

While vented roof assemblies are designed to dry to the exterior, unvented roof assemblies are designed to dry to the interior. That's why an unvented roof assembly should never include interior polyethylene. (If a building inspector insists that you install some type of interior "vapor barrier," you can always install a smart vapor retarder like MemBrain to satisfy your inspector.) For more information on the theory behind roof assemblies and wall assemblies with exterior rigid foam, see "Calculating the Minimum Thickness of Rigid Foam Sheathing" on p. 155.

A (SOMEWHAT) CONTROVERSIAL APPROACH

What if you need to insulate an existing low-slope roof with attic access on only one side of the building? This type of attic might be 3 ft. high on the high side, but might taper down to only 6 in. or 8 in. on the low side.

Doing it the right way probably requires some ceiling demolition and a spray-foam contractor (if the work is performed from the interior) or else requires new roofing (if the work is performed from the exterior). Either approach is expensive, so some contractors have figured out a way to insulate this kind of roof without demolishing the ceiling and without installing new roofing.

Bill Hulstrunk is the technical manager at National Fiber, a manufacturer of cellulose insulation. "With that type of attic, we crawl in and do as much air-sealing as possible on the side with good access," Hulstrunk told me. "Then there is a point where the attic gets too confined and you can't crawl in there to do any air-sealing.

So we'll dense-pack the side of the attic with limited access, and then we'll blow in loose-fill cellulose on the side of the attic where there was enough access for air-sealing work. It is always a good idea to have some vents on the side walls, above the top of the insulation, to provide some connection between the air above the loose-fill insulation and the outside. If we have done a good job with the air-sealing, we have reduced the amount of moisture that will get up there. But in case there is some moisture that gets through, it's good to have some way to allow the moisture to be able to make its way to the exterior."

Hulstrunk's approach receives qualified endorsement from Bruce Harley. In his book, *Insulate & Weatherize*, Harley wrote, "Even an excellent dense-pack job can allow some air movement. In an unvented cathedral ceiling or flat roof, this can deposit moisture at the roof deck,

Minimum Required R-Value for Rigid Foam Insulation

	Minimum R-value of rigid foam installed above roof sheathing	Minimum thickness of rigid foam (assuming EPS)	2012 IRC requirements for minimum R-value of the entire roof assembly	R-value of the air-permeable insulation installed on the interior side of the sheathing	Minimum percentage of the roof's total R-value that needs to come from the rigid foam layer
Zones 1–3	R-5	1.5 in.	R-38	R-33 (9 in.)	13%
Marine Zone 4	R-10	2.5 in.	R-49	R-39 (11 in.)	20%
Zones 4A and 4B	R-15	4 in.	R-49	R-34 (9½ in.)	31%
Zone 5	R-20	5 in.	R-49	R-29 (8 in.)	41%
Zone 6	R-25	6.5 in.	R-49	R-24 (6½ in.)	51%
Zone 7	R-30	7.5 in.	R-49	R-19 (5½ in.)	61%
Zone 8	R-35	9 in.	R-49	R-14 (4 in.)	71%

especially in a home with high humidity. There are two basic strategies to avoid increasing the risk of condensation and potential damage to the roof deck: using foam insulation to control condensing temperatures, and ensuring an opening from the unvented cavities into a larger, vented space. The first approach—using continuous foam insulation—is the only proven, code-approved method for an unvented roof . . . . The second approach is to provide a partial venting path for the closed dense-pack area . . . . If one end of the dense-packed area is open to a vented attic space (preferably the top), any wetting effects appear to be balanced by drying toward the vented space. This approach can also be used under low-slope roofs (for example, a row house or shed dormer), where access near the low side is impossible. Experience has shown that up to one-third of the total attic area can be dense-packed without venting, provided that the remaining attic space is vented normally. Note that this method does not conform to standard code requirements but has been accepted by many local building officials. And I would consider this approach much more risky in climate zones 6 to 8 [than in warmer zones]."

When I interviewed Harley about using dense-packed cellulose in low-slope roofs, he was cautious. "I am not comfortable trying to dense-pack an entire attic cavity, especially where it gets deeper in some areas, and therefore harder to dense-pack well," Harley told me. "The risks are just too high. There are examples of dramatic and expensive failures. There are lots of questions: How effectively did you really dense-pack over areas where there may be air leaking? Are there small flaws in the cellulose? What is the moisture load in the house? We don't really have control over that."

REPAIRING A PROBLEMATIC ROOF

What if you are called in to repair problems in an existing building with a low-slope roof that shows signs of moisture?

"We fix the problem roofs—the ones that get moldy—one of two ways," Joe Lstiburek told me. "The usual way we repair them is from the inside. We take out the gypsum ceiling and the insulation, and we spray 2 in. or 3 in. of closed-cell spray foam on the inside of the roof sheathing and the inside of the short walls. We encapsulate the mold. Then we repair the ceiling and we blow the space full of cellulose. If the space is too deep to fill with cellulose, we sometimes blow low-density spray foam over the high-density spray foam, because low-density foam is cheaper than high-density."

The second way to fix this type of roof is from the exterior. "We'll install two 2-in. layers of polyiso on top of the sheathing, then a layer of OSB, and we'll screw it all down and install the roofing. From the inside, we'll install fiberglass batts up against the roof sheathing, held in place with metal pins. That's a foolproof method."

Harley still endorsed limited use of the dense-packing method, as long as a list of conditions is met: "For a common rowhouse in Chicago or Philadelphia, in climate zone 5, in a building with effective code-compliant venting of the attic space, we have seen pretty good results from an approach that includes dense-packing the lowest part of the attic," Harley said. "But never more than one-third of the total attic area."

indows perform multiple functions. They must be transparent enough to admit natural light and to provide a view. They need to reduce the rate of heat flow from indoors to outdoors during the winter and from outdoors to indoors during the summer. In some climates, they should admit as much solar heat gain as possible; in other climates, they should reduce solar heat gain as much as possible (while still providing light and a view, of course). Finally, some windows need to open, to admit fresh air when needed or to allow occupants to escape the building during a fire, and these operable windows need to be as airtight as possible when closed.

6

WINDOWS

You've chosen a window manufacturer, you've selected the frame material, and you've decided on casements rather than double-hungs. But how do you specify glazing?

Everybody has an opinion on windows, and there's a lot to talk about. Which frame material do you prefer: wood or fiberglass? Do you like double-hungs, sliders, or casements? Who provides better warranty service, Marvin® or Pella®? Window selection is a big topic. We'll start by focusing on glazing.

WHY WINDOWS MATTER

Windows are crucial to a home's thermal performance and the comfort of occupants. In a cold climate, the wrong windows will act like holes in a home's thermal envelope, leaking tremendous amounts of heat. In contrast, the best performing windows can actually collect more heat than they lose during the winter months, turning your walls' weakest link into an asset.

In a hot climate, windows with the wrong type of glazing are often the leading cause of summer overheating—they're probably the main reason your air-conditioner struggles to keep your home cool on summer afternoons. That's why the right type of glazing can transform an unlivable room into a pleasant oasis.

If you are building a new home, the cost to upgrade from run-of-the-mill windows to high-performance windows is relatively small, and the incremental cost can easily be justified by future energy savings. Upgrading to better windows will never be cheaper than during new construction. If an existing home has bad windows, however, the cost to replace every window with new high-performance windows is often prohibitive. After all, the cost to replace an existing window will always be

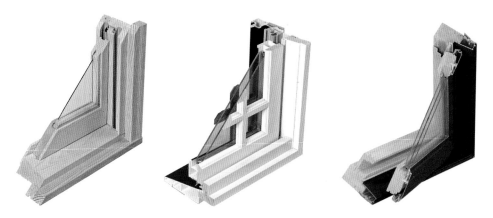

GLAZING OPTIONS. Sealed air spaces reduce heat flow. The more insulating spaces in the glass unit, the better the performance; triple-glazed windows (shown at right in aluminum-clad wood) are among the most energy efficient you can buy. Also shown are single-glazed solid wood (left) and double-glazed insulated fiberglass (center).

significantly more than the incremental cost to upgrade to better windows when the house is being built.

GLAZING BASICS

Old-fashioned single-glazed windows have been relegated to garages and barns. These days, the vast majority of new residential windows come with either double or triple glazing.

Most double- and triple-glazed windows are fitted with insulated glazing units (IGUs). The typical IGU consists of two panes of glass connected by a spacer at the perimeter. The spacer establishes the distance between the panes and seals the gap; it needs to be gastight so the gas between the panes (often argon or krypton) doesn't escape and so moisture can't enter. Warm-edge spacers—for example, the Super Spacer®, the Inex™ spacer, the Intercept® spacer, or the Swiggle Seal® spacer—are better at reducing heat flow through the perimeter of the window than old-fashioned aluminum spacers.

IGUs can also be produced from three (or, very rarely, four) layers of glass.

ABOUT LOW-E COATINGS

In most of the United States and Canada, low-e windows are now standard for new homes. A low-e coating is an almost invisible layer of metal that is applied to one side of the glass by the glass manufacturer. The effect of a low-e coating is to lower the U-factor of the glazing; that is, it slows heat transfer.

Most low-e windows have double-pane IGUs with a low-e coating on one side of one pane. In almost all cases, the low-e coating faces the air space between the panes, so that the coating is protected from abuse. (It should be noted, however, that hard-coat or pyrolytic low-e coatings are tough enough to be used on single-pane storm windows.)

Low-e coatings don't just reflect heat in one direction; they work in both directions. Because the addition of a low-emissivity coating adjacent to an air space has the effect of lowering the U-factor (that is, raising the R-value) of the air space, a low-e coating helps slow heat transfer from the interior to the exterior during winter and also helps slow heat transfer from the exterior to the interior during summer.

Low-e triple glazing can have either one or two low-e coatings. (If a triple-glazed IGU has two low-e coatings, it's sometimes referred to as "double-low-e" glass.) It's also possible to order triple glazing without any low-e coatings; such windows may allow more solar heat gain on sunny days, but they will lose more heat at night than a triple-glazed window with a low-e coating.

Knowing that a window has low-e glazing tells you almost nothing about its solar heat gain coefficient (SHGC). A low-e window might have a low SHGC, making it a good choice for a house in Florida, or a high SHGC, making it a good choice for a house in Minnesota. Just because a window is low-e, doesn't mean it's good at reducing solar gain.

Argon and krypton gas

Filling the space between the panes of an IGU with argon gas instead of air improves the performance of the glazing by lowering the unit's U-factor. Most low-e glazing units are filled with argon gas.

The optimal thickness of the space between panes of argon-filled glazing units is ½ in. Increasing or decreasing the thickness of this space degrades performance. For krypton, the optimal space is thinner—only ⅜ in.—so krypton, a much more expensive gas than argon, is usually

READING THE LABELS

There are two important numbers you need to know when choosing glazing: the U-factor and the SHGC. The U-factor measures the rate of heat flow; it's the inverse of R-value. In all climates, a low U-factor is better than a high U-factor.

The SHGC tells you how much heat enters a building through the window when the sun is shining. When it comes to SHGC, there is no simple rule to guide you. If you live in a sunny climate with high air-conditioning bills, you probably want windows with a low SHGC, especially on the east and west sides of your house. (North windows don't see much sun, and south windows are relatively easy to shade, at least during summer when the sun is high in the sky between 10:00 a.m. and 3:00 p.m.)

If you live in a cold climate with high heating bills, traditional advice suggests that you probably want windows with a high SHGC, especially on the south side of your house. Note, however, that recent research suggests that this traditional advice is flawed. For more information on this issue, see "Reassessing Passive Solar Design Principles" on p. 252. Selecting the best glazing for each orientation is best done with an energy modeling program like RESFEN or the PHPP.

World's Best Window Co.

Millennium 2000+
Vinyl-Clad Wood Frame
Double Glazing · Argon Fill · Low E
Product Type: **Vertical Slider**

NFRC — National Fenestration Rating Council® — CERTIFIED

ENERGY PERFORMANCE RATINGS	
U-Factor (U.S./I-P)	Solar Heat Gain Coefficient
0.35	**0.32**

ADDITIONAL PERFORMANCE RATINGS	
Visible Transmittance	Air Leakage (U.S./I-P)
0.51	**0.2**
Condensation Resistance	
51	

Manufacturer stipulates that these ratings conform to applicable NFRC procedures for determining whole product performance. NFRC ratings are determined for a fixed set of environmental conditions and a specific product size. Consult manufacturer's literature for other product performance information.
www.nfrc.org

A window's U-factor and SHGC numbers appear on the familiar National Fenestration Rating Council (NFRC) label found on most new windows. Note that the NFRC reporting requirements require U-factors and SHGCs to be whole-window measurements—that is, measurements that include the window frame—not glazing-only measurements. You can't compare a whole-window U-factor with a glazing-only U-factor. If a window salesperson brags about a certain U-factor or SHGC, be sure to ask whether the advertised number measures the performance of the whole window or only the glazing.

reserved for applications where the total glazing unit thickness must be minimized.

Don't be tempted to buy glazing without argon or krypton gas. Like a low-e coating, argon gas is a cost-effective upgrade. In almost any location in the United States, argon gas and low-e coatings will quickly yield energy savings exceeding their cost.

BUYING LOW-SHGC WINDOWS IS EASY

The vast majority of low-e windows sold in the United States have low-SHGC glazing. These windows perform well in Texas and Florida, but they may not always be a good idea up north.

The main reason that low-SHGC windows dominate the market is that window manufacturers prefer to stock a single type of glazing from Florida to the Canadian border, to simplify the management of their inventory.

If you live in a sunny climate, low-solar-gain double glazing makes sense. Popular options include:

- LoE^2-270® from Cardinal
- ClimaGuard™ 55/27 from Guardian®
- Solarban® R100 from PPG IdeaScapes®

BUYING HIGH-SHGC WINDOWS IS HARD

If you want to buy a high-SHGC window, you'll probably need to do some research before placing your order. Many window reps are ignorant about glazing options, so be prepared to educate the sales staff (or go over their heads) to get what you want.

Several glass manufacturers make high-SHGC double glazing. Good bets include:

- LOF Energy Advantage™ from Pilkington
- LoE-179 from Cardinal
- Sungate® 500 from PPG
- ClimaGuard 75/68 from Guardian

When ordering your windows, you can mention these products by name.

Until recently, few U.S. window manufacturers were able to supply high-solar-gain windows. Even those who were able to supply them often erected hurdles that made special orders difficult. (These hurdles included technical ignorance, high prices, and in some cases an outright refusal to supply special-order glazing.) That's why U.S. builders looking for high-SHGC windows often seek out Canadian window manufacturers, many of whom have an excellent understanding of the technical advantages of high-solar-gain windows for cold climates.

During the past few years, however, some U.S. manufacturers have begun to market high-solar-gain glass. For example, Pella now offers a glazing option called NaturalSun; it's a high-solar-gain double glazing from Cardinal. The center-of-glass specs for NaturalSun glazing are pretty good: a SHGC of 0.70 and a U-factor of 0.27. This glazing results in a whole-window SHGC of 0.51 and a whole-window U-factor of 0.32.

Visible transmittance

Although I've focused my attention on glazing U-factor and SHGC, there's another number that matters: visible transmittance, or VT. A high VT is better than a low VT, unless there is reason to believe that glare will be a problem. Windows with a low VT are less likely to cause glare than windows with a high VT.

Every time you add another layer of glazing to a window, the VT goes down. When the VT drops below 0.40, everything seen through the window begins to look a little gray.

What about triple glazing?

In general, neither glass manufacturers nor window manufacturers have "branded" any particular type of triple glazing. As a result, those interested in triple-glazed windows are forced to compare U-factors and SHGC numbers. For more guidance on buying triple-glazed windows, see "Choosing Triple-Glazed Windows" on p. 170.

WHAT NUMBERS SHOULD I AIM FOR?

In you are in a hot climate, you probably want a double-glazed low-solar-gain window. Look for these specs:

- A whole-window SHGC of 0.28 to 0.37. Lower is better than higher.
- A center-of-glass SHGC of 0.20 to 0.27. Lower is better than higher.
- A whole-window U-factor of 0.30 or less. Lower is better than higher.
- A center-of-glass U-factor of 0.24 or 0.25. Lower is better than higher.

If you are in a cold climate, you may want a double- or triple-glazed high-solar-gain window. If you settle for a double-glazed window, look for these specs:

- A whole-window SHGC of 0.42 to 0.55. Higher is better than lower.
- A center-of-glass SHGC of 0.59 to 0.76. Higher is better than lower.

- A whole-window U-factor of 0.30 to 0.39. Lower is better than higher.
- A center-of-glass U-factor of 0.27 to 0.29. Lower is better than higher.

If you can spring for a triple-glazed window, look for these specs:

- A whole-window SHGC of 0.33 to 0.47. Higher is better than lower.
- A center-of-glass SHGC of 0.50 to 0.63. Higher is better than lower.
- A whole-window U-factor of 0.19 to 0.26. Lower is better than higher.
- A center-of-glass U-factor of 0.16 to 0.22. Lower is better than higher.

Balancing U-factor and solar heat gain

Since 1977, when Sweden introduced its stringent energy code, almost all new homes in Sweden have been equipped with triple-glazed windows. Here in the United States, where energy codes are more lax, triple-glazed windows are still rare. For a minority of U.S. builders, however—especially cold-climate builders of superinsulated homes—triple-glazed windows are considered essential. Because few U.S. manufacturers offer high-solar-gain triple-glazed windows, most Americans get these windows from Canadian manufacturers.

EXTRA GLASS KEEPS out the cold. Triple-glazed Canadian windows like this fiberglass casement window from Thermotech have U-factors as low as 0.17.

LOOK FOR A LOW U-FACTOR AND A HIGH SHGC

In any climate, a window with a low U-factor performs better than one with a high U-factor. The lower the U-factor, the better.

Many cold-climate builders prefer windows with a high SHGC and a high VT. After all, solar gain helps heat a house during the winter. During the summer, when solar heat gain is less desirable, a properly sized roof overhang will shade south-facing windows during the hottest hours of the day—at least on a building's south side.

For cold-climate builders following a traditional passive solar approach, most low-U-factor windows have a SHGC that is unacceptably low. Designers of cold-climate houses have to balance conflicting needs—the need for windows with a very low U-factor and as high a SHGC as possible. Most builders end up choosing triple-glazed windows with a U-factor ranging from 0.19 to 0.26 and a SHGC ranging from 0.39 to 0.47.

The higher the VT, the better. Windows with a low VT look gray and depressing. To get an idea of what range you're looking for, consider the advice of Robert Clarke, a technical specialist at Serious Energy and the former president of Alpen windows. According to Clarke, any window with a VT below 0.40 "would not be ethical to sell as clear glass."

When comparing U-factor, SHGC, and VT specifications among manufacturers, be careful. While leading manufacturers

Casement Window Specifications

Window manufacturer	Glazing	Whole-window U-factor	Whole-window SHGC	Whole-window VT
Accurate Dorwin, high SHGC	AFG 1E2 triple + argon	0.24	0.47	0.48
Accurate Dorwin, low SHGC	AFG 2 Ti-AC40 triple + argon	0.17	0.24	0.39
Duxton, high SHGC	Cardinal 179 triple with 2 low-e	0.21	0.39	
Duxton, low SHGC	AFC Ti-AC50 triple	0.19	0.24	0.38
Fibertec, high SHGC	Pilkington LOF with 1 low-e	0.26	0.41	0.46
Fibertec, low SHGC	Guardian RLE 7138 triple + krypton	0.18	0.28	0.37
Inline, high SHGC	Pilkington LOF hard-coat low-e + argon	0.22	0.39	0.43
Inline, low SHGC	Cardinal 272 soft-coat low-e + argon	0.20	0.23	0.39
Paradigm, foamed frame	Guardian RLE 7138 triple + argon	0.22	0.23	0.38
Thermotech, high SHGC	Pilkington LOF EA2 triple, 2 low-e	0.19	0.42	0.43
Thermotech, high SHGC	Pilkington LOF EA2 triple low-iron glass, 2 low-e	0.19	0.44	0.44
Thermotech, high SHGC	Clear triple glazing	0.29	0.47	
Thermotech, low SHGC	AFG Ti-R triple, 2 low-e	0.17	0.25	0.40

provide whole-window values (as required by NFRC labeling rules), less reputable manufacturers often trumpet glazing-only numbers. These glazing-only numbers often seem to show much better thermal performance than whole-window numbers, but they are misleading. To avoid comparing apples to oranges, insist on whole-window specifications that include the window frames.

SUPPLIERS OF TRIPLE-GLAZED WINDOWS

The five leading Canadian manufacturers of triple-glazed windows with pultruded fiberglass frames are Accurate Dorwin, Duxton, Inline Fiberglass, Fibertec, and Thermotech®.

New England builders looking for less-expensive triple-glazed windows have sometimes settled for triple-glazed vinyl windows from Paradigm Windows in Maine. Like almost all of the triple glazing offered by U.S. manufacturers, however, all of Paradigm's triple glazing has a very low SHGC.

Another U.S. manufacturer of high-performance windows is Alpen Windows of Boulder, Colorado. Although Alpen doesn't offer triple-glazed windows, it sells low-U-factor windows with Heat Mirror® glazing. (Heat Mirror glazing has two panes of glass with one or more

VINYL FRAMES HELP to reduce cost. Paradigm Windows of Portland, ME, offers vinyl casement windows with foam-injected frames. Unfortunately, the windows have a low SHGC.

suspended plastic films between the inner and outer panes.)

Assembling manufacturers' information on U-factors, SHGC, and VT is time-consuming. To help out window specifiers everywhere, I created the table on p. 171, which shows the specifications for casement windows from seven manufacturers. The table does not include any European window brands—for example, windows from Intus, Makrowin, Optiwin, or Zola—because most European manufacturers do not provide NFRC ratings.

Can a house with plastic components be considered green?

Should vinyl building materials be banned from green homes? Some environmentalists think so. There seem to be three categories of building materials that particularly irk the anti-PVC crowd: vinyl siding, vinyl windows, and vinyl flooring. Since there are alternatives to all of these materials, these environmentalists argue, green homes shouldn't include any of them.

Vinyl-framed windows now outsell windows with wooden frames, aluminum frames, or fiberglass frames. Moreover, in many areas of the country, vinyl siding outsells all other types of residential cladding, and PVC is by far the most common material used to manufacture residential drain pipes. While these facts probably distress anti-vinyl crusaders, they provide evidence that these vinyl building products outperform competing products in some ways. Vinyl building products fill a niche. Vinyl is durable, weather-resistant, low-maintenance, and affordable.

The anti-vinyl position rests on several arguments:

- The raw materials used to manufacture vinyl—chlorine and fossil fuels—are associated with environmental problems.

- Some of the chemicals present in vinyl as a contaminant—especially dioxin—raise environmental concerns.

- Workers in plants that manufacture PVC resin face health risks.

- Some vinyl products include plasticizers that may be released into indoor air, potentially damaging occupants' health.

- When vinyl building products wear out, they aren't always disposed of in an environmentally appropriate way.

- When buildings catch fire, vinyl building products release toxic smoke, endangering firefighters.

- A life-cycle assessment of vinyl's environmental impacts may indicate that vinyl is less desirable than some alternatives.

All of the above arguments have been used by anti-vinyl groups. Some of the points are indisputable, while others are debatable. On some points, evidence points to an opposite conclusion than the one reached by anti-vinyl crusaders. On other points, the evidence is inconclusive, and more research is needed before we can reach firm conclusions.

LIFE-CYCLE ASSESSMENTS

Environmental life-cycle assessments attempt to weigh all of the pluses and minuses of building materials so that one product can be compared to another. It's important to remember than any life-cycle assessment is only partially scientific, and involves more judgment than calculation.

The U.S. Green Building Council (USGBC) has issued at least two reports on PVC building materials—a 2004 draft report, followed by a 2007 final version called "Assessment of Technical Basis for a PVC-Related Materials Credit for LEED."

In the 2004 draft report, the authors wrote, "Using current data for Life-Cycle

Assessment (LCA) and risk assessment, our analysis of the chosen building material alternatives shows that PVC does not emerge as a clear winner or loser. In other words, the available evidence does not support a conclusion that PVC is consistently worse than alternative materials on a life cycle environmental and health basis.... Therefore, the current body of knowledge as analyzed in this report ... does not support a credit in the LEED rating system for eliminating PVC or any other material."

According to the best available evidence, many vinyl building materials are preferable to available alternatives. The authors of the 2007 USGBC report concluded, "The evidence indicates that a credit that rewards avoidance of PVC could steer decision makers toward using materials that are worse on most environmental impacts, except for the case of resilient flooring, in which sheet vinyl and VCT are worse than the alternative materials studied for most environmental impacts."

END-OF-LIFE DISPOSAL

The environmental effects of disposing of worn-out vinyl materials are hard to pin down. The authors of the 2007 USGBC report wrote, "Data on end-of-life emissions are highly uncertain and therefore there is a wide range of exposure possibilities; if end-of-life emissions are close to the upper end of our range, then PVC is among the worst materials studied for health risk, but if end-of-life emissions are close to the lower end of our range of possible values, then PVC is among the mid or better materials studied for health risk in the product categories of window frames, pipe, and siding."

According to the 1994 *Environmental Building News* (*EBN*) article on vinyl, "Except for the space taken up, landfilling PVC is not usually a problem. Attesting to the stability of PVC in landfills is the fact that most landfill liners are made from PVC."

WORKER SAFETY

Although there are valid reasons for concerns over the health of workers in plants that manufacture PVC resin, it's important to note that workers' exposure to dangerous emissions in these plants have dropped in recent decades.

According to the 1994 *EBN* article, "In 1971 a rare cancer of the liver, angiosarcoma, was traced to vinyl chloride exposure among PVC workers, and strict workplace exposure limits were established by the Occupational Safety and Health Administration (OSHA). These restrictions necessitated radical changes in the manufacturing environment—all polymerization vats had to be sealed and controlled .... To the credit of the chlorine and PVC industries and government regulatory bodies, ... vast improvements have been made in manufacturing processes over the past twenty years, and many of the worst environmental offenders (DDT, dieldrin, and CFCs, for example) are already gone or on their way out. The residual vinyl chloride gas in PVC products has been reduced to (perhaps) insignificant levels, compared with two decades ago. The environmental and health risks associated with PVC are greatest at the two ends of its lifetime: during manufacturing and disposal (if by incineration). Most PVC products are safe to use and some offer significant durability, cost, and maintenance advantages compared with competing products."

Builders who prefer wood windows to vinyl windows need to acknowledge an important truth: you can't have wood windows without logging, and logging is a dangerous profession—more dangerous than working in a chemical plant.

According to "America's Most Dangerous Jobs," a September 23, 2005, article posted on a website hosted by CNN, "The highest rates of fatal injuries—the most per worker employed—occurred among loggers, pilots, and fishermen. Loggers recorded 85 fatalities in 2004, a rate of 92.4 deaths for every 100,000 workers, more than 22 times the rate among all workers. Loggers deal with tremendous weights when they fell trees and it's not always possible to know exactly where a tree will fall or when. Too, they often work on steep hillsides, in poor weather, and in a hurry."

I'm not advocating that green builders specify vinyl windows to reduce injuries to loggers. (The loggers I know enjoy their work, and don't want to see their industry shrink.) I'm just pointing out the fact that workers in many industries face risks.

Moreover, the installation of siding and windows also carries risks—whatever material the products are made of. According to a government report, "Construction accounted for the second most fatal work injuries of any industry sector in 2011."

Avoiding vinyl

Many elements of the anti-vinyl argument are emotional and inconsistent. Those who aim to build a plastic-free home rarely argue in favor of plastic-free computers or plastic-free cell phones. Similarly, very few people who are injured or sick insist on treatment in a plastic-free hospital—and considering the dependence of modern surgery and patient care on plastic materials, that's a very good thing.

Anyone who gets excited by the thought of owning a Prius needs to acknowledge that plastic materials are often extremely useful. According to one source, more than 50% of a typical vehicle's volume is composed of plastics.

Only a small percentage of homeowners really want a plastic-free house. Most who do will end up compromising, since it's hard to wire a house without vinyl-insulated electrical cable. If a few Luddites manage to build a plastic-free house, it's likely to resemble homes built 150 years ago. It's an achievable but impractical goal. Writing in *EBN* in 1994, Malin and Wilson concluded, "For builders and architects, our recommendation is not to avoid vinyl altogether, but to seek out better, safer, and more environmentally responsible alternatives."

WHAT REALLY MATTERS

So, does it really matter if your window frame is made of vinyl or something else? Perhaps. If you hate the idea of having any vinyl in your house, it obviously matters. If you can afford alternative materials, you should specify exactly what you want. When it comes to an environmental analysis, however, the bottom line on vinyl is uncertain.

Many of us fret about the environmental effects of our daily decisions, but we tend to focus on issues that don't matter very much. Meanwhile, we manage to get the big things wrong. We may fret over whether we have properly separated recyclables from our trash, or fret over whether to choose a plastic bag or a paper bag when we go shopping. We may admonish family members who leave the water running while brushing their teeth. And when we build a new home, we wonder whether wood windows make more sense than vinyl windows.

But the biggest environmental impacts made by American families concern our profligate use of energy and our voracious appetite for raw and manufactured materials. The best thing we can do to lower our environmental impact is to stop shopping.

Instead of wondering whether you should buy vinyl siding or fiber-cement siding, you might consider whether there is any way to live in an old apartment building rather than to build a new house.

When walls have exterior foam, where do the windows go?

Builders in northern states and Canada often specify exterior wall foam for new construction as well as for residing jobs on existing houses. Installing rigid foam on exterior walls reduces thermal bridging through studs and (as long as the foam is thick enough) greatly reduces the chances of condensation or moisture accumulation in wall cavities. Current trends favor thicker and thicker foam; many cold-climate builders now routinely install 4 in. or 6 in. of EPS, XPS, or polyiso on exterior walls.

INNIES OR OUTIES?

Builders installing thick exterior wall foam can install windows two ways: with the window flanges in the same plane as the back of the siding—so-called outie windows—or with the window flanges in the same plane as the OSB wall sheathing —so-called innie windows. Either way will work.

Let's consider a wall with 2×4 studs, OSB sheathing, 4 in. of exterior foam, $\frac{3}{4}$-in.-thick vertical strapping, and fiber-cement lap siding. How should the windows be installed?

Outies, step by step

A builder who prefers outie windows would do it this way:

1. Window rough openings are oversize by $1\frac{1}{2}$ in. in both dimensions.

2. Each rough opening is lined with a frame made of $\frac{3}{4}$-in. by $8\frac{3}{4}$-in. plywood strips, creating a window buck. On the interior, the frames are installed flush; on the exterior, the frames project out

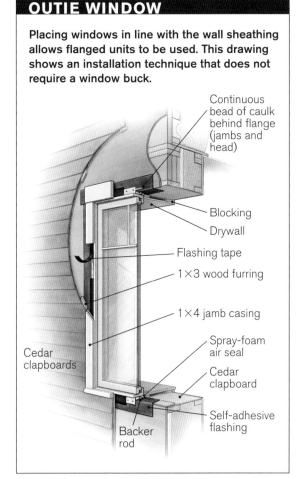

OUTIE WINDOW

Placing windows in line with the wall sheathing allows flanged units to be used. This drawing shows an installation technique that does not require a window buck.

Continuous bead of caulk behind flange (jambs and head)

Blocking

Drywall

Flashing tape

1×3 wood furring

1×4 jamb casing

Spray-foam air seal

Cedar clapboard

Cedar clapboards

Self-adhesive flashing

Backer rod

$4\frac{3}{4}$ in. beyond the outside face of the OSB sheathing (that is, $\frac{3}{4}$ in. beyond the outside face of the foam).

3. Once the exterior foam is installed, a frame of $\frac{3}{4}$-in. strapping, fastened flat to the foam, is installed around each plywood window projection. The outer face of the $\frac{3}{4}$-in. strapping is flush with the outer edge of the plywood frame.

4. The bottom of the plywood window buck is flashed with peel-and-stick flashing, just like a conventional rough opening.

5. Windows are installed in the plywood bucks; they are attached to the studs (through the plywood) with metal masonry clips (masonry brackets).

6. Peel-and-stick flashing is installed on the sides and top of the window, covering the window flanges and extending back to the foam.

7. Plastic housewrap is installed over the foam. The housewrap laps over the peel-and-stick flashing. Under the windows, peel-and-stick flashing laps over the housewrap.

INNIE WINDOW

Windows set into the wall are better protected from the elements, but they require careful flashing details to prevent water entry at the jambs and sill.

- Blocking
- Drywall
- Spray-foam air seal
- Self-adhesive flashing
- Drainage mat
- Wood-shake siding
- Self-adhesive flashing
- 5/8-in. plywood sheathing
- Cedar clapboard
- Backer rod

8. Vertical strapping is installed on top of the foam and the housewrap. Siding is attached to the vertical flashing.

Innies, step by step

On the other hand, a builder who prefers innie windows would do it this way:

1. Plastic housewrap is installed over the OSB sheathing.

2. The windows are installed conventionally, with the flanges on top of the OSB sheathing. The plastic housewrap is integrated with the window flashing.

3. The exterior foam is installed on top of the housewrap.

4. Vertical strapping is installed on top of the foam.

5. Exposed foam edges facing the window are protected with peel-and-stick flashing.

6. The exposed foam under the window sill is cut at a slope and protected with flashing made of a durable waterproof material; copper is ideal.

7. The exterior of the window is trimmed out with water-resistant jamb extensions made of cedar or cellular PVC.

INNIES VS. OUTIES

The innie vs. outie debate has been going on for decades. Back in 1984, here's what builder John Hughes of Edmonton, Alberta, had to say about the debate in an article for *Fine Homebuilding*: "It's possible to locate windows and doors anywhere on these broad sills, but most people like to keep windows flush with the new exterior wall. This creates a wide sill inside the house, looks good on the outside, and eliminates the necessity of installing a broad, weather-resistant exterior sill."

Both innie and outie windows have strong advocates. When I reported on the innie-versus-outie controversy for an article in the July 2002 issue of *Energy Design*

WHERE DOES THE HOUSEWRAP GO?

Let's say you're building a house with plywood or OSB sheathing. You plan to install 2 in. or 4 in. of rigid foam on the exterior of the wall sheathing, followed by vertical rain-screen strapping and siding. Where does the housewrap go?

Depending on who you talk to, you get two different answers.

- It goes between the rigid foam and the vertical strapping.
- It goes between the sheathing and the rigid foam.

I've heard a variety of arguments in favor of each position. For example, I've been told the housewrap belongs between the foam and the strapping, "because that way it's easier to integrate with the flashing at the logical drainage plane." On the other hand, I've been told the housewrap belongs between the sheathing and the foam, "because that way it protects the sheathing," or "to prevent the housewrap from flapping in the wind," or even "to protect the housewrap from extreme temperatures which might degrade the plastic."

Both sides of this argument have merit. If you have a strong opinion favoring either position, it's safe to say that either approach can work well, as long as the housewrap is properly integrated with all of the window flashing, door flashing, and the flashings protecting other penetrations.

Simplifying the decision

If this quandary has you discombob- ulated, though, here's an easy way through the thicket:

- If you are installing innie windows, your housewrap should go under the foam.
- If you are installing outie windows, your housewrap should go over the foam.

Integrating housewrap with innie windows

Innie windows are installed just like they are on a house without exterior foam. The housewrap covers the plywood or OSB sheathing, and the window is installed with your favorite flexible-flashing details. The foam is installed later, and there's no reason to integrate the free-draining rain-screen gap with any of the other flashing details on the wall.

All you have to do is come up with exterior jamb extensions—including a sloped secondary sill tucked under the sill that comes with the window—to cover the edges of the foam at the window and door openings. It's perfectly reasonable to argue that these exterior jamb extension details don't really have to be watertight, just resistant to weathering, durable, and attractive.

Integrating housewrap with outie windows

Outie windows are usually installed with the window flanges in the same plane as the back of the siding. This generally requires the installation of a plywood box in each window rough opening; the box extends x inches beyond the plywood or OSB sheathing, with x = the thickness of the foam + the thickness of the rain-screen strapping.

After the foam is installed but before the housewrap goes up, you need to install a picture frame of strapping lumber (installed flat to the foam) around each rough opening. The outer face of the strapping should be flush with the outer edge of the plywood frame. Then you install your window.

The housewrap goes up next, on top of the foam. At each window head, the housewrap is creased and extended out over the picture frame, and then down over the window flange or the flexible flashing at the window head. At the windowsill, the flexible flashing protecting the rough sill extends over the housewrap. Then the rain screen strapping is installed over the housewrap.

The method I've described is just one way to install housewrap over exterior foam. Of course, there are many variations to these installation and flashing details.

Can I just skip the housewrap?
Some builders argue that rigid foam is a perfectly good WRB, so foam-sheathed walls don't need any housewrap at all.

If you decided to go this route, be sure to do your research before proceeding. It's important to note:

- Not all brands of rigid foam have been approved for use as a WRB.
- Rigid foam can be used as a WRB only if you follow the fastening and seam-sealing details listed in the ICC-ES report used to obtain acceptance for your brand of foam to be used as a WRB.
- Some building experts note that over a period of years, rigid foam may shrink, raising the question of whether an installation of taped foam will remain waterproof over the long term.

YOU SAY UNDER, I SAY OVER.

It's possible to install housewrap or asphalt felt between the wall sheathing and a layer of exterior foam, as shown in this detail. It's also possible to install the WRB on the exterior side of the foam.

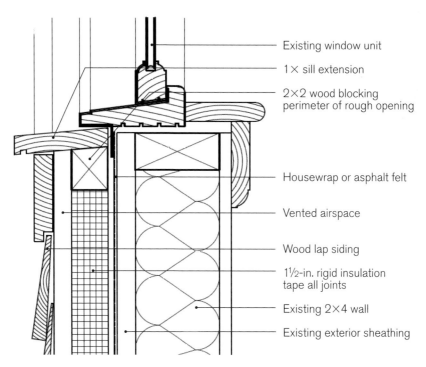

Existing window unit

1× sill extension

2×2 wood blocking perimeter of rough opening

Housewrap or asphalt felt

Vented airspace

Wood lap siding

1½-in. rigid insulation tape all joints

Existing 2×4 wall

Existing exterior sheathing

Drawing courtesy of Green Building Advisor

Update (*EDU*), building scientist Joe Lstiburek came out in favor of outie windows. "It looks cooler that way," he explained. Since the vast majority of residential windows are installed as outies, there's no doubt that outie windows look "normal" to most Americans.

However, Chris Makepeace, a certified engineering technologist at Alberta Infrastructure in Edmonton, AB, favored innie windows. "The window should be totally supported by the structure of the wall," Makepeace told me. "If the window is toward the inside, then the bulk of the window frame is able to 'see' the interior heat, and the window is at a more constant temperature year round. If we extend the window farther to the exterior, we increase the water leakage potential."

Jack Hébert, president of the Cold Climate Research Center in Fairbanks, AK, also preferred innie windows. "It creates a pocket where you don't get as much wind across the face of the window," Hébert told me.

Thorsten Chlupp, a builder in Fairbanks, AK, agreed with Hébert that innie windows are best: "Windows can be installed either at the face of the sheathing—in a recess—or out at the face of the wall. From a performance standpoint, a recess is better, because the window is somewhat protected from wind-washing and the interior glass is more easily warmed by the heat in the room. By contrast, windows installed at the face of the wall are in an interior recess, separating them from the warm air inside (especially if a curtain is drawn) and exposing the outer layer of glass to cold wind. I've observed that in extremely cold weather—when it's 25°F below zero, for example—frost tends to form inside windows installed at the face of the wall, whereas frost rarely occurs on inset windows. I've installed windows both ways, but because of the frost problem I now do only recessed installations. A recessed installation is more complicated because the sides of the recess must be covered with exterior jamb extensions. On vinyl-sided homes, we make the extensions from 20-gauge metal coil stock. The bottom is sloped to shed water, and there are flanges on both edges—an inner flange that gets fastened to the sheathing and an outer flange that laps over the 1×4 strapping that we install on top of the EPS around the window. We've also made extensions from wood and cellular PVC. These solid extension jambs are glued and screwed at the corners and fastened to the wall over a thick bead of sealant. We either toe-screw them to the framing or fasten them from the inside with metal clips."

According to Massachusetts architect Betsy Pettit, each approach has advantages and disadvantages. "With innie windows, you have to return the exterior trim and extend the windowsills," Pettit noted. "By the time you do that work, innie windows aren't the most economical approach. However, innie windows should last longer, because they'll receive less rain deposition. The innie approach puts the windows in the right location."

Builders deciding between innie and outie windows should remember these points:

• The WRB (for example, housewrap) can be under the foam or over the foam. A third option is to omit the housewrap and use taped foam as the WRB. In most cases, innie windows require a WRB under the foam, while outie window require a WRB over the foam. (For more information on the question of where to locate the WRB, see "Where Does the Housewrap Go?" on p. 178.)

• No matter where the windows are located, flashing details need to tie the perimeter of the window into the WRB.

An engineer investigating ways to optimize the design of net-zero-energy homes concludes that inexpensive triple-glazed windows are good enough

An architectural cliché from the 1970s —the passive solar home with large expanses of south-facing glass—is making a comeback. In recent years, we've seen North American designers of Passivhaus buildings increase the area of south-facing glass to levels rarely seen since the Carter administration.

What's the explanation for all this south-facing glass? We're told that there's no other way for designers to meet the energy limit for space heating required by the Passivhaus standard: namely, a maximum of 15 kwh per square meter per year.

Struggling to meet this goal, many Passivhaus designers have found that the typical triple-glazed windows sold in North America have U-factors that aren't quite low enough (or SHGCs that aren't quite high enough) for their designs to meet the standard. Because of this, these designers often end up specifying very expensive triple-glazed windows from Germany or Austria.

WHAT ABOUT COST-EFFECTIVENESS?

These Herculean efforts to meet the Passivhaus standard rarely pay attention to cost-effectiveness. Even when designers find it necessary to invest in measures that yield lower energy savings than a photovoltaic array of the same price, they plow ahead because they have to meet the numbers dictated by the PHPP software.

These investments in very expensive building materials are probably a waste of money. An excellent paper by Gary Proskiw, "Identifying Affordable Net Zero Energy Housing Solutions," looks into the cost-effectiveness of large expanses of south-facing glazing as well as the cost-effectiveness of low-U-factor windows. Proskiw, a mechanical engineer from Winnipeg, MB, who specializes in residential energy issues, concluded that heroic window measures don't pay worthwhile dividends.

Proskiw's paper focused on ways to optimize the design of a net-zero-energy (NZE) house. While the paper mostly focused on Canadian climates, it considered one U.S. home (the NZE house built by Habitat for Humanity® in Wheat Ridge, CO) in its analysis.

THE VALUE OF EXTRA SOUTH-FACING GLAZING

Proskiw asked an interesting question: Should the designer of a superinsulated home add extra south-facing windows "to increase solar gains and reduce the space heating load"? He tackled the question by analyzing the cost of this measure and then comparing the cost to the energy benefit.

For the purpose of his analysis, he considered an 1,800-sq.-ft. NZE house located in Winnipeg. He assumed that the base-case house had R-44 exterior walls and south-facing glazing with an area equal to 6% of the floor area. According to his analysis, the cost to build an R-44 wall is $170 per square meter ($15.80 per sq. ft.). What if the designer chose to add another south-facing window—one measuring 1 square meter (10.76 sq. ft.)?

Proskiw estimated that a triple-glazed, low-e, argon-filled fixed window measuring 1 square meter costs $488. Proskiw estimated that the net cost of adding this window to the house would equal the cost of the window minus the cost of the displaced wall area; he calculated the incremental cost this way: $488 – $170 = $318. (Proskiw knew that this calculation method underestimates the cost of adding a window because it ignores the costs associated with framing the rough opening, the cost of the header, and the cost of trimming the opening; however, if these costs are included, Proskiw's argument is only strengthened.)

The base-case house had a modeled energy consumption of 1,462 kwh per year. Adding the extra window resulted in a modeled energy consumption of 1,443 kwh per year. In other words, the extra window saved only 19 kwh per year, which Proskiw valued at $1.90. He calculated that the payback period for this measure is 167 years. "Given that the life expectancy of an insulated glazing unit (IGU) is about 25 years, it is clear that inclusion of the extra 1 square meter of south facing window area can never be economically justified," Proskiw wrote. "From a design perspective, these results indicate that increasing the amount of window area in a NZE house, *as an energy saving measure*, has to be examined extremely carefully since it is unlikely to be economic relative to other options."

According to energy expert Marc Rosenbaum, adding a south-facing window measuring 1 square meter (gross area) on one of his Massachusetts house designs

(a house from the Eliakim's Way development on Martha's Vineyard) would save 120 kwh a year (worth about $12 a year, according to Proskiw's method). If the window could be installed for an incremental cost of $318—(the actual incremental cost is likely to be higher)—the simple payback period would be 26 years.

WHAT ABOUT INVESTING IN REALLY GOOD WINDOWS?

Proskiw also compared two different types of triple-glazed window:

- The less expensive option ($360 per square meter) was a "relatively conventional triple-glazed unit with an insulated spacer." This window did not include argon gas or any low-e coatings.

- The more expensive option ($488 per square meter) was a "triple-glazed unit with one low-e coating, two argon fills, and an insulated spacer." The incremental cost for this window was $488 – $360 = $128.

Proskiw assumed that the window measured 1 square meter and faced south. The energy savings attributable to the glazing upgrade was 8 kwh per year, which Proskiw valued at $0.80. The upgraded glazing had a simple payback period of 160 years.

EXPENSIVE GLAZING DOESN'T MAKE ECONOMIC SENSE

Proskiw wrote, "The reason the two window upgrades fared so poorly, from an economic perspective, is that the space heating load in a NZE house is very small compared to any other type of house. By adding window area or upgrading window performance, the space heating load is reduced but it is already so small that there is little opportunity for further savings."

He went on to note, "The preceding discussion used the incremental analysis

PASSIVHAUS NUMBER 1. Completed in 2004, Katrin Klingenberg's house in Urbana, IL, was the first single-family residence in the United States to be certified as complying with the Passivhaus standard. The house is known as the Smith house.

of costs and benefits to illustrate the economics of adding glazed area and of upgrading windows in a Net Zero Energy House. Although it used single examples, the process could be easily used for other windows in other houses. A more rigorous analysis, using a wider range of windows, houses, locations, etc., would yield similar results in most cases."

What's the lesson for designers of super-insulated homes? "Since windows and their upgrade options are so expensive, the investment would often be better spent on improving the energy performance of some other conservation or renewable energy option," Proskiw concluded.

INEXPENSIVE TRIPLE-GLAZED WINDOWS ARE FINE

One way to summarize Proskiw's findings: Builders of superinsulated homes in cold climates should choose affordable (usually triple-glazed) windows rather than exotic windows with extremely low U-factors.

"From an energy perspective and based on the incremental costs and energy savings, window selection should be based solely on the need to control condensation," Proskiw wrote. In most cases, that means that you should choose glazing with a warm-edge spacer. "Further, the window area should be limited to that necessary to meet the functional and aesthetic needs of the building. As such, south facing glazing area should be restricted to 6% [of the conditioned floor area] (to control overheating) and total window area should also be limited to that required for functional and aesthetic considerations. On a broader level, these results indicate that our long held belief in the merits and value of passive solar energy as a key component of Net Zero Energy House design need to be carefully reexamined and likely challenged."

Proskiw summed up the situation this way: "When one square meter of window area is added to a house, two things happen: the gross space heating load is increased (since the window has a lower R-value than the wall area which it replaced) and the passive solar gains are increased. Unfortunately, the increased space heating load is present 24/7 during the heating season. The extra passive gains are also available, but can only be utilized during a portion of the heating season (unless overheating is allowed to occur). As the house becomes more energy efficient, that 'portion' becomes increasingly smaller."

It's often hard to decide whether to replace them, repair them, or leave them just the way they are

If you're trying to lower your energy bills, you have probably plugged many of your home's air leaks and have added insulation to your attic floor. Now you may be wondering, "What should we do about our old windows?" Unfortunately, there is no clear answer to this question. Sometimes it makes sense to leave old windows exactly the way they are. Sometimes it makes sense to repair the windows' weatherstripping and add storm windows. And sometimes it makes sense to replace old windows with new energy-efficient windows.

Before providing a framework to help you decide what to do, it's important to address a few basic questions about window replacement.

REPAIR OR REPLACE? Just because a window is old and lacks high-performance glazing, doesn't mean it isn't worth preserving.

WILL NEW WINDOWS SAVE ENERGY?

Here's the good news: If you install new energy-efficient windows, your energy bills will go down. Here's the bad news: Your bills won't go down as much as the window salesman promised. In fact, your new replacement windows will save you so little money on your energy bills that the payback period for this investment may be more than 100 years—far longer than the new windows are likely to last.

Of all the data-crunchers who have looked closely at energy savings attributable to window replacement, none is more credible than Michael Blasnik, a Boston-based energy consultant with access to utility bill data for millions of U.S. homes. "I've looked at a lot of window replacement data," Blasnik explained in 2012 at the Building Energy 12 conference in Boston. "I've heard window salespeople say that you can save 50% on your heating bills if you replace all your windows. In fact, the amount of energy saved by replacing all of the windows in a home is generally on the order of 1% to 4% of the heating energy usage."

Exaggerated marketing claims by companies selling replacement windows have exasperated energy experts for decades. "Window replacement has a 200- to 300-year payback period," said Blasnik. "A Wisconsin study found that a lot of the expected energy saving is lost by the reduction of solar gain. Most replacement windows have low-solar-gain glazing, so maybe half the energy saving is gone due to the reduction in solar gain. I tell people, go ahead and replace your windows if you want, but don't expect significant energy savings." In short, says Blasnik, "the measure is not cost-effective."

WHAT IF I LEAVE THEM JUST THE WAY THEY ARE?

While many older homes still have their original single-glazed windows, almost all such homes (especially those in cold climates) have had triple-track storms installed by now. Single-glazed windows with exterior triple-track storm windows don't perform quite as well as new double-glazed windows, but their performance is surprisingly close. The annual difference in energy bills may amount to just $1 or $2 per window.

Before embarking on an expensive plan to fix or replace your windows, ask yourself three questions:

• Do your windows have storms?

• Do the windows operate smoothly?

• Does the existing weatherstripping do an adequate job of keeping out drafts?

If the answer to all three questions is yes, you may not need to do anything at all.

OK—I WANT TO FIX UP MY WINDOWS

Let's assume that your windows don't include any lead paint (see the sidebar above). If you want to improve the energy performance of your windows, it's fine to do so. Just don't expect you will save enough energy to justify your investment.

If you've decided to invest in improvements, you have two choices: repair or replace. Why would you decide to repair old windows instead of replacing them? There are several possible reasons:

WHAT ABOUT LEAD PAINT?

If your family includes children under the age of six, or anyone who may be getting pregnant soon, and your house was built before 1978, you need to determine whether your existing windows have lead paint.

You can test the existing paint with a do-it-yourself test kit or you can hire an abatement company to test your paint. If your windows have lead paint, and your family includes vulnerable members, you should consider lead abatement work or window replacement by a contractor familiar with lead-safe practices.

To learn more about these issues, visit

▪ The EPA web page on lead hazards.

▪ The HUD web page on lead hazards: "About Lead-Based Paint."

▪ The New York State Department of Health web page on lead hazards: "What Homeowners Need to Know About Removing Lead-Based Paint."

• You value the look of your historic windows, and you want to preserve them.

• You are worried that new windows won't last as long as restored historic windows.

• You care more about the character of the house than achieving the lowest energy bills on the block.

• Your house is located in a neighborhood controlled by a historic preservation commission.

When this topic has come up on GBA, many readers have posted cogent arguments in favor of repairing historic windows. For example, here's what James Morgan, a designer in Carrboro, NC, had to say: "The laws of physics, when consulted on the big energy picture, tell us that for a historic building (with usually

WINDOW SHADES AND WINDOW QUILTS

If you want to improve the energy performance of existing windows, and you don't care about cost-effectiveness, you might want to install interior insulating shades or window quilts. For these devices to save energy, you have to remember to pull down the shades or window quilts in the evening, and open them in the morning. (During winter, if you forget to open them during the daytime, you might miss out on desirable solar gain.) Some homeowners don't mind these tasks; others hate them.

According to GBA technical director Peter Yost, "Field testing indicates that insulated cellular shades with sealing sidetracks contribute about R-4 to the window .... We have just installed such shades in our home and I have to admit some winter nights go by with more than one shade stacked in its stored position with an R-value of about 0; and optimally deploying the shades on cloudy versus sunny cold winter days is more than a bit challenging, even for us folks with home offices."

WEIGHING COST AND CHARACTER. Don't jump to conclusions—repairing old windows often makes more economic sense than replacing them.

rather limited fenestration), glazing U-factors are a relatively minor consideration compared to all the other usual energy retrofit suspects."

The authors of an oft-cited 1996 study ("Testing the Energy Performance of Wood Windows in Cold Climates") concluded, "Replacing an historic window does not necessarily result in greater energy savings than upgrading that same window. The decision to renovate or replace a window should not be based solely on energy considerations, as the differences in estimated first year savings between the upgrade options are small."

How can I repair my old windows?

Repairing an older window can easily cost as much as replacing it—or more, if the work includes certified lead abatement.

According to a *Fine Homebuilding* article, "Should Your Old Wood Windows Be Saved?," repairing old windows is usually cheaper than replacement. "Restoring and upgrading old windows isn't cheap, but much of the expense is paid in sweat if you're willing to do the work yourself ....According to [window specialist Jade] Mortimer, a professional may charge around $200 for a complete restoration and upgrade of each window—maybe more, depending on the damage. However, if you do the work yourself, you can generally expect to pay less than $100 for materials. A storm window can cost as little as $80 or in excess of $300. Again, the upgrade can cost much less if you build your own."

In most cases, repairing an older double-hung window will require removal of the interior stops and parting beads; inspection and repair of the sash weights, sash cords, and pulleys; installation of new weatherstripping and (in some cases) sash locks; repair of the window putty; and new paint.

LOW-E STORM WINDOWS

If your older single-pane windows already have storm windows, it makes sense to keep the storms you have. Of course, storm windows are effective only if they are closed during the winter. (A surprisingly high percentage of triple-track storm windows are left open all winter long.)

If you live in a cold climate, and your windows don't have storms, it makes sense to install low-e storm windows. There are two basic types of low-e coating: sputtered (also called soft-coat) and pyrolitic (also called hard-coat). While either type of low-e coating is suitable for use in a sealed insulated glazing unit, only pyrolitic coatings are hard and durable enough for storm windows. When used on a storm window, the low-e coating faces the interior. Because most pyrolitic coatings have a higher SHGC than most sputtered coatings, pyrolitic coatings are particularly appropriate for cold climates.

STORM WINDOWS. When you're considering window upgrades for operational or energy-efficiency purposes, in many cases installing or replacing storm windows can offer more bang for the buck than installing full replacement windows.

HOT CLIMATE CONCERNS

Old single-glazed windows are, by definition, high-solar-gain windows. On a sunny winter day, that's good news. However, on a hot summer day, it's bad news, especially if the windows face west. If you live in a hot climate, you probably worry more about your cooling costs than your heating costs. Solar gain through windows is a major factor affecting cooling loads, so it makes sense to address solar gain in rooms that overheat.

Excess solar gain can be addressed by providing improved shading (for example, with a trellis or an awning) or by installing solar control window films. Another (expensive) option is to install replacement windows with low-solar-gain glazing.

Research has shown that an old single-glazed window fitted with a low-e storm window performs as well as a new double-glazed low-e window. According to a classic 2007 study by Craig Drumheller, the average payback period associated with the installation of new low-e storm windows on older homes in Chicago is 4.3 years.

If you are intrigued by low-e storm windows, there is a caveat: This type of storm window works well when installed over single-glazed windows but should never be installed over newer double-glazed low-e windows. According to an article in *Environmental Building News*, "Modeling performed for LBNL by sustainability consultant Thomas Culp, Ph.D. has uncovered the potential for serious overheating problems when low-e storms are added to low-e windows: in hot weather, in direct sunlight, temperatures up to 185°F (85°C) may be reached. That kind of heat can cause premature aging or failure of the insulated glazing unit's seals."

NEW REPLACEMENT WINDOWS

It sometimes makes sense to install new replacement windows in an older home—as long as you realize that you'll never see enough savings in your energy bills to justify the high cost of the work. If you decide to install new replacement windows, choose a reputable contractor to perform the work. It should go without saying that the contractor should have a good understanding of moisture management issues and methods for flashing rough openings. Unfortunately, not all window replacement contractors fall into this category.

Remember, building codes appropriately require every bedroom to have at least one window that is large enough to provide egress in an emergency. It's important to verify that your window replacement contractor understands this part of the building code. A bedroom window with a small rough opening may require a casement rather than a double-hung to meet egress requirements.

COMFORT IS WORTH PAYING FOR

What's the bottom line? If you live in a cold climate, and your house has older single-pane windows and no storms, you should invest in low-e storm windows. If you live in a hot climate, you may want to invest in window film to reduce solar gain.

It's hard to justify any other improvements to existing windows on the basis of energy savings. That said, many people want to repair or replace older windows for other reasons. If your older windows are drafty, or if you skin feels cold when you sit beside a window on a winter night, you may be happy to spend $400 or $500 per window for improved comfort.

The traditional HVAC triad addresses heating, ventilation, and air-conditioning. Every energy-efficient house in North America needs a heating system and a ventilation system, and many (but not all) also need an air-conditioning system.

Ignored by the HVAC designation is a fourth element of indoor comfort: humidity control. The main way to avoid a common wintertime problem—low indoor humidity—is to ensure that the home's building envelope has as few air leaks as possible. The main way to avoid high indoor humidity during the summer is to operate an air-conditioner, although this approach may need to be supplemented in some climates by the use of a stand-alone dehumidifier.

7

HVAC

Most forced-air heating systems are still poorly designed and installed

M any different appliances can be used to heat a house, including boilers, water heaters, heat pumps, and wood stoves. However, most homes in the United States are heated by a forced-air furnace. These devices are connected to ducts that deliver heated air to registers throughout the house. Different types of furnaces are manufactured to burn a variety of fuels, including natural gas, propane, oil, and firewood. The most common furnace fuel in the United States is natural gas.

In Europe, where furnaces are almost unheard of, most homes are heated by a boiler that distributes heat through hot-water pipes. Unlike Europeans, however, most Americans insist on central air-conditioning in their homes. It's easier to provide whole-house air-conditioning in a home with a duct system. Once you have a duct system for cooling, it's cheaper to install a furnace for winter heating than to install a boiler with a separate distribution system.

Even though the smallest available furnaces are often oversize for a high-performance home, furnaces still have virtues that are hard to ignore. They are inexpensive, widely available, and easily serviced by local HVAC contractors. For many North American homes, they are a logical way to supply space heat.

DEFINING AFUE

When it comes to fuel efficiency, residential furnaces in the United States are divided into two main categories: medium-efficiency furnaces and high-efficiency furnaces.

Furnace efficiency is usually calculated using a laboratory procedure that measures an appliance's annual fuel utilization efficiency, or AFUE. This calculation accounts for heat losses up the chimney, heat losses through the appliance jacket, and heat losses due to on-and-off cycling, but it doesn't account for electricity use (fan energy use) or heat lost through the distribution system (ductwork). AFUE can be calculated for boilers as well as furnaces and is used for appliances that burn many different types of fuel.

Low-efficiency and medium-efficiency furnaces

The usual definition of a low-efficiency furnace is one that is less than 75% efficient. The reason you can no longer buy a low-efficiency furnace is that the federal government now requires residential gas-fired furnaces to have a minimum efficiency of 80%. (The minimum efficiency for oil-fired furnaces is 83%, except for oil-fired furnaces designed for installation in mobile homes, which have a minimum efficiency of 75%.)

Medium-efficiency furnaces have efficiencies in the range of 80% to 82%. The line between mid-efficiency and high-efficiency furnaces is not arbitrary, but marks the division between appliances with distinct operating characteristics. Mid-efficiency furnaces are designed to keep flue gases hot enough to avoid any condensation of flue-gas moisture, while high-efficiency furnaces deliberately

Furnaces use natural gas, propane, oil, wood, wood pellets, or electricity, and are fired when a remote thermostat detects that the temperature in a room has fallen below a preset level. Once in operation, the burner fires in a combustion chamber and warms a heat exchanger. A blower pushes air over the heat exchanger or coils, and hot air flows through a series of ducts and enters a home's living spaces through registers in the floors, walls, or ceiling. Ducts also supply return air to the furnace, and combustion gases exhaust through a chimney or direct vent system.

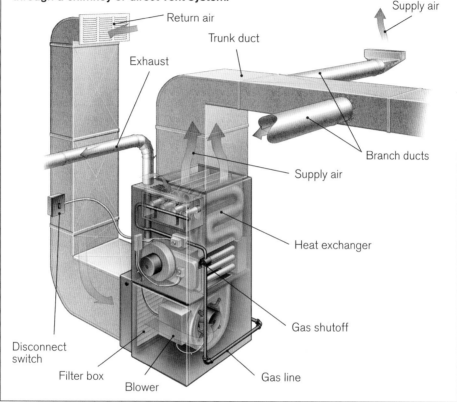

encourage the condensation of flue-gas moisture.

It is technically difficult to manufacture a furnace with an efficiency between 83% and 89%, so none are available in that range. Furnaces with "in-between" efficiency have sporadic condensation of flue gases, and this condensation causes corrosion problems. Furnaces with an efficiency of 90% or more wring so much heat out of the flue gases that the furnace exhaust can be vented through PVC pipe,

a material that is more resistant to corrosive condensate than the stainless-steel vent pipe that would have to be used for the hotter flue gases that would occur in a furnace with an efficiency in the tricky 83% to 89% range.

High-efficiency furnaces

High-efficiency furnaces (also called condensing furnaces) have AFUE ratings that range from 90% to about 97%. These furnaces have a secondary heat exchanger

ıe moisture in the escaping flue
; condensed. This phase change
water vapor to liquid water releases
ı.. improving the unit's efficiency.
Condensing furnaces must be hooked
up to a drain that can dispose of the
liquid condensate.

A high-efficiency furnace costs more
than a mid-efficiency furnace. However,
the venting system for a high-efficiency
furnace may cost less than the chimney
required for a mid-efficiency furnace.
Most condensing furnaces burn either
natural gas or propane. While condensing
oil-fired furnaces exist, the devices have
a mixed reputation. According to some
HVAC specialists, oil-fired condensing
furnaces require frequent cleaning.

SINGLE-STAGE, TWO-STAGE, AND MODULATING FURNACES

The simplest furnaces are single-stage
furnaces with single-speed blowers. If
the furnace is rated with an output of
60,000 Btu/hr, that is the furnace's output
whenever it is running.

More sophisticated two-stage furnaces
can operate at two different output levels.
Most of the time, these furnaces operate
at a lower Btu/hr output; the higher
output is needed only on the coldest days
of the year.

Modulating gas furnaces are more sophisticated than two-stage furnaces. They
include an automatic fuel valve that varies
the amount of fuel delivered to the burner.
Many modulating furnaces also include
a variable-speed blower motor (usually
an electronically commutated motor, or
ECM) which (like the automatic fuel
valve) ramps up and down in response to
heating demand. Because modulating furnaces can match the heating demand precisely, they provide more even heat than
single-speed furnaces that operate with a
stop-and-go jerkiness.

Oil-burning furnaces are less flexible than
gas furnaces. While it's fairly easy to
design a gas valve that varies the amount
of fuel delivered to the burner, oil burners
have a nozzle that is optimized for a
single firing rate at a fixed Btu/hr output.
That's why oil furnaces are usually single-stage furnaces.

Condensing furnaces are power-vented, so
they include at least two fans: an air-
handler fan that distributes warm air
through the home's ductwork, and a power-
vent fan to move exhaust gases through
the flue pipe. Most, but not all, condensing furnaces are sealed-combustion furnaces, meaning the burners pull outside
air into the combustion chamber through
plastic ducts to feed the fire's needs.
Sealed-combustion furnaces don't use any
indoor air for combustion. The main
advantage of a sealed-combustion furnace
(compared to an old-fashioned atmo-
spherically vented furnace) is that a
sealed-combustion furnace is much less
likely to suffer from backdrafting problems. (Backdrafting occurs when a powerful exhaust fan—for example, a range
hood fan—depressurizes a house enough
to draw combustion fumes down the
chimney and back into the house.)

DUCTING MISTAKES

During the 1950s and 1960s, fuel was
so inexpensive in the United States that
most heating contractors routinely
installed leaky ductwork. In many areas
of the country, contractors still install
ductwork in vented crawl spaces or vented
attics; because these locations are outside
of a home's conditioned envelope, the
conditioned air that escapes from leaky
ductwork in these locations is gone for
good. To make up for the fact that leaky
duct systems waste large amounts of
energy, HVAC installers usually install
oversize furnaces with huge blowers.

In the 1980s, energy-efficiency advocates responded to the nation's leaky duct crisis by establishing training programs to encourage HVAC installers to seal duct seams. After three decades of training, these programs are beginning to bear fruit in some areas of the United States. Unfortunately, the gospel of airtight ductwork hasn't reached every corner of the country, and many HVAC contractors are still installing ductwork the way their grandfathers did in 1964.

Here is a list of the most common duct design and duct installation errors:

• Trying to design a duct system without performing a room-by-room heat loss calculation. For more information on this issue, see "Using Manual J For Load Calculations" on p. 82.

• Locating ducts outside of a home's thermal envelope (for example, in a vented attic or vented crawl space).

• Failing to provide a return-air pathway from every room in the house back to the furnace.

• Undersizing return air ducts. (Return air ducts should be at least as large as supply air ducts.)

• Using framing cavities like stud bays or panned joist bays instead of ducts to move supply air or return air.

• Failing to seal duct leaks.

FURNACES LEAK TOO

Unfortunately, furnaces and furnace plenums often leak as much as some duct systems. If your furnace is located inside your home's conditioned space, these leaks may not matter very much. But if your furnace is located in a garage or vented attic—a bad idea, by the way— leaky furnaces waste energy.

Brand-new furnaces and air handlers are delivered from the factory with leaky

DUCTING TIPS

Every branch duct running to a register needs a balancing damper. These dampers are adjusted as part of the commissioning process to make sure that each room gets the design air flow.

In general, undersize ducts cause more problems than oversize ducts. If your duct system is undersize, air flow will be constricted and the furnace may not be able to remove heat fast enough to prevent damage to the heat exchanger.

Return air ducts need to be as large as or larger than supply air ducts. Most residential HVAC systems have undersize return ducts; when in doubt, make them bigger.

Galvanized ducts are always preferable to flex ducts. The corrugations in flex ducts cause turbulence that reduces airflow through the duct; moreover, flex duct is hard to keep straight and well supported. For maximum efficiency, ducts should be as straight and as short as possible, with a minimum of elbows. Whether you choose galvanized ducts or flex ducts, make sure to install enough duct hangers to prevent sagging.

Traditionally, supply registers were usually located near exterior walls, in an attempt to counteract the chilling effect caused by winter infiltration and the radiational cooling that occurs when warm bodies lose heat to cold window glass. If you are building a tight house with thick insulation and high-quality windows, however, it's possible to install supply registers on interior walls. This strategy results in shorter duct runs that operate more efficiently than longer ducts extending to a building's exterior walls.

It should go without saying that duct seams should be sealed with mastic and duct systems should be checked for leakage with a Duct Blaster.

Here's a checklist of the steps you need to take to create an efficient, high-performance forced-air heating system:

- Perform a room-by-room heating load and cooling load calculation.
- Avoid the temptation to buy an oversize furnace. Specify a furnace that meets your home's design heating load, without tacking on a "safety factor."
- If you live in a cold climate, specify a condensing furnace.
- Locate the furnace in the center of your basement or in a mechanical room near the center of your house.
- Design the duct system using Manual D.
- Locate all ducts within the home's thermal envelope.
- If the house has high-performance windows and a low rate of air leakage, locate supply registers on interior walls.
- Keep duct runs short and straight, with as few elbows as possible. It's better for ducts to be slightly oversize than undersize.
- Minimize the use of flex duct. If flex duct is installed, support it with an adequate number of hangers, and make sure the duct runs aren't twisted, crushed, or pinched.
- Design a return air system with multiple return air grilles rather than a single central return.
- Plan for a return air path from every conditioned room back to the furnace's return air plenum.

seams. As typically installed, furnaces also have leaks between the furnace and the plenums. In a study conducted by the Florida Solar Energy Center® (FSEC®), 69 furnaces and air handlers were measured for leakage. On average, 5.3% of system airflow was leaking at the furnace or air handler. (Of course, additional leakage occurred in the homes' duct systems.)

Commenting on the research, Philip Fairey, FSEC's deputy director, noted, "In most cases the units as shipped from the factory contain seams that leak. Some factory seams are gasketed, but in many cases they could be better." The solution: feel for air leaks, and seal any accessible seams with aluminum tape or mastic.

Don't forget to consider other options

After reading this chapter, you may know more about furnaces than you used to. Before specifying a furnace for your next project, however, remember that other options exist. An increasing number of high-performance homes are heated and cooled with two or three ductless mini-split heat pumps (see p. 215).

For an energy-efficient forced-air system, seal seams with mastic and test with a Duct Blaster

For years, Americans who would never put up with leaky plumbing pipes have been willing to accept leaky ducts. While water damage is hard to ignore, the damage caused by leaky ducts is more subtle. Yet leaky ducts not only waste huge amounts of energy but can also lead to comfort complaints, moisture problems, mold, and rot.

Most green certification programs require builders to pay attention to duct tightness. Now that duct testing requirements are starting to appear in building codes, more and more builders are asking questions about the ins and outs of duct leakage testing.

DUCT BASICS

Most green builders already know their duct basics:

• Duct leaks are very common; in many homes, duct leaks are responsible for significant energy losses.

• For ducts located in an unconditioned attic, any leaks in the supply system tend to depressurize a house, while return-system leaks tend to pressurize a house. Either condition can cause problems.

• Duct leaks outside of a home's thermal envelope waste more energy than duct leaks inside a home's thermal envelope.

• Even if ducts are located inside of a home's thermal envelope, duct leaks can still connect to the outdoors. For example, supply system leaks in a ceiling between the first and second floors of a two-story home can pressurize the joist bay, forcing conditioned air outdoors through cracks in the rim joist area.

• It's much easier to seal duct seams during new construction than in an existing house.

CODE REQUIREMENTS FOR DUCT SEALING

Although model codes have included duct-sealing requirements for years,

---

A GOOD DUCT SYSTEM:

• Has been designed to meet ACCA Manual D requirements, with each duct carefully sized to provide the airflow needed to meet room-by-room heat loss and heat gain calculations.

• Has been designed so that duct runs are as short and straight as possible.

• Does not use building cavities (for example, panned joists or stud bays) as ducts.

• Locates all ducts within the home's thermal envelope.

• Includes ducts or air paths that allow return air to flow back to the air handler from every room with a supply register.

• Has all seams sealed with duct mastic.

• Has been tested for duct leakage.

enforcement has been spotty or nonexistent. For example, a 2001 study of 80 new homes in Fort Collins, CO, found that the number of homes that complied with code duct-tightness requirements was zero. Astonishingly, the average duct leakage in the studied homes was 75% of total system airflow.

Another 2001 study found that Massachusetts Energy Code requirements for duct sealing were widely ignored. Researchers who inspected 186 new Massachusetts homes reported that "serious problems were found in the quality of duct sealing in about 80% of these houses."

The 2012 IRC requires (in section M1601.4.1) that "All joints, longitudinal and transverse seams, and connections in ductwork shall be securely fastened and sealed with welds, gaskets, mastics (adhesives), mastic-plus-embedded-fabric systems or tapes." Hardware-store duct tape is not an approved tape.

Mandatory testing

Builders need to get up to speed on duct testing because recent code changes require that all residential duct systems except those that are located entirely within a home's thermal envelope need to be tested for leakage.

Like the 2009 IRC, the 2012 IRC requires duct leakage testing unless the duct system is located entirely inside of the home's thermal envelope. The new code has increased the stringency of the duct leakage thresholds. The code permits builders to test a duct system in one of three ways:

• One option is a so-called rough-in test *before* the air hander is installed. While the 2009 code had a threshold of 4 cfm per 100 sq. ft. of conditioned floor area for this test, the 2012 code has lowered this threshold to 3 cfm.

• Another option is a so-called rough-in test *after* the air handler is installed. While the 2009 code had a threshold of 6 cfm per 100 sq. ft. of conditioned floor area for this test, the 2012 code has lowered this threshold to 4 cfm.

• The third option is a so-called post-construction test. While the 2009 code had a threshold of 12 cfm per 100 sq. ft. of conditioned floor area for this test, the 2012 code has lowered this threshold to 4 cfm.

TESTING FOR DUCT LEAKAGE

Energy auditors have developed several methods for testing duct tightness. These methods vary from fast and dirty to time-consuming and accurate. Builders interested in tight duct systems should familiarize themselves with the range of available duct testing options:

• Using only a blower door;

• Using a blower door and a pressure pan;

• Using a Duct Blaster;

• Using a Duct Blaster and a blower door;

• Using a theatrical fog machine.

A fast, rough test

In *Residential Energy* (Prentice Hall, 2013), authors John Krigger and Chris Dorsi describe a quick (but not particularly accurate) method for estimating duct leakage: "The simplest way to estimate duct leakage in cfm50 is to perform two blower-door tests: one with the home's registers sealed with paper and tape, and one without. Subtracting the two readings provides a very rough estimate of total duct leakage." Because of the inherent inaccuracies of this method, it is rarely used.

The pressure-pan method

A pressure pan is a diagnostic tool consisting of a metal pan (similar to a cake pan) connected by a tube to a manometer (that is, a pressure gauge). The device is used to temporarily cover a forced-air register to measure the pressure exerted on the pan by a blower door. To conduct a pressure-pan test, you need a pressure pan and a blower door. Here are the basic steps:

• A blower door is used to depressurize the home to 50 Pascals.

• The air handler fan is turned off.

• The tester then blocks each register (one at a time) with the pressure pan and records the reading of the pressure-pan manometer. (The manometer shows the pressure created by air leaking into the duct system.) Typical readings of the duct system pressure (with respect to the house pressure) range from 1 Pascal to 45 Pascals.

• The higher the reading, the leakier the duct run.

In a *Home Energy* magazine article, "Pressure Pans: New Uses and Old Fundamentals" (January/February 1998), Jeffrey Siegel and Bruce Manclark explained, "A duct system at 0 Pascal is entirely within the pressure envelope of the house and has no leaks to the outdoors. A system approaching 50 Pascals is essentially outside the pressure envelope, meaning that it has catastrophic leakage to the outdoors."

It's important to note that the pressure pan readings don't really provide measurements of duct leakage; rather, they provide a method for comparing the relative leakiness of several duct runs in the same home. That hasn't prevented some energy experts from recommending thresholds for pressure-pan measurements. According to Krigger and Dorsi, "Registers of newly installed ducts should read less than 0.5 Pascals and existing duct registers should read less than 1 Pascal after being sealed."

In "Duct Improvement in the Northwest," (*Home Energy* magazine, January/February 1996), author Ted Haskell provided

this advice for existing homes: "Houses with fewer than three pressure-pan readings above 2 Pascals are unlikely to be cost-effective to seal."

The pressure-pan test has two virtues. First, it is fast—especially when an auditor is already conducting a blower door test. Second, it identifies which of a home's duct runs are the leakiest, so that a contractor knows where to focus duct-sealing efforts. However, many ex-

PRESSURE-PAN TESTS find leaks. Used in conjunction with a blower door, pressure-pan testing is a fast way to determine if a house's ductwork is leaky.

disadvantage of the pressure-pan test is that it is more art than science . . . . The one exception is when homes have very similar duct geometry and installation, as is the case with manufactured homes or identical homes in a subdivision."

The Duct Blaster test

The most common method for testing the tightness of a duct system is the duct-blower test (also known as the Duct Blaster test). A duct blower resembles a miniature blower door; the most common brand is the Duct Blaster, manufactured by the Energy Conservatory in Minneapolis. Here are the steps:

- All supply registers and return grilles are sealed with polyethylene and tape.

- The air handler fan is turned off.

- The Duct Blaster is set up and attached to the duct system (near the furnace or at a large return-air grille).

- The manometer's reference probe is inserted into the air handler plenum.

- The Duct Blaster is turned on to pressurize the duct system to 25 Pascals (a pressure that represents typical operating pressures for forced-air systems). The airflow through the Duct Blaster fan (which is displayed in cubic feet per minute on the Duct Blaster's manometer) equals the flow escaping through leaks in the duct system. The results are reported as cfm at 25 Pascals, or cfm25.

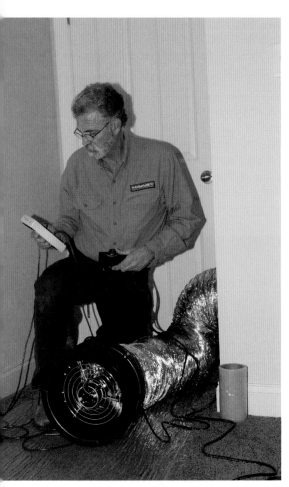

TESTING DUCTS with a duct blower. A duct blower can be connected to a residential duct system at a large return-air grille or near the furnace. Once the duct system has been pressurized or depressurized to 25 Pascals, the air flow of the fan gives an indication of the duct system's leakiness.

perts warn contractors not to jump to conclusions based only on the pressure readings recorded during a pressure-pan test.

As with many other diagnostic tests—infrared scanners come to mind—it takes an experienced auditor to interpret the results of a pressure-pan test. "Pressure-pan readings are difficult to interpret, and the same number can reflect quite different leakage rates in different houses," wrote Siegel and Manclark. "The

Although this test reveals the leakiness of the duct system, it doesn't tell the tester where the leaks are located; nor does it quantify what percentage of the leakage is leakage to the outdoors. Moreover, it doesn't tell us how much a duct system leaks under normal operating conditions—conditions that may differ from Duct Blaster pressurization to 25 Pascals. According to Krigger and Dorsi, "Leakage ranges from less than 50 cfm25 for a fairly tight duct system to more than 500 cfm25 for a very leaky duct system."

Builders hoping to comply with the 2012 IRC duct-testing requirements will need Duct Blaster test results showing total duct leakage equal to or less than either 3 cfm or 4 cfm (depending on whether it is a rough-in test or a postconstruction test) per 100 sq. ft. of conditioned floor area.

Using a Duct Blaster to test duct leakage to the outdoors

Energy auditors often want to know how much of a duct system's leakage is leakage to the outdoors. Leakage to the outdoors can occur when air escapes through a leak in a duct installed in an unconditioned attic. It is also possible for a portion of the leakage through a duct that seems to be within a home's thermal envelope is actually leakage to the outdoors, because such leaks can pressurize joist bays, forcing conditioned air through rim-joist cracks.

One quick-and-dirty indication that a duct system has sizable leaks to the outdoors occurs when an auditor notices obvious air flow from forced-air registers during a blower-door test. Because the house is strongly depressurized, the airflow represents exterior air; and because it's coming from the duct system, the airflow is a sign that the duct system has leaks that connect with the outdoors.

To determine how much duct leakage is leakage to the outdoors, a tester needs a blower door and a Duct Blaster. Here are the steps:

• A blower door is set up in an entry door.

• All supply registers and return grilles are sealed with polyethylene and tape.

• The air handler fan is turned off.

• A pressure tap is temporarily installed in the duct system to measure the pressure of the duct system with respect to the house.

• Another manometer or tube is set up to measure the outside pressure with respect to the ducts.

• The Duct Blaster is set up and attached to the duct system (usually near the furnace).

• The blower door is turned on and the house is pressurized to 25 Pascals.

• The Duct Blaster is turned on to pressurize the duct system; the Duct Blaster fan is adjusted until there is no pressure difference between the ducts and the house. At that point, all of the air going through the Duct Blaster is going outdoors through duct leaks. The airflow indicated on the Duct Blaster's manometer (in cfm) quantifies that duct leakage to the outdoors.

Obviously, duct leaks to the outdoors represent heating or cooling energy that is lost.

Testing ducts with a fog machine

To find the location of duct leaks, nothing beats a theatrical fog machine. Gary Nel-

FOG PINPOINTS LEAKS. Forced into the ductwork by the duct blower, theatrical fog can track down both big and small leaks. It's also a good way to silence HVAC installers convinced that their ducts are sufficiently sealed.

son, the founder of the Energy Conservatory, describes the method: "You tape up all the registers and you pressurize the ducts. Then you introduce fog into the Duct Blaster—you aim the fog nozzle at the fan blades, without letting the fog get drawn into the vent holes in the motor, and you watch where the fog pours out. For more information on this technique, see "Pinpointing Leaks with a Fog Machine" on p. 113.

SEALING THE LEAKS THAT MATTER MOST

The mechanics of duct sealing are beyond the scope of this chapter, but it's worth noting:

• Duct seams need to be mechanically fastened (using sheet-metal screws for galvanized ducts and compression straps for flex duct) before being sealed.

• For sealing most duct leaks, mastic works better than any tape. (Bruce Manclark calls tape "the Band-Aid of the HVAC industry.")

• Mastic is messy, so wear old clothes when you apply it.

• Install mastic "as thick as a nickel."

• Cracks or seams wider than ⅛ in. need to be repaired with fiberglass mesh as well as mastic.

It's important to prioritize duct-sealing efforts so that the most important leaks are addressed first. As Philip Fairey, the deputy director of the Florida Solar Energy Center, likes to say, "Duct leakage is like real estate—it's all about location, location, location."

In existing homes, it's surprisingly common to find disconnected duct components—takeoffs that are coming loose from ducts or ducts disconnected from register boots—in attics or basements. Such disconnected ducts can waste tremendous amounts of energy.

• Leaks connected to the outdoors are more important than leaks inside the home's thermal envelope.

• Holes that see high pressures—in other words, holes near the air handler—are more important than distant holes that see relatively low pressures. Bruce Manclark's mantra is, "Follow the pressure: boots for show, plenums for dough."

• Most furnaces have many bad leaks close to the blower fan, including leaks in the furnace jacket seams, leaks between the furnace and the plenums, and leaks between the duct takeoffs and the plenums.

• Supply system leaks waste more energy than return system leaks.

For decades, plumbers have routinely tested newly installed supply and drain pipes. Meanwhile, most HVAC contractors have gotten away with leaky, untested duct systems. However, the tide is now turning. In the future, testing residential duct systems for leaks will become a routine part of residential construction.

Make sure you choose products that provide durable sealing

Most residential duct systems have numerous leaks that waste energy and lead to room-to-room pressure imbalances. Unfortunately, though, few building inspectors outside of California bother to enforce existing code requirements that residential duct seams be sealed with mastic or high-quality duct tape.

ALL ABOUT MASTIC

Most energy-conscious builders seal duct joints with mastic. Mastic is a gooey, nonhardening material with a consistency between mayonnaise and smooth peanut butter. Duct joints should always be secured with #8 sheet-metal screws before seams are sealed with mastic.

Mastic is spread over duct seams with a disposable paintbrush, putty knife, or your fingers. (If you spread mastic with your fingers, wear rubber gloves.)

Gaps in ductwork or plenums that are over $\frac{1}{16}$ in. or $\frac{1}{8}$ in. wide can be sealed with mastic as long as the gap is first reinforced with fiberglass mesh tape. If you're using mastic to seal seams in fiberglass board ductwork, use fiberglass mesh tape for all joints.

Sources of mastic

Manufacturers of mastic include Hardcast® (Versa-Grip™ 181 mastic), McGill AirSeal (Uni-Mastic™ 181), Polymer Adhesives (AirSeal 22), RCD Corporation® (#6 Mastic®), and ITW TACC (Glenkote® mastic).

DUCT MASTIC SEALS leaky seams. Mastic can be applied to leaky duct seams with a paint brush or gloved fingers.

ALL ABOUT DUCT TAPE

Because common hardware-store duct tape—technically known as cloth-backed rubber-adhesive duct tape—fails quickly when used on ducts, most energy-conscious builders seal duct joints with mastic. Although mastic works well on galvanized steel ductwork, it is messy to apply and awkward to use on clamped flex duct joints.

According to the IRC, any tape used on duct board or flex duct must be labeled in accordance with UL 181A or 181B. In most regions of the United States, however, local inspectors have little or no interest in the leakiness of residential ducts, and duct tape labels are rarely checked for UL compliance.

"I've been to wholesale distributors in Ohio, and I don't see them displaying anything with UL markings," said Mark Pulawski, former cloth tape market manager for Intertape Polymer Group®, a duct tape manufacturer in West Bradenton, FL. "When I ask them, 'Where are your UL products?' they say, 'We don't sell any of those.' They hold up a roll of [cloth] duct tape, and they say, 'This is what the guys use.'"

Does UL 181 duct tape perform any better?

In some areas, however, building inspectors insist that duct tapes sport a UL 181 label. Yet the UL 181B standard alone is no guarantee of long-term tape performance. "The UL 181 listing is more of a smoke-and-flame listing," said Bob Davis, an energy consultant for Ecotope in Seattle. "The testing doesn't have much to do with whether it will work as a duct sealant."

At least four different types of tape have met the UL 181B standard, including some cloth-backed rubber-adhesive duct tapes, foil-backed tapes with acrylic adhesive, oriented polypropylene (OPP) tapes, and foil-backed butyl tapes. Unfortunately, according to tests performed at Lawrence Berkeley National Laboratory by Max Sherman and Iain Walker, a UL 181 listing is no guarantee that a tape will last any longer than unlisted cloth duct tape.

"In California, the duct-tape industry wanted the code to approve the use of UL 181-listed products," said Walker. "But in our lab tests we have found that the UL 181 products fail. Just because it is UL 181 listed does not mean that it performs any better than non-UL 181 listed products. The listed tapes may be of a higher quality—the mechanical properties of the tape are better—but they are not any better in terms of longevity at high temperature. Under those conditions the UL 181 tapes failed as well as the non-UL 181 tapes."

More important than a tape's UL 181 label is the material category into which it falls. At least two new types of duct tape—butyl duct tape and OPP duct tape—may offer better performance than cloth duct tape, without the messiness of mastic.

Oriented polypropylene tape

For sealing the inner core of flex duct to metal collars, as well as to repair the outer jacket of flex duct, many contractors have begun using OPP tape, which is a film-backed (as opposed to cloth-backed) tape resembling packing tape. (Housewrap tape is a type of OPP tape.) The tape has a smooth backing and an acrylic adhesive, said to be more tenacious than rubber adhesive. The backing can be manufactured in a variety of colors, including a shiny "metallized" plastic finish. "In new construction in California, we're seeing more and more contractors using OPP tape and a clamp to seal the core of the flex duct to a metal collar," said Walker.

At least three manufacturers make UL 181B-FX listed polypropylene duct tape: Intertape Polymer Group (manufacturer of AC698 tape), Shurtape® Technologies (manufacturer of DC 181 tape), and Berry Plastics (manufacturer of FlexFix® tape).

Manufacturers of OPP tape take pains to distinguish their product from the gray stuff. Although their DC 181 is a tape designed for use on ducts, Mark Hooks, a product manager at Shurtape Technologies, insisted that "it's not a duct tape."

As long as joints sealed with OPP tape are clamped, it will probably perform better than cloth duct tape.

Butyl duct tape

Foil-backed butyl tape performs much better than cloth duct tape, although it isn't cheap. Hardcast, the manufacturer of Versa-Grip 181 duct mastic, sells several types of butyl duct tape; one of them, Foil-Grip™ 1402, has a UL 181B listing.

Foil-Grip 1402 consists of 12 mils of butyl adhesive (similar to the adhesive used in some flexible window flashings) with a 2-mil aluminum-foil top layer. Hardcast recommends Foil-Grip butyl tape for use with galvanized steel duct, duct board, or flex duct. The manufacturer claims that Foil-Grip 1402 is rugged enough to use outdoors or below grade.

Berry Plastics sells a butyl-adhesive duct tape under two different brands (Nashua® and Polyken®). Nashua 558CA is basically the same product as Polyken 558CA. The tape consists of a butyl adhesive on a polyethylene-coated cloth backing; it has a UL 181 BFX listing for use with flex duct.

Like OPP tape manufacturers, butyl tape manufacturers want to differentiate their

product from duct tape. "We don't like to use the word *tape*," said David Barnes, a technical service representative at Hardcast. "We're trying to overcome all of the perceptions associated with duct tape."

Butyl tapes have fared well in the Lawrence Berkeley tests. "The butyl tapes come with a metal foil backing as opposed to the cloth backing," said Walker. "The cloth-backed tapes are the ones we see shrinking and failing. The butyl tapes have much more adhesive on them, so they will take longer to dry out and will stay flexible longer. In our testing we've done several different orientations over the years, and we haven't found any failures in the butyl tape."

CHOOSING BETWEEN TAPE AND MASTIC

Because all duct-sealing products, including mastic and all types of duct tape, have disadvantages, deciding on the best duct-sealing strategy is tricky. Chuck Murray, an energy specialist with the Washington State University Energy Program, sees no reason to abandon mastic. "I haven't seen a tape yet that I like for use in a crawl space," said Murray. "But we continue to monitor the situation."

One of mastic's chief advantages is that, unlike some tapes, it performs well without clamping. Yet mastic will not prevent a joint from opening up. "Mastic is not a mechanical fastener—you still need sheet-metal screws, and scrap metal or fiberglass drywall mesh for big holes," noted Davis. "You need to be sure that everything will hold together on its own merits. But, unlike with tapes, you don't have to worry about whether the surfaces are clean."

Most installers don't bother to clean their joints before applying a sealant, and Davis feels that mastic holds up better under the circumstances. Yet mastic manufacturers, like duct tape manufacturers, generally require joints to be clean. "You need to clean the joint with soap and water and a rag," said David Barnes from Hardcast. "The same surface prep is required no matter which sealing system is used."

High-quality duct tape—not mastic—should be used to seal holes in a furnace or air handler. As energy expert Bruce Harley noted, "Mastic would render the cabinet unserviceable."

SCREW BEFORE SEALING. Peel back any insulation to examine the duct connection. Here, a broken elbow had to be repaired with sheet-metal screws before sealing.

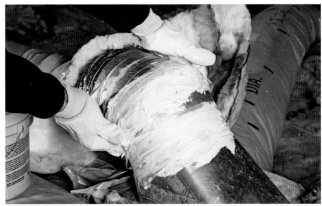

MASTIC, THEN FIBERGLASS. After spreading a thin layer of mastic, embed a length of fiberglass mesh in the mastic.

MORE MASTIC. After the mesh tape is applied, spread more mastic over the surface.

MAKING GOOD DUCT JOINTS

Here are some tips for creating durable, airtight duct seams:

- Duct seams need to be mechanically fastened (using sheet-metal screws for galvanized ducts and compression straps for flex duct) before being sealed.

- To secure seams in round galvanized ducts up to 12 in. in diameter, use at least three #8 screws per joint. To secure ducts over 12 in. in diameter, use five screws per joint.

- For securing joints in rectangular galvanized duct, use at least one screw per side.

- In most locations, mastic is preferable to tape.

- Mastic is messy, so wear old clothes when you apply it.

- Install mastic "as thick as a nickel."

- Cracks or seams wider than $1/16$ in. or $1/8$ in. need to be repaired with fiberglass mesh as well as mastic.

- Don't forget to seal collar connections between plenums and duct take-offs.

Sealing joints in flex duct

Flex duct sections are usually connected with a beaded metal sleeve or coupling. Here's the procedure for sealing flex-duct connections:

- The duct boot or coupling should be inserted at least 2 in. into the end of the duct. The fitting should be attached to the inner sleeve of the flex duct with a drawband (clamp) or #8 screws.

- Seal the joint between the inner section of duct and the fitting with high-quality duct tape or mastic.

- Seal the exterior vapor-barrier sleeve with a drawband and tape.

KEEPING DUCTS INDOORS

Five ways to bring ducts inside a home's conditioned space

If you live in New England, you know that furnaces are installed in basements. But any New Englander who moves to Oregon soon learns that furnaces are installed in garages. And anyone who retires to Texas discovers that furnaces are installed in unconditioned attics. Of course, there are many other examples of similar regional differences in construction practices. But this is one regional difference that matters. New Englanders have it right: furnaces and ductwork belong inside a home's conditioned space, not in the great outdoors.

If you build in a region where ducts are usually installed in unconditioned attics or ventilated crawl spaces, it's time to get with the program and learn how to bring your ducts indoors, where they belong.

THE PROBLEM ISN'T TRIVIAL

Unconditioned attics, vented crawl spaces, and garages are cold in winter and hot in summer. Because most duct systems are leaky and poorly insulated, duct systems installed outside a home's conditioned envelope waste tremendous amounts of energy.

According to Dave Roberts and Jon Winkler, engineers at the National Renewable Energy Laboratory, ducts in unconditioned attics waste about 20% of the output of a furnace or air-conditioner. These researchers reported that during peak conditions, the losses are even greater. Roberts and Winkler wrote that in Houston, Phoenix, and Las Vegas, "The average DSE [distribution system efficiency] for the three locations on the design day, which would be considered the day of the

season when cooling demand is highest, is 72%. This means that on the hottest day of the summer, 28% of the air-conditioner output is ultimately lost."

These calculations assume that attic duct connections are all intact. However, as any home inspector knows, attic ducts are often crushed, ripped, or completely disconnected. Because homeowners rarely visit all the nooks and crannies of their attics, these problems can remain uncorrected for years.

WHERE DOES THE FURNACE GO?

It's no longer acceptable to locate a furnace or air handler in the garage or an unconditioned attic. So where should the furnace go? If you want to install your furnace inside your home's conditioned envelope, it can be located in a basement, in a sealed crawl space, in an unvented conditioned attic, or in a centrally located mechanical room.

If you're building a house with a basement, you're all set.

A crawl space isn't a great place for a furnace, because the location is awkward for anyone who has to change a filter or perform maintenance. A conditioned attic will work, but access is to an attic is almost as awkward as to a crawl space.

Many sources advise that a furnace or air handler can be installed in a closet—and that's true. However, every time I see a furnace or air handler crammed into a closet, I cringe. In general, the equipment barely fits. Because the space is so tight, filter changes are usually awkward, and any alterations to the equipment are almost impossible. And if the homeowner later decides to install an HRV or an electronic air cleaner, where is the new equipment supposed to go?

A furnace doesn't belong in a closet; it belongs in a mechanical room. You can put the mechanical room anywhere you want—on the first floor or second floor—but make it big. Calculate the area you think you need, and then double it. Ideally, the mechanical room should be in a central location so that duct runs are short. Because the furnace is inside the home, it should be a sealed-combustion unit. Choose one that's quiet, and install a solid-core door on the room to reduce sound transfer.

WHERE DO THE DUCTS GO?

The location of your ducts is partly determined by the location of your furnace or air handler. There are five basic approaches. Ducts can be installed:

- In a basement or a sealed crawl space;
- In an unvented conditioned attic;
- In open-web floor trusses;
- In soffits (or dropped ceilings);
- In a chase (an "inverted soffit") designed into special roof trusses.

Putting ducts in a basement or sealed crawl space

Builders in the Northeast have been locating ducts in basements for decades. As long as the basement has insulated walls, this is an excellent approach. What's not to like? The ducts are inside the home's conditioned space. In a basement, your HVAC installer can stand up straight and see what he or she is doing.

In a crawl space, however, the quality of the installation may drop because your HVAC installer will probably be eager to finish the job and crawl out of there.

Putting ducts in an unvented conditioned attic

If you are used to installing ducts in attics, you can keep doing it that way—as long as you insulate the sloped roof instead of

KEEP DUCTWORK IN conditioned spaces. Because leaky ducts in vented attics and crawl spaces waste more energy than leaky ducts inside the building, energy-conscious builders and designers keep all ductwork within the conditioned space, typically inside drywall enclosures with taped joints.

the attic floor and make sure that the attic is unvented.

Putting ducts in open-web floor trusses

If you are building a two-story house, it often makes sense to locate ducts in open-web floor trusses. If you go this route, remember the following:

• It's easy for duct leaks to pressurize the joist bays, so be sure that your rim joist is carefully air sealed to keep conditioned air indoors.

• You'll need to order deep joists—in most cases, your joists will be 16 in. deep. When designing your stairs, be sure to account for these deeper joists.

• If you are building a tight, well-insulated house with high-performance windows, supply registers can be located near the center of the home instead of at the home's perimeter. That keeps duct runs short.

• Installing ducts in open-web floor trusses won't work without close communication and coordination between all the trades. If the HVAC contractor runs the ducts

OPEN-WEB FLOOR trusses. If you order properly sized open-web floor trusses, your HVAC contractor should have enough room to install ductwork between floors.

without proper coordination, the plumber will scream, "Where am I supposed to run my drains?" and the electrician will scream, "Where do I put the can lights?"

Putting ducts in soffits or dropped ceilings

In a single-story home, it often makes sense to install ducts in soffits or a dropped ceiling. This works especially well in a home with a central hallway flanked by bedrooms on both sides. In a house with a more complicated floor plan, duct soffits can be built along the top of any wall. Ideally, the home will be designed with 9-ft. ceilings, so that there's plenty of room to drop the ceiling height where necessary.

For this approach to work, it's essential to complete installation of the soffit's air barrier before the ducts are installed. If the drywall crew can't come to the site twice, the soffit "ceiling" will probably be sealed by the framing crew, perhaps with OSB and caulk (or better still, plywood and high-quality tape). If this step of the job is done poorly, however, the house will have a major air leak. Of course, any leaks in the supply ductwork will pressurize the soffit, greatly increasing the air leakage rate.

Putting ducts in a chase built into a special roof truss

It's possible to order a roof truss designed to accommodate a duct chase near the attic floor. Some truss manufacturers refer to this type of truss as a "plenum truss." When these trusses are used, the resulting chase has many names, including "raised HVAC coffer" and "inverted soffit."

If you're building a house with 8-ft. ceilings, these special roof trusses make more sense than site-built soffits. Like a site-built soffit, a chase-within-a-roof-truss must be carefully air sealed before

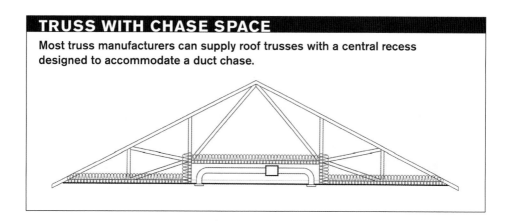

TRUSS WITH CHASE SPACE

Most truss manufacturers can supply roof trusses with a central recess designed to accommodate a duct chase.

the ducts are installed, which means the drywall hangers and tapers have to come twice or your framing crew has to be trained to do the required air sealing.

These roof trusses obviously create a bump in the attic floor, complicating the work of the insulation crew. If the chase has vertical walls, be sure the vertical insulation is protected by an attic-side air barrier.

There's no free lunch

Let's say that you have always installed ducts in unconditioned attics. What would happen if you were to move the ductwork inside the home's conditioned space?

• It may be possible to downsize the air conditioner and furnace.

• Room-to-room temperature differences will probably be reduced, improving occupant comfort.

• Homeowners will see a significant drop in their energy bills.

However, it's important to be realistic. Bringing the ducts inside the conditioned envelope is usually a headache for the builder, and the necessary details raise costs. Open-web trusses will probably cost more than I-joists, and deep joists may require a longer stairway. For a successful job, the general contractor will need to budget time for facilitating coordination between all of the trades, including the framers, HVAC contractor, plumber, electrician, and drywallers.

REMEMBER, YOU STILL NEED TO SEAL DUCT SEAMS

In years past, it was common to read that "as long as ducts are installed inside a home's conditioned envelope, you don't have to seal the duct seams." These days, however, most energy consultants insist that HVAC contractors seal duct seams with mastic, even when all the ducts are inside. There are at least two good reasons for this practice:

• If ductwork is leaky, remote registers may get weak air flow, leading to comfort complaints.

• Duct leaks in soffits or joist bays can pressurize the soffit or the joist space, forcing conditioned air outdoors through cracks in the rim-joist area.

For most superinsulated homes, a furnace is overkill

If you build a small, tight, well-insulated home—in other words, a green home—it won't need much heat. Because typical residential furnaces and boilers are rated at 40,000 Btu/hr to 80,000 Btu/hr, they are seriously oversize for a superinsulated home, which may have a heating design load as low as 10,000 Btu/hr to 15,000 Btu/hr.

Builders have been struggling for decades with the question, What's the best way to heat a superinsulated home? Your solution will depend in part on your answers to a couple of other questions:

• Are you comfortable heating the house from a single point source? If you are, the best solution might be a wood stove, pellet stove, or a direct-vent space heater. These solutions work best in compact homes with open floor plans. Of course, the tighter the home's envelope and the thicker the insulation, the more likely that indoor temperatures will remain fairly consistent from room to room.

• Do you want an all-electric house? Green builders have diverging views on this question. Builders of NZE homes often avoid gas- and oil-fired appliances, preferring to balance energy loads with electricity produced on site by a photovoltaic (PV) array.

Of course, most homes still depend on grid-powered electricity, and if your local electric utility generates power from fossil fuel, then it makes little environmental sense to heat with electricity. From a carbon-production standpoint, it's usually better to burn fuels on site rather than in a remote power plant.

WHAT NOT TO INSTALL

Before moving on to right-size solutions, it's worth mentioning that it rarely makes sense to install radiant-floor heat in a superinsulated house. For well-built homes, an in-floor radiant system is usually overkill. Although these expensive systems are a good way to heat a poorly insulated house, they are usually a waste of money in a tight house. Moreover, many radiant floor systems include energy-wasting circulators that operate for 24 hours a day during the heating season.

A TWO-STAGE FURNACE MAY MAKE SENSE

Some builders of superinsulated homes have concluded that there's nothing wrong with a conventional natural gas furnace. The engineers at the Building Science Corporation in Westford, MA, often specify a two-stage natural gas furnace (for example, the Goodman® GMH95-045). Unlike a one-stage furnace, which has only two firing modes—on or off—a two-stage furnace with an ECM blower operates efficiently even under partial load conditions.

The Goodman GMH95-045 is available on the web for between $839 and $1,050. According to Building Science principal John Straube, production builders can install a heating system using this furnace for about $2,500.

USING A FURNACE. Some builders of small, well-insulated homes still specify a conventional furnace, such as the Goodman GMH95-045, a two-stage natural-gas furnace.

RIGHT-SIZE HEATING SYSTEMS

What if you don't want a gas furnace—perhaps because your house lacks a gas connection or because the smallest available furnace is still too big for your needs? Here are three other options:

• Electric resistance baseboard heat;

• A direct-vent space heater;

• A ductless minisplit air-source heat pump.

Electric resistance baseboards

If your home has an impeccable envelope, and you've pared your heating load to the bare minimum, it may make sense to heat your house with electric resistance heat. That's how Katrin Klingenberg, the founder of the Passive House Institute U.S., heats her 1,450-sq.-ft. house in Urbana, IL.

It's possible to buy a 1,500-watt (4,714 Btu/hr) baseboard heater on the web for $90. If your house has a design heating load of 14,000 Btu/hr, you could heat it with three baseboard heaters ($270 plus installation). The main drawback to this solution is that in most areas of the country, electric resistance heat is expensive to operate.

Direct-vent space heaters

Many compact homes are easily heated by a direct-vent space heater. Installed on an exterior wall, these heaters require a wall penetration to accommodate two concentric vents. The outer pipe (the donut) brings in combustion air for the sealed-combustion burner, while the inner pipe is the exhaust flue. It's possible to buy direct-vent heaters that burn natural gas, propane, or kerosene.

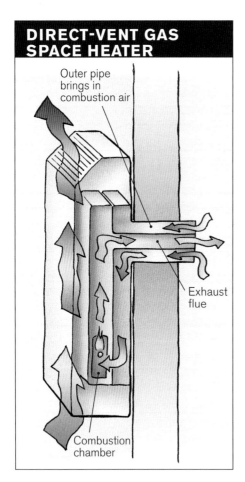

DIRECT-VENT GAS SPACE HEATER

Outer pipe brings in combustion air

Exhaust flue

Combustion chamber

Direct-vent space heaters are affordable. A quick web search reveals that a natural gas Empire® DV215SG heater (15,000 Btu/hr input) can be purchased for around $750. Other options include the Rinnai® EX11C (8,800 Btu/hr output) for about $1,000 and the Monitor™ GF1800 (16,000 Btu/hr output) for $1,150. If you want a heater that requires no electricity, you might choose the Robur® TS2000 (7,400 Btu/hr input) for about $509.

The first NZE house in the country—a superinsulated Habitat for Humanity house in Wheat Ridge, CO—is heated with a natural gas direct-vent space heater in the living room, supplemented by electric resistance heaters in each bedroom.

Ductless minisplit air-source heat pumps

If you've traveled to Mexico, the Caribbean, or the Mediterranean, you've probably seen ductless minisplit air-conditioners. A ductless minisplit includes an outdoor unit (the condenser) and at least one wall-mounted indoor blower (a fan-coil unit); the two units are connected by copper tubing that circulates refrigerant.

A ductless minisplit is a type of air-source heat pump, so it can be used for heating as well as cooling. In recent years, Japanese manufacturers (including Daikin, Fujitsu, and Mitsubishi) have significantly improved the heating efficiency of ductless minisplits. These units can now be used for heating in very cold climates—even in Vermont, where winter temperatures reach –20°F. According to Andy Shapiro, an energy consultant from Montpelier, VT, Japanese heat pumps are much more sophisticated than U.S.-made equivalents. "The Japanese are eating our lunch with these units," Shapiro told me.

DUCTLESS MINISPLIT HEAT PUMP

Wall-mounted blower unit

Condenser unit

These ductless minisplits are so efficient and dependable that they are the heating system of choice for many low-energy buildings, including Passivhaus buildings. Shapiro used ductless minisplits for a heating system he designed for the NZE gymnasium at the Putney School in Putney, VT. He calculated that the capital cost for the building's ductless minisplits and a PV array big enough to power them was cheaper than a ground-source heat pump system—even though the ductless minisplits require a bigger PV array. At the Putney School, the ductless minisplit system cost $100,000 less than a ground-source heat pump system, while requiring only $35,000 more in PV modules than would have been required to power the ground-source system.

According to Shapiro's estimate, which is based mostly on manufacturers' specifications, a ductless minisplit heating system can be expected to operate at an average coefficient of performance (COP) of 2.3—that is, 2.3 times as efficient as an electric resistance heater. Shapiro's monitoring data reveal that the typical water-to-water ground-source heat pump system has an average COP of about 2.5. (Remember, the higher COPs claimed by ground-source heat-pump manufacturers are artificially high because they exclude pumping energy.) According to Shapiro, water-to-air ground-source heat pumps may have COPs as high as 3.5.

DUCTLESS MINISPLITS IN MASSACHUSETTS

Carter Scott used a Mitsubishi Mr. Slim® system with a nominal heat output rating of 28,000 Btu/hr to heat a NZE home he built in Townsend, MA. The 1,232-sq.-ft. home has a design heating load of only 10,500 Btu/hr (see "Just Two Minisplits Heat and Cool the Whole House" on the facing page). The installed cost of the ductless minisplit system—including one indoor unit downstairs and another one upstairs—was $5,250, a price that includes both heating and air-conditioning. According to the home's architect, Ben Nickerson, at an outdoor temperature of 0°F, the Mitsubishi unit still cranks out 10,000 Btu/hr at a COP of 1.8.

CAN I REALLY DEPEND ON A HEAT PUMP?

If you're worried that a heat pump won't be adequate when the thermometer bottoms out in January, remember:

• The coldest temperature of the year is reached for only a few hours a year.

• Tight, superinsulated homes lose heat very slowly, even during power outages. As long as a cold snap doesn't last for many days, most superinsulated homes won't lose much heat.

• In very cold temperatures, turning off the ventilation system will help a building stay warm.

• If you're really worried about prolonged subzero cold snaps, one or two electric resistance baseboard units provide cheap insurance.

Carter Scott has built 30 homes in Massachusetts without any heat in the bedrooms

arter Scott was one of the first builders bold enough to build a cold-climate home heated by only two ductless minisplit units (one in the downstairs living room, and one in the upstairs hallway). Skeptics predicted that the unheated bedrooms would be cold and uncomfortable. Yet Scott was confident that the home's excellent thermal envelope—with high-R walls, triple-glazed windows, and low levels of air leakage—would keep the homeowners comfortable even when the bedroom doors were closed.

Scott owns a construction company called Transformations in Townsend, MA. He built his pioneering two-minisplit house in Townsend in 2008; the inclusion of a 5.7-kw roof-mounted photovoltaic array made it into a zero-energy house.

DUCTLESS MINISPLIT FOR A NET-ZERO ENERGY HOUSE

Heating and cooling is provided by a ductless minisplit system with a nominal output of 21,000 Btu/hr. The 12-in.-thick R-49 walls are framed with double 2×4 walls and insulated with 3 in. of closed-cell spray foam and 9 in. of cellulose. The R-75 roof is insulated with 5 in. of closed-cell spray foam and 13 in. of cellulose. All windows are triple-glazed.

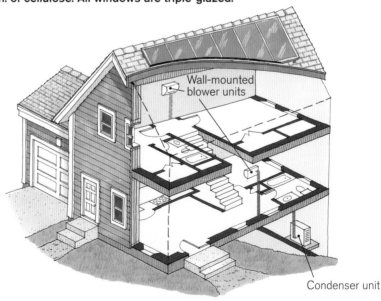

Wall-mounted blower units

Condenser unit

The skeptics' cold bedroom predictions were unfounded. "We have since built several houses in which the upstairs mini-split unit isn't even being used until the outdoor temperature drops below 20°," Scott said. "Typically the response from homeowners is, 'Wow, these houses have even indoor temperatures' and 'these houses are quiet.' And the fact that there are no utility bills makes people excited."

CARTER SCOTT'S FIRST NZE HOUSE

A ductless minisplit is a type of air-source heat pump that can provide space heating as well as air-conditioning. Most of the ductless minisplits sold in the United States are manufactured in Japan; the best known brands are Daikin, Fujitsu, and Mitsubishi.

The first zero-energy house built by Scott's company was designed by archi-tect Ben Nickerson. Here are the home's specifications:

• Area: 1,232 sq. ft.;
• Basement ceiling insulation (unconditioned basement): 3 in. of closed-cell spray foam plus R-30 fiberglass batts (total R-50);

• Wall framing: 12-in.-thick double-stud walls;

• Wall insulation (flash and fill): 3 in. closed-cell spray foam plus 9 in. cellulose (R-50);

• Sloped ceiling insulation (flash and fill): 5 in. closed-cell spray foam plus 13 in. cellulose (R-64);

• Windows: Paradigm triple-pane krypton-filled low-e windows;

• Siding: Vinyl;

• Design heat load: 10,500 Btu/hr;

• Space heating: Two Mitsubishi Mr. Slim ductless minisplit units (one 12,000 Btu/hr unit downstairs, and one 9,000 Btu/hr unit upstairs); installed cost, $5,250;

• Mechanical ventilation: Lifebreath® 155 ECM energy-recovery ventilator;

• Domestic hot water: Sun Drum® solar thermal system with electric resistance backup;

• PV system: 5.7-kw roof-mounted array (Evergreen Solar® PV modules) and Fronius IG 5100 inverter (cost before incentives: $33,000).

In 2009, this home won the second prize in a utility-sponsored contest called the Zero Energy Challenge.

ZERO-ENERGY HOUSE. From the outside, the only clue that this home is unusual is the large photovoltaic array on the south-facing roof. The entire home is heated by two ductless minisplit units.

DUCTLESS MINISPLIT. The indoor unit of a ductless minisplit heat pump is a small fan-coil unit. The indoor unit is connected to the outdoor unit with insulated copper tubing that carries the refrigerant.

When the temperature is below zero, Mitsubishi ductless minisplits still perform

For Scott, heating a house measuring 1,700 sq. ft. to 2,000 sq. ft. with two ductless minisplits is no longer an experimental method. It's standard operating procedure—one he's used on 30 houses.

Although he has considered using Fujitsu or Daikin minisplit units, Scott continues to specify units from Mitsubishi. He usually specifies the MUZ-FE12NA outdoor unit and the MSZ-FE12NA indoor unit; this pairing is rated at 12,000 Btu/hr. Even at an outdoor temperature of 0°F, these units can put out 10,000 Btu/hr of space heat at a COP of 1.8. Mitsubishi minisplits will still deliver heat when the outdoor temperature drops to –13°F.

Scott pays his HVAC contractor less than $6,000 to install two minisplit units in one of his homes.

After Scott heard that the owner of a home he had built (a custom home in Princeton, MA) had turned off the upstairs heating unit because the downstairs unit adequately heated the whole house, he decided to try an experiment. At his next house, Scott installed just one ductless minisplit. "We thought that maybe we could just use one unit downstairs. But I didn't think of cooling. The cooling didn't rise to the second floor, and the house was hot upstairs in the summer. We went back to the house and installed a minisplit unit upstairs. So if you want AC on the second floor, you need an AC unit up there."

Since he learned his lesson, Scott always includes a minisplit unit on each floor of his two-story homes.

Anyone interested in following in Scott's footsteps needs to remember that the success of his two-minisplit approach depends in part on compact rectangular designs. Stretched-out houses on a single floor, designs with ells, or designs that include a bonus room over the garage aren't amenable to the two-minisplit solution.

WHAT ABOUT VENTILATION?

Scott's first zero-energy house in Townsend included a Lifebreath ERV—an effective but costly ventilation solution. As a builder of spec homes on his way to becoming a production builder, Scott has always focused on affordability. That's why the standard ventilation system included with his homes is often a simple exhaust-only system. However, he offers a variety of ventilation options to customers who are willing to pay extra.

"The baseline ventilation system we offer is a Panasonic® exhaust fan in each bathroom," said Scott. "They cost us $250 each installed. The next step up—an available option—would be a Panasonic ERV that exhausts and supplies from the same

We now have enough information on the use of ductless minisplits to heat and cool cold-climate homes to set out some rules of thumb. The rules of thumb that I present here are based on the work of Carter Scott, energy consultant Marc Rosenbaum, and researchers Kohta Ueno and Honorata Loomis, to whom I am indebted.

1. Design your building to have an excellent thermal envelope

If you want to heat and cool your building with just one or two point-source heaters, you want an above-average thermal envelope. That means that the building needs a very low rate of air leakage, above-code levels of insulation, and high-performance windows.

2. Consider snow loads when placing outdoor units

If you live in snow country, your outdoor unit needs to be protected by a roof—but not a roof that inhibits air flow—or needs to be wall-mounted at least 4 ft. or 5 ft. above grade. It's better to locate the outdoor unit on the gable end of a house than under the eaves.

3. Most two-story homes need at least two ductless minisplits

A single ductless minisplit unit located on the first floor of a two-story house is often capable of heating the whole house. However, a first-floor unit is incapable of cooling the upper floor. In a two-story house, if you want both heating and cooling, you will need at least two ductless minisplits: one downstairs and one upstairs. The downstairs unit will do most of the heating, and the upstairs unit will do most of the cooling.

4. Big windows can make things tricky

If you are heating your house with one or two point-source heaters, it's a good idea to avoid oversize windows if you want to minimize room-to-room temperature differences. The temperature in a bedroom can be within 4 F° or 5 F° of an adjacent hallway or common room as long as the heat flow rate through the exterior walls and windows is no greater than the heat flow rate through the uninsulated partition walls. Corner bedrooms are more of a challenge than bedrooms near the center of a building, and bedrooms with big windows are more of a challenge than bedrooms with reasonably sized windows.

During winter, large windows lose a lot of heat at night and on cloudy days. During summer, large windows can cause heat-gain problems on sunny days, especially if the windows face east or west.

5. Bonus rooms need special consideration

A bonus room—for example, a bedroom over a garage—cannot be heated and cooled by a ductless minisplit head located outside of the room. Bonus rooms usually have five out of six surfaces facing outdoor temperatures, so this type of room needs its own thermostat.

Bonus rooms violate a basic tenet of good building envelope design—namely, to create a compact shape. If you want your building to be energy efficient—and if you expect to heat and cool the building with just one or

location. That's $500 installed. A little better would be the Fantech® VHR 704 HRV with one exhaust location and one supply location. Better than that would be the Fantech SHR 1504 HRV, which could exhaust three bathrooms and supply all of the bedrooms. The next bump up would be the Lifebreath ERV, which is about $2,500."

two minisplits — you need a compact design with as few bump-outs and ells as possible.

6. In climate Zone 5 and warmer locations, you don't have to worry about cold-weather performance or lack of capacity

All reports are consistent on this point: cold-weather ductless minisplits from Mitsubishi and Fujitsu are performing well at outdoor temperatures that are lower than the units are rated for. (Mitsubishi provides performance data on some of its ductless minisplit models at outdoor temperatures as low as −13°F; many users report that these units are performing well at −20°F.) Rosenbaum reported, "In temperatures below design temperatures, the units have enough capacity to heat the houses even though we don't size them with an intentional safety factor."

According to researchers Ueno and Loomis, "The MSHPs [minisplit heat pumps] seldom hit maximum power draw, indicating substantial excess capacity even during worst-case winter conditions (much colder than local design temperatures). These results are consistent with the installed capacity of the equipment: the oversizing (compared to calculated loads) typically ranged from 150% to 200%. Although oversizing cooling equipment is commonly criticized, oversizing of heat pumps (for wintertime loads) can be beneficial. This is particularly true for MSHPs that modulate their capacity, as their highest efficiency is obtained when the unit is running at the lower end of their capacity range."

Of course, it's still important to perform a heating and cooling load calculation before specifying a minisplit, and it's still important to choose equipment designed to perform at typical outdoor temperatures in your climate. Here's the point: Occasional comfort complaints arise from heat distribution issues, not appliance capacity problems.

7. One ductless minisplit head can serve a maximum of about 1,100 sq. ft.

This rule of thumb was proposed by Ueno and Loomis. To clarify, this is based on distribution issues and room-to-room temperature differences, not on limitations to the heating or cooling capacity of the equipment.

8. Leave bedroom doors open during the day

If you want to heat your house with a ductless minisplit located in a living room or hallway, you'll need to leave your bedroom doors open during the day. When the bedroom doors are closed at night, bedroom temperatures may drop 5 F° between bedtime and morning.

If family members don't want to abide by this approach or don't want to accept occasional low bedroom temperatures during winter, then supplemental electric resistance heaters should be installed in the bedrooms.

9. Ductless minisplit units should run 24 hours per day

Turning your ductless minisplit on and off, or controlling it with a setback timer, will result in higher rather than lower energy bills. These units are designed to modulate, and operate at higher efficiencies when they run continuously than when they are turned off and on.

LETTING GO OF SOLAR THERMAL

As Scott continues to aim for high performance at the lowest possible cost, he has tweaked a few of his specifications. These days, Scott is installing more open-cell spray foam in his walls, and less cellulose, for two reasons: the spray foam provides a better air seal, and his insulation contractor offers open-cell foam for the same price as cellulose.

To reduce costs, he has switched from triple-glazed vinyl windows from Paradigm to triple-glazed vinyl windows from Harvey®. When I asked Scott about the quality of Harvey windows, his answer made it clear that the windows' best feature was the low price. "The quality of Harvey triple-pane windows is improving," Scott told me. "They now come with a hole midway up the jambs, which we pin to the studs. This keeps them opening and closing above 85°. We are also careful not to put more than ½ in. of low-expanding foam to seal around the windows. Harvey will sell me an R-5 window at an unbeatable price. In quantity, I'm getting the windows for just a few dollars more than our old double-pane windows."

In the past, Scott tried a variety of approaches for heating domestic hot water, including solar hot water systems. His favorite water heater is now the Navien® 180 on-demand tankless unit fueled by propane or natural gas. "An $8,500 solar hot water system doesn't make any sense compared to the $1,800 Navien. The fuel use cost with the Navien is so low that there really isn't much money to be saved doing anything different."

GROUND-SOURCE HEAT PUMPS ARE TOO EXPENSIVE

Before he discovered ductless mini-split units, Scott built three homes with ground-source heat pumps (GSHPs). Now that he knows about minisplits, however, he has no intention of installing another GSHP.

When I asked him why, his response was simple. "The first ground-source heat pump system I installed cost $38,000. The second one cost $40,000. The third one had a direct-exchange loop and cost me $22,000," he said. "But I can install two minisplits for less than $6,000. And the whole system efficiencies are about the same, as far as I can tell. Even if the ground-source units have a slightly higher COP, it's not enough to warrant the extra money."

Most green builders include some type of mechanical ventilation system in every home they build. That's good. Because green buildings usually have very low levels of air leakage, mechanical ventilation is usually essential. Unfortunately, several research studies have shown that a high number of mechanical ventilation systems are poorly designed or installed. Among the common problems:

- Ventilation fans with low airflow because of ducts that are undersize, crimped, convoluted, or excessively long.

- Ventilation systems that ventilate at too high a rate or for too many hours per day, resulting in a severe energy penalty.

- Ventilation systems that waste energy because they depend on inappropriate fans (for example, 800-watt furnace blowers).

It's disheartening to learn that many green homes waste energy because of poorly designed ventilation systems that were improperly commissioned.

THE ASHRAE STANDARD

ASHRAE's residential ventilation standard (Standard 62.2) sets the minimum ventilation rate at 7.5 cfm per occupant plus 3 cfm for every 100 sq. ft. of occupiable floor area. Systems complying with ASHRAE 62.2 have ventilation rates that are relatively low; for example, a 2,000-sq.-ft. house with three occupants requires 83 cfm of mechanical ventilation. That's about as much airflow as is provided by a typical bath exhaust fan. Because ventilation airflows are typically quite low, ventilation ductwork needs to be impeccably sealed. If ventilation ductwork is leaky, fresh air won't reach its intended destination.

Prominent building scientists are now debating the merits of the ASHRAE 62.2 ventilation rate. Max Sherman, former chairman of the ASHRAE 62.2 committee, defended the existing ASHRAE formula. On the other hand, Joseph Lstiburek, the well-known building scientist and gadfly, argued that the existing ASHRAE ventilation rate is too high, resulting in unnecessarily high energy costs—especially in hot humid climates, where the introduction of high volumes of outdoor air increases the need for cooling and dehumidification.

Lstiburek and Armin Rudd, a fellow engineer at the Building Science Corporation, advised designers of Building America houses to ventilate at a lower rate. "These [Building America] homes have roughly 50 to 60 percent of the ventilation rate required by ASHRAE standard 62.2," Rudd wrote. "The lack of complaints by occupants indicates that the systems are working to provide indoor air quality acceptable to the occupants."

The "great rate debate" is far from settled.

WHAT ARE MY VENTILATION CHOICES?

After two decades of experimentation, builders have narrowed ventilation choices down to four main options:

- The simplest system is an exhaust-only ventilation system based on one or more bath exhaust fans.

DO WE REALLY NEED MECHANICAL VENTILATION?

As more and more local building codes include ventilation requirements, fewer builders are able to get away with building new homes without mechanical ventilation. However, a few die-hard holdouts defend homes without mechanical ventilation.

One reason homes without mechanical ventilation systems work better than expected is that many common household appliances act just like exhaust-only ventilation systems. Such appliances include:

- Power-vented water heaters (50 cfm);
- Clothes dryers (100 cfm to 225 cfm);
- Central vacuum cleaners (100 cfm to 200 cfm);
- Wood stoves (30 cfm to 50 cfm).

When these appliances are operating, fresh outdoor air enters a house through random cracks to replace the air that is exhausted. However, homes without ventilation systems are homes of the past. The building science community has reached a consensus: build tight and ventilate right.

- For better fresh air distribution, choose a central-fan-integrated supply ventilation system.
- For the lowest operating cost, choose an HRV or an ERV connected to a dedicated duct system.
- If you don't relish the thought of installing complicated ventilation ductwork, consider installing one or more pairs of innovative Lunos fans from Europe.

CAN I INSTALL A SUPPLY-ONLY VENTILATION SYSTEM IN A COLD CLIMATE?

Some builders worry that a supply-only ventilation system (for example, central-fan-integrated supply ventilation) won't work in a cold climate, because the ventilation fan will drive interior air into building cavities where moisture can condense.

This worry is needless. As energy expert Bruce Harley explained, "The upper portions (walls and ceilings) of every home—typically most of the second floor in two-story homes—already operate under positive air pressure in cold weather, due to the stack effect. The relatively small airflow of most supply-only ventilation systems (75 cfm to 150 cfm) will have little effect on this situation other than to shift the neutral pressure plane down slightly, in all but the very tightest of homes .... In cold climates, I believe that distributed, supply-only ventilation such as that supplied by a ducted distribution system controlled by an AirCycler®, or other ducted low-flow supply ventilation, is vastly preferable to single or multi-port exhaust-only systems, except in extremely tight homes (in which case balanced supply and exhaust ventilation is the best choice)."

WHAT'S WRONG WITH EXHAUST-ONLY SYSTEMS?

As Harley's comments make clear, many energy experts (including Lstiburek) disparage exhaust-only ventilation systems. The main argument against exhaust-only ventilation systems—for example, a Panasonic bath exhaust fan controlled by a timer—is that they don't provide adequate distribution of fresh air. As a result, some rooms have plenty of fresh air while other rooms remain stuffy.

According to some ventilation experts, ASHRAE 62.2—which currently lacks any provision requiring fresh-air distribution—should be revised to include a distribution requirement. Armin Rudd has wrote, "I think distribution of ventilation air is an important issue. Bringing in ventilation air and hoping that it will provide adequate indoor air quality throughout the whole house is just a hope and a prayer."

Research shows, however, that in some homes, especially small homes with an open floor plan, exhaust-only ventilation systems work well. If the exhaust fan is well chosen—my own favorite is the Panasonic WhisperGreen™ fan, which uses only 11.3 watts to move 80 cfm—exhaust-only ventilation systems have very low installation and operating costs. If you choose this type of ventilation system, it's important to remember to undercut the bathroom door.

DO I NEED PASSIVE AIR INLETS?

Most homes with exhaust-only ventilation systems don't require any passive fresh air inlets in the walls. Unless the house is unusually airtight, fresh air will find its way into the home through random cracks.

A 2000 Vermont study ("A Field Study of Exhaust-Only Ventilation System Performance in Residential New Construction In Vermont") by Andy Shapiro, David Cawley, and Jeremy King, investigated whether passive fresh air inlets make any sense. The researchers studied 43 new homes (22 of which had passive fresh air vents) with exhaust-only ventilation systems. They wrote, "When the EOV [exhaust-only ventilation] fan was operating, 35% of the vents were exhausting inside air, 48% were supplying outside air, and 17% of the vents were not moving air." The explanation? "The pressures induced by fans in these [studied homes] . . . were low relative to pressures induced on

a house by natural forces, including wind and temperature-driven stack effect."

Note that there is an exception to this guideline: If your house approaches Passivhaus levels of airtightness (1 air change per hour at 50 Pascals or less), an exhaust-only ventilation system may be starved for makeup air. Most Passivhaus homes have a balanced ventilation system (an HRV or an ERV). Builders of very tight homes who prefer to install an exhaust-only ventilation system should consider the installation of one or two passive air inlets.

There's an easy way to check whether your exhaust fan is starved for makeup air: simply measure the exhaust air flow. If you are aiming for 50 cfm of exhaust air flow, and that's what you're getting, then everything is fine. If 50 cfm of air is leaving your house, that means that 50 cfm of outdoor air is simultaneously entering your house.

CENTRAL-FAN-INTEGRATED SUPPLY VENTILATION

For years, the engineers at the Building Science Corporation have been singing the praises of central-fan-integrated supply ventilation systems. These systems can be used only in homes with forced-air heating or cooling systems. The systems include three important components:

• A duct that introduces outdoor air to the furnace's return-air plenum;

• A motorized damper in the fresh air duct;

• An AirCycler control to monitor the runtime of the furnace blower and to control the motorized damper.

The AirCycler control (also known as a fan cycler) prevents both underventilation and overventilation. When the AirCycler notices that the furnace fan hasn't operated for a long time, the control turns on the fan to prevent underventilation. When the control notices that the fan has been operating continuously for a long time, the control closes the motorized damper to prevent overventilation.

During the swing seasons—spring and fall—the furnace blower will need to operate occasionally for ventilation purposes, even when there is no call for heat or cooling. In most climates, about 15% of the annual blower run time for such systems will be devoted to ventilation only. If the system is properly commissioned, the furnace will supply a 7% outside air fraction during ventilation mode.

The big downside to central-fan-integrated supply ventilation is that the installer needs to understand how to design and commission the system. HVAC contractors capable of this task are rare. Unless the designer of a central-fan-integrated ventilation system takes great care when specifying the furnace and programming blower operation, such a system can have unreasonably high operating costs.

A well-designed central-fan-integrated supply ventilation system needs a furnace with an energy-efficient ECM blower. Such furnaces cost between $1,000 and $1,500 more than conventional furnaces. If you end up using a furnace with a conventional blower motor—that is, one that draws 700 watts to 800 watts—the ventilation system will incur a big energy penalty. (For purposes of comparison, a Panasonic exhaust fan draws 11.3 watts, and most HRVs draw 100 watts or less.)

Duct systems and fans designed for heating and cooling are not optimized for ventilation. While ventilation airflow is typically in the range of 50 cfm to 100 cfm, furnace fans move as much as 1,200 cfm to 1,400 cfm. One study (Robb Aldrich, Chicago, 2005) found that a poorly designed central-fan-integrated supply ventilation system in a house with an 800-watt furnace fan used 347 kwh of electricity for ventilation during a swing-season month. During the same month, an identical home with an exhaust-only ventilation system used only 6% as much electricity for ventilation. Although the researchers were somewhat worried that the exhaust-only ventilation system might be ineffective, the data were reassuring: all of the rooms had very acceptable carbon dioxide readings.

WILL COLD OUTDOOR AIR DAMAGE MY FURNACE?

Some builders worry that central-fan-integrated supply ventilation systems won't work in a cold climate, where cold outdoor air might damage the furnace. According to Armin Rudd, such concerns are baseless—as long as the ventilation system is well designed.

Assuming a high outdoor air fraction (15%) and a low outdoor temperature (−30°F), a furnace equipped with a supply-only ventilation system will experience mixed return-air temperatures no colder than 55°F, as long as the thermostat is set to 70°F. Even in Chicago, such systems work well.

DO I REALLY NEED THE AIRCYCLER AND MOTORIZED DAMPER?

To reduce costs, some builders install the lazy man's version of a central-fan-integrated supply ventilation system—one that includes a passive fresh air duct to the return-air plenum, but without a motorized damper or AirCycler control. What's wrong with this approach?

- During the swing seasons, when the furnace fan isn't operating, the house won't get enough fresh outdoor air, and homeowners may complain of stuffiness.

- During the rest of the year, when the furnace fan is operating regularly, the house will be overventilated, resulting an a severe energy penalty. During winter, all that unnecessary cold air will need to be heated; during the summer, all that unnecessary hot air will need to be cooled and dehumidified.

AN HRV WITH DEDICATED VENTILATION DUCTWORK

The best ventilation performance and lowest operating cost comes from an HRV or ERV with dedicated ventilation ductwork. Such a "gold standard" system should be designed to pull stale air from bathrooms and laundry rooms, while introducing fresh air to the living room and bedrooms.

Although HRVs and ERVs save energy compared to exhaust-only or supply-only ventilation systems, they are expensive to install. The high cost of these systems raises questions about their cost-effectiveness, especially in mild climates. To learn more about this issue, see "Are HRVs Cost-Effective?" on p. 232.

For ventilation purposes, either an HRV or an ERV can work well in any climate. The presumed advantage of ERVs over HRVs in hot, humid climates is not based on research or field data. As Max Sherman wrote, "Almost all hot, humid climates have hours when it is dryer outside than inside, and then ERVs actually make the [indoor] moisture problem worse. The net effect is that ERVs are about a wash [compared to HRVs] for humidity control in those climates." (For more information on this topic, see "HRV or ERV?" on p. 226.)

LUNOS FANS

The Lunos fan is a new type of ventilation fan from Germany. Installed in pairs, the wall-mounted ventilation fans automatically alternate between exhaust mode and supply mode. Because each fan includes a ceramic core, they are able to recover heat from the exhaust air stream. These fans are particularly useful for retrofit applications or for any situation where the installation of ductwork would be awkward.

THE GOLD STANDARD for residential ventilation. The most effective ventilation systems include an HRV or ERV—similar appliances that transfer heat (but not air) between a ventilation system's exhaust and supply air streams. Shown here is a top-of-the-line unit from RenewAire®.

How to choose the right mechanical equipment for a balanced ventilation system in your home

Every tight home needs a mechanical ventilation system. Most builders choose one of three ventilation options:

- An exhaust-only ventilation system;
- A central-fan-integrated supply ventilation system;
- A balanced ventilation system using an HRV or an ERV.

A balanced ventilation system with an HRV or an ERV is the preferred ventilation system for a Passivhaus building. Although balanced ventilation systems are expensive to install, they have the lowest operating cost of any ventilation option—assuming, of course, that the designer or installer hasn't made any blunders. (Sadly, this can be an optimistic and risky assumption.)

The purpose of an HRV or an ERV is to deliver fresh air to a home's interior. Neither appliance is designed to provide makeup air for combustion appliances or kitchen exhaust fans. HRVs and ERVs are not space-heating devices, heat-delivery devices, or energy-saving devices. The more hours that an HRV or ERV operates, the more energy it uses—electrical energy to operate its fans, as well as heating or cooling energy to make up for the conditioned air that these devices expel from a home.

WHAT THEY DO AND HOW THEY WORK

An HRV's fans pull fresh air into a home while simultaneously exhausting stale air from the home. In most installations, the fresh air is delivered to the living room and bedrooms, while the stale air is removed from bathrooms, laundry rooms, and sometimes the kitchen.

Both the fresh air stream and the stale air stream flow through the HRV. The core of the appliance allows some of the heat from the warmer air stream (the stale air in winter, the fresh air in summer) to be transferred to the cooler air stream. In winter, in other words, the appliance "recovers" some of the heat that would have otherwise been exhausted. This heat transfer occurs without any mixing of the two air streams.

An ERV does everything that an HRV does. In addition, an ERV allows some of the moisture in the more humid air stream (usually the stale air in winter and the fresh air in summer) to be transferred to the air stream which is dryer. This transfer of moisture—called enthalpy transfer—occurs with very little mixing of the two air streams. (The cross contamination rate for one well-regarded ERV, the UltimateAir RecoupAerator®, is 9.6%.)

HOW AN HRV WORKS

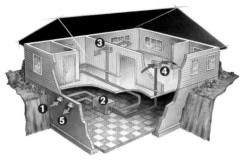

An insulated shell increases the efficiency of the HRV by keeping hot or cold air in the unit.

Particulate filters wrap the heat exchanger. HRV filters should be cleaned every six months.

1 A fan draws fresh outdoor air into the HRV.

4 Conditioned indoor air is pulled into the HRV, where it heats or cools incoming air.

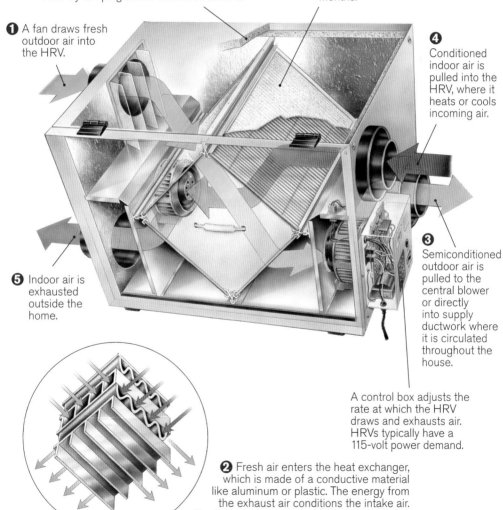

5 Indoor air is exhausted outside the home.

3 Semiconditioned outdoor air is pulled to the central blower or directly into supply ductwork where it is circulated throughout the house.

A control box adjusts the rate at which the HRV draws and exhausts air. HRVs typically have a 115-volt power demand.

2 Fresh air enters the heat exchanger, which is made of a conductive material like aluminum or plastic. The energy from the exhaust air conditions the intake air. Air streams are separated to keep exhausted contaminants from entering incoming air.

WHY VENTILATE A HOUSE?

Before we can clarify the choice between an HRV and an ERV, we have to consider the question, Why should a house be ventilated? As it turns out, the question has several answers, including:

- To provide enough fresh air to keep the occupants healthy.
- To remove odors.
- To dilute indoor pollutants.
- To lower the indoor relative humidity.

Most of the goals listed in the above box are easy to understand. (Even so, establishing an optimal ventilation rate to achieve these goals is a contentious issue.) However, using ventilation to achieve the last of these four goals—lowering the indoor relative humidity—gets problematic.

To prevent moisture damage to a house, lower humidity levels are always preferable to higher humidity levels. In other words, dry is always better than damp. However, some people begin to complain if the indoor relative humidity is too dry—say, 20% or below. (Of course, people have lived healthy lives for thousands of years in climates where the relative humidity is often below 20%, so it's not at all clear that low humidity levels are unhealthy.)

Ventilation can reduce the indoor relative humidity only if the outdoor air is dryer than the indoor air. Because cold air can't hold as much moisture as warm air, ventilating a house helps lower the indoor relative humidity only when it's cold outside (or on dry days during spring and fall). In most parts of the United States, ventilation during hot weather actually introduces more moisture into the house—that is, it tends to raise rather than lower the indoor relative humidity.

What do manufacturers recommend?

Unfortunately, you can't depend on HRV and ERV manufacturers to tell you whether your home is better off with an HRV or an ERV. Many manufacturers' websites include misstatements:

- Both Fantech and Lennox® advise customers that the only relevant criterion is climate.

- The Broan® website falsely claims, "An HRV ... is used only in the cold months of the year to resolve high moisture problems in the home. An ERV ... can be used all year round to provide fresh air for your home."

OTHER MYTHS

These myths—that the choice between an HRV and an ERV depends only on climate and that HRVs can't be used during the summer—are only two of the many red herrings encountered by builders in search of accurate information on HRVs and ERVs. Other commonly repeated myths include the following:

- ERVs can't be used in cold climates because their cores will freeze.

- In a humid climate, an ERV can act as a dehumidifier or can help address high indoor humidity.

Both of these statements are false. (Freeze-up problems were solved years ago by the development of controls with a defrost cycle.)

VENTILATING IN HOT, HUMID CLIMATES

When an HRV or ERV ventilates an air-conditioned house during the summer, the cool exhaust stream absorbs heat from the incoming fresh air. In other words, the incoming outdoor air is cooled by the outgoing exhaust air. This is possible only in an air-conditioned house. If there's no air-conditioning, the exhaust air won't be cool, so there is little opportunity for heat exchange to occur.

If the house has an ERV, some of the moisture from the incoming outdoor air is transferred to the exhaust air. This reduces, but does not eliminate, an undesirable moisture source. (In hot, humid climates, the increased moisture load caused by summer ventilation is an unavoidable drawback to any type of ventilation.)

In a hot, humid climate, it makes more sense to install an ERV than an HRV—but not for the reason that many people assume. "ERVs are not intended to reduce indoor relative humidity during the summer," explained Daniel Forest, the vice president of R&D for Venmar®, a manufacturer of HRVs and ERVs.

Operating an ERV during the summer in Houston, TX, doesn't lower the indoor relative humidity; rather, it makes the situation worse. The best that can be said is that, from a moisture-load perspective, operating an ERV is less bad than operating an HRV, assuming, of course, that the home is equipped with a dehumidifier.

The main reason to prefer ERVs over HRVs in Houston is that the additional moisture introduced by the ERV—a latent load that the air-conditioner must contend with—is less than the moisture that would have been introduced by an HRV. While HRVs and ERVs both cause increased energy use, the energy attributable to ERV operation is less.

High humidity in tight houses

In Houston, a tight, well-insulated house is more likely to have problems with high indoor humidity than an older leaky house. In a tight home, an air-conditioner doesn't run anywhere near as often as in a leaky home, especially during the swing seasons (spring and fall). If the air-conditioner is rarely on, there are fewer opportunities for the HVAC equipment to dehumidify the interior air. Of course, adding mechanical ventilation only makes the situation worse.

The solution to this problem is not an ERV. The solution is a stand-alone dehumidifier.

Two researchers from the Lawrence Berkeley National Laboratory, Iain Walker and Max Sherman, wrote a paper ("Humidity Implications for Meeting Residential Ventilation Requirements") that includes a discussion of the effects of residential ventilation in Houston. They noted, "The use of an ERV did not change the humidity distribution in a hot, humid climate compared to a continuous exhaust system."

Elaborating on this finding in an e-mail, Sherman told me, "It is true our results show little value in ERVs in hot, humid climates, but it is important to understand why . . . . Almost all hot, humid climates have hours when it is dryer outside than inside and then ERVs actually make the moisture problem worse. The net effect is that ERVs are about a wash for humidity control in those climates . . . . On the other hand, if there were independent humidity control (such as...a stand-alone dehumidifier), then ERVs pay big dividends in terms of energy savings in hot, humid climates. To say it another way, the whole idea of an ERV is not to change the indoor humidity (and temperature) with ventilation. So if the indoor humidity is good already, the ERV reduces energy costs. If it is bad already, the ERV is not likely to help."

WHAT ABOUT COLD CLIMATES?

Many people assume that HRVs make more sense than ERVs in cold climates. However, the situation isn't that simple. Whether the interior of a cold-climate home is humid or dry during winter depends on several factors, including:

- The leakiness of the building envelope.
- The ventilation rate of the ventilation equipment.
- The number of square feet per occupant.
- The behavior of the occupants.

At one extreme would be a large, leaky, Victorian house occupied by two elderly people who rarely cook and have few houseplants. At the opposite extreme would be a small, tight home occupied by a six-person family who eats home-cooked meals and takes frequent showers.

IS THE HOUSE DRY OR DAMP?

In most cases, an old leaky Victorian home doesn't need an HRV or an ERV. (It makes little sense to install a $4,000 ventilation system in a home that already has a high air-exchange rate.) But even if we narrow our focus to new homes with tight envelopes, we find that winter humidity levels vary widely. Big homes with few occupants tend to be dry during the winter. Small homes with many occupants tend to be humid during the winter. These two types of homes may need different ventilation systems (or may need to be ventilated at different rates).

According to Don Fugler, a senior researcher at the Canada Mortgage and Housing Corporation, some Canadian houses can benefit from an ERV. "Although I have never promoted ERVs, we've started to see situations where an ERV may make more sense," said Fugler.

"In a new, energy-efficient house with no major moisture sources in a very cold climate—a prairie climate—the code-required level of ventilation will dry out your house way too much."

Another building scientist, Terry Brennan of Camroden Associates in Westmoreland, NY, agreed with Fugler that the answer to the question, "HRV or ERV?" is, "It depends." Brennan said, "Where I have monitored indoor relative humidity—usually in houses that are typically 2,400 sq. ft. or smaller—HRVs maintain 30% or 35% RH, so I would say they didn't need enthalpy. But in a bigger house with only two people, it might be different. Of course, it depends on how airtight the house is."

OTHER WAYS TO ADDRESS HUMIDITY AND DRYNESS

It's possible to overthink the choice between an HRV and an ERV. After all, there are other ways to address humidity problems in houses. In fact, these other factors tend to overwhelm performance differences between HRVs and ERVs.

For example, regardless of the type of ventilation equipment in your home, you can adjust your interior relative humidity during winter by adjusting your ventilation rate. If your house is too humid—usually indicated by the presence of condensation or frost on your windows—just increase the ventilation rate. In other words, run your fan for more hours per day.

If your house is too dry—usually indicated by dry skin or static electricity problems—just reduce your ventilation rate. (Be careful, however—if you reduce the ventilation rate too much, you risk undermining other important ventilation functions like odor removal.)

THE BOTTOM LINE

If you want to install an HRV or an ERV, which should you choose? Here are some guidelines:

- For a small, tight house in a cold climate—especially a house with a large family—choose an HRV.

- For a large house in a cold climate—especially a house with few occupants—choose an ERV.

- In a hot, humid, climate, an ERV will cost a little less to operate during summer than an HRV.

- In mixed climates, choose either appliance.

However, these guidelines aren't set in stone. For example, Paul Raymer, a ventilation expert and former member of the ASHRAE 62.2 committee, is skeptical of the idea that large homes with few occupants could benefit from an ERV. "For big homes, an ERV might have little or no impact [on indoor relative humidity]—unless it was a big ERV," said Raymer. "And you generally don't need as much ventilation air in a big house with few occupants."

In fact, the difference in performance between these two types of appliances is so slight that many builders ignore climate, house size, and occupancy, and instead make their choice based on energy efficiency.

Remember, stupid installation details will undermine the efficiency of even the best equipment. It makes little sense to install a high-efficiency HRV or ERV by connecting it to the plenums of a furnace with an inefficient blower motor. If your furnace blower comes on every time your HRV operates, then the efficiency of the HRV motor is irrelevant. That's why anyone who goes to the expense of purchasing an HRV or ERV should insist on an installation with dedicated ventilation ductwork, not an installation that tries to use existing furnace ductwork.

If you live in a hot, humid climate, and you're worried about high indoor humidity during summer, reduce your ventilation rate. (Building scientist Joseph Lstiburek has made the somewhat controversial recommendation that homeowners in hot, humid climates should ventilate at a lower rate than the level recommended by ASHRAE 62.2.) Finally, if your indoor relative humidity is too high during the summer, you probably need a dehumidifier. Ventilation won't solve this problem.

MAYBE YOU DON'T REALLY NEED AN HRV

Finally, it's worth mentioning that it's possible to have a well-ventilated home without an HRV or an ERV. It's much cheaper to install a central-fan-integrated supply ventilation system controlled by a fan cycler. If you choose this route, be sure that your furnace has an energy-efficient ECM blower.

Compared to a simple exhaust fan, a heat-recovery ventilator saves energy, but it probably won't save enough to justify the high cost of the equipment

From 1977 (when the Saskatchewan Conservation house was built) until 2004 (when the first U.S. Passivhaus was built), North American builders completed hundreds of superinsulated homes. In those days, anyone interested in rating the performance of these homes was probably interested in just one metric: annual energy use.

In recent years, however, with the increasing attention paid to the Passivhaus standard, some builders of superinsulated homes are walking along a narrower path. Any builder interested in achieving the Passivhaus standard soon learns that a low energy bill is no longer sufficient to gain accolades.

A HIGH-QUALITY ventilation system isn't cheap. A residential ventilation system that includes a Zehnder HRV like the one in this photo costs more than $5,000.

UNEXAMINED POSTULATES

This narrow Passivhaus path has several restrictions; I call them "unexamined Passivhaus postulates." Like postulates in geometry, Passivhaus postulates need not be proven; they just are. Here are four of the postulates:

• It makes sense to deliver space heat through ventilation ductwork.

• It's more important to achieve 15 kwh per square meter per year and 0.6 ACH50 than to calculate whether these goals are cost-effective.

• The output of a PV system should not be considered in one's annual energy calculations.

• Every house needs an HRV.

These Passivhaus postulates are not equally binding—for example, North American designers have chosen to ignore the postulate affirming that space heat should be delivered through ventilation ductwork. (Although the principle is widely ignored, it is still prominently featured on the Passipedia page that establishes the definition of a passive house.) When I interviewed Dr. Wolfgang Feist in December 2007, he used the same definition for a Passivhaus that is enshrined on Passipedia: "As long as you build a house in a way that you can use the heat-recovery ventilation system —a system that you need anyway for indoor air requirements—to provide the heat and cooling, it can be considered a Passivhaus."

Each of the four postulates listed above deserves to be examined more closely than it has up until now because each of these postulates forces Passivhaus designers to follow a narrower path than the one followed by the North American designers of superinsulated homes who worked from 1977 to 2004. Here, I'll address just one of the unexamined Passivhaus postulates: the one holding that every house needs an HRV.

DOES THE PASSIVHAUS STANDARD REQUIRE AN HRV?

The question as to whether the Passivhaus standard requires an HRV is complicated. As far as I know, every Passivhaus in the United States includes an HRV or an ERV.

The requirement for an HRV is explained in a rule book published by the Passivhaus Institut in Darmstadt, *Certification Criteria for Residential Passive House Building*. The book contains "Documents necessary for Passive House certification," a list that includes "HRV commissioning report. The results must at least include the following ... name and address of the tester, time of adjustment, ventilation system manufacturer and type of device, adjusted volume flow rates per valve for normal operation, mass flow/volumetric flow balance for outdoor air and exhaust air (maximum disbalance of 10%)."

According to this document, it seems clear that an HRV is required, not optional.

As it turns out, however, the Passivhaus standard doesn't require the use of an HRV. According to Floris Keverling Buisman, a certified Passive House consultant in New York City, "PHI [The Passivhaus Institut] does not require an HRV .... Why it is generally recommended is that it will be very hard to get your heating (or cooling) demand below 15kwh/m2·year without an HRV in most climates. The tricky part is that if you would like to get certified (voluntarily) you need to conform to all the Passivhaus criteria, which includes comfort—which is defined by ISO 7730 .... If your supply air is more than 3.5°C (6.3°F) lower than the room temperature, your building in my understanding would no longer be comfortable and certifiable by PHI as a Certified Passive House. This is why you need an HRV with a high recovery rate in most climates."

For most Passivhaus builders, the net result of these requirements is that it is very difficult or impossible to install an exhaust-only or supply-only ventilation system. In essence, the Passivhaus standard pushes builders in the direction of an HRV.

Other ventilation approaches are cheaper

While HRVs do an excellent job of ventilating a house, there are less expensive approaches: either an exhaust-only ventilation system or a supply-only ventilation system. Thousands of superinsulated homes successfully use one of these two approaches.

The main advantage of an HRV is that it recovers some of the heat that would otherwise leave the building with the exhaust air. However, an HRV is an expensive gadget, which raises the question, Does this gadget recover enough energy to justify its high cost? The answer depends on your climate. In a very cold climate, an HRV can recover enough heat to justify its high cost. In moderate climates, however, an HRV doesn't make much sense.

This analysis raises an interesting question: why have Passivhaus proponents embraced one expensive gadget—the HRV—but rejected another expensive gadget—the PV module? Hint: The answer has nothing to do with cost-effectiveness. In most U.S. climates, an investment in PV modules provides a greater energy return than an equivalent investment in an HRV (or, for that matter, an investment in thick subslab foam).

MODELING HRV ENERGY SAVINGS

John Semmelhack, an energy consultant and certified Passivhaus consultant in Charlottesville, VA, has taken a fresh look at the question of HRV cost-effectiveness and reported his findings in a paper titled, "An Energy and Economic Modeling Study of Exhaust Ventilation Systems Compared to Balanced Ventilation Systems with Energy Recovery," which he presented on September 28, 2012, at the seventh annual North American Passive House conference in Denver.

Semmelhack was well aware of the disadvantages of HRVs: "These systems are relatively costly to install compared to other ventilation options, are somewhat complex for owners to operate and maintain, and require a significant amount of fan energy for operation (200–400 kwh/year, about 4–8% of total site energy for a modest-sized, all-electric Passive House). By contrast, well-designed exhaust ventilation systems are less expensive to install, are easier to maintain, and require significantly less fan energy for operation."

Because he has consulted on several Passivhaus projects, Semmelhack knows exactly how much it costs to install an HRV. He wrote, "In North American Passive Houses, ventilation and space conditioning are often decoupled, requiring separate distribution systems and typically higher upfront cost. It is common for a stand-alone Passive House ventilation system to have an installed cost of $4,000 to $7,000 or more."

Of course, HRVs recover heat that would otherwise be lost. Semmelhack's energy modeling exercise showed that "both the ERV and HRV ... save energy compared to an exhaust ventilation system in every case in the study." Although this fact is well known, very few architects and builders have actually calculated how much energy is saved by an HRV compared to a simple exhaust-only ventilation system.

The answer, as it turns out, is not much—unless you live in a very cold climate. In mild climates, a PV array is a better investment than an HRV. Semmelhack wrote, "The amount of site energy saved by the ERV/HRV systems is much lower in the milder climates (330–600 kwh/year) than the colder climates (800–1,100 kwh/year). The lower energy savings in the milder climates leads to poor cost-effectiveness when compared to other energy-saving or energy-producing options such as extra insulation or a photovoltaic system."

Details of Semmelhack's modeling exercise

Semmelhack used the PHPP to model a single-family three-bedroom house measuring 1,800 sq. ft. He assumed that the house was heated with an air-source heat pump (for example, a ductless minisplit system), and he assumed that the house achieved a Passivhaus level of airtightness (0.6 ACH50).

He modeled the house in six different climates (San Francisco; Atlanta; Charlottesville, VA; Portland, OR; Chicago; and Burlington, VT). The mildest climate he looked at (San Francisco) has 3,200 heating degree days, while the coldest climate (Burlington) has 7,300 heating degree days.

In each climate zone, he modeled the performance of the house with three different ventilation systems: an UltimateAir 200DX ERV, a Zehnder Comfo 350 HRV, and a Panasonic FV-08VKS3 exhaust fan with variable airflow settings and passive air inlets. The electricity use of each appliance was assumed to be as follows: 0.58 watts/cfm for the UltimateAir ERV, 0.30 watts/cfm for the Zehnder HRV, 0.12 watts/cfm for the Panasonic exhaust fan. When installed in Chicago and Burl-

ington, the HRV and ERV were assumed to have electric defrost systems.

The ventilation rate was assumed to be 56 cfm continuous for the HRV and ERV, and 64 cfm for the exhaust-only ventilation system "to account for occupant on-demand use of other exhaust appliances: other bath fans (50 cfm $\times$ 2 hours/day), range hood (100 cfm $\times$ 1 hour/day) and clothes dryer (125 cfm $\times$ 1 hour/day)."

By using PHPP software, Semmelhack was able to model aspects of HRV performance that aren't captured by some other energy-modeling programs. He wrote, "The energy analysis included annual heating demand and latent cooling demand for ventilation and infiltration, ventilation fan energy use, defrost energy use, and space conditioning energy use for ventilation and infiltration."

WHAT DO I GET FOR MY INVESTMENT IN AN HRV?

To determine whether an HRV is cost-effective in a given climate, Semmelhack had to determine two numbers: the amount of energy saved and the incremental cost of the equipment compared to an exhaust-only ventilation system.

Semmelhack assumed that the capital costs to install the three studied ventilation systems were as follows:

• The system with an UltimateAir ERV cost $4,125 (including ERV, ductwork, fittings, registers, labor, and markup).

• The system with a Zehnder HRV cost $5,375 (including HRV, ductwork, fittings, registers, labor, and markup).

• The system with Panasonic fans cost $2,102 (including three bath fans, one kitchen range hood, ductwork, fittings, labor, and markup).

Some readers will probably note that an exhaust-only ventilation system could be installed for less than Semmelhack assumed; if so, this fact would only strengthen Semmelhack's conclusions.

Using these figures, Semmelhack calculated that the UltimateAir ERV represented a $2,023 upcharge from an exhaust-only system, while a Zehnder HRV represented a $3,273 upcharge. He assumed that the lifetime of the ventilation equipment was 20 years.

Using the PHPP energy modeling spreadsheet, Semmelhack calculated the total amount of energy saved over 20 years for the ERV option and the HRV option, compared to the baseline system (the Panasonic exhaust-only system). The energy savings had a cost, of course: The cost of the saved energy over 20 years was equal to the upcharge for the expensive equipment.

Semmelhack concluded, "The cost/kwh saved for the [UltimateAir] 200DX ranged from as low as $0.12/kwh in Burlington to as high as $0.31/kwh in San Francisco. The cost/kwh saved for the [Zehnder] Comfo 350 ranged from as low as $0.17/kwh in Burlington to as high as $0.41/kwh in Atlanta."

For purposes of comparison, Semmelhack calculated that the energy generated by a photovoltaic system in Charlottesville costs the owner $0.13/kwh, while the energy saved by an attic insulation upgrade in Charlottesville costs the owner $0.17/kwh. Semmelhack concluded, "Based on this analysis, the ERV and HRV systems are not cost-effective (compared to the reference points) in terms of energy savings in the milder climates, and are only moderately cost-effective as the house 'migrates' to a cold climate (Burlington)."

Passivhaus blinders lead to irrational results

In his paper, Semmelhack took the bull by the horns and questioned why the Passivhaus standard requires the use of an HRV. He wrote, "Based on the poor cost-effectiveness of ERV/HRV systems in the milder climates, it seems irrational that these mechanical systems should be a 'de facto' requirement for meeting the annual heat demand requirement for [Passivhaus] certification."

In his PowerPoint presentation at the Denver conference, Semmelhack was blunt. "Typical Passive House HRV/ERV systems do not appear to be particularly cost-effective in the milder climates." He continued, "We should remove our Passive House blinders and take a closer look at other ventilation options .... PHIUS certification metrics should not have a de-facto mandate for cost-ineffective mechanical systems."

As PV systems continue to drop in price, the Passivhaus preference for HRVs rather than PV systems gets harder and harder to justify.

HRVS HAVE SEVERAL BENEFITS

Defenders of HRVs will probably bristle at Semmelhack's analysis, pointing out that an HRV provides better comfort and delivers fresh air more evenly than does an exhaust-only system. This is undeniable, and some homeowners may be happy to pay thousands of dollars for these benefits. Others, however, are likely to find that a simple exhaust-only ventilation system meets all of their ventilation needs.

UNEXAMINED POSTULATES COME AT A COST

The energy-efficiency pioneers who built superinsulated homes from 1977 to 2004 were fairly nimble. They experimented with a variety of approaches to superinsulation, searching for innovative specifications that worked to lower energy consumption.

Compared to these nimble pioneers, Passivhaus designers are dragging around a ball and chain. (Note to Passivhaus designers: If you bend down and look closely at the device fastened to your ankle, you'll see a small inscription: "Made in Germany.") The requirement to include an HRV—which many designers interpret as a requirement for an expensive HRV from Europe—is making Passivhaus designers less nimble than other builders.

Years ago, Amory Lovins predicted that superinsulation techniques would allow builders to "tunnel through the cost barrier." The concept was later championed by Wolfgang Feist, who predicted that Passivhaus buildings would require less expensive HVAC equipment than ordinary buildings. As it turns out, most Passivhaus builders in the United States haven't been able to tunnel through the HVAC cost barrier—in part because of the burden of unexamined Passivhaus postulates.

There is at least one builder in the United States who seems to have managed to tunnel through the HVAC cost barrier, however. I'm thinking of Massachusetts builder Carter Scott. Scott usually specifies simple exhaust-only ventilation systems.

The Passivhaus Standard is a construction standard for super insulated buildings developed in Germany in the early 1990s. The standard requires buildings to have a very low rate of air leakage and a very low rate of energy use. Complying with the Passivhaus standard results in an energy-efficient building, but some critics maintain that the level of energy savings isn't high enough to justify the added costs of compliance.

8

THE PASSIVHAUS STANDARD

The history of a superinsulation standard

More and more designers of high-performance homes are buzzing about a superinsulation standard developed in Germany, the Passivhaus standard. The standard has been promoted for two decades by the Passivhaus Institut, a private research and consulting center in Darmstadt, Germany.

The institute was founded in 1996 by a German physicist, Dr. Wolfgang Feist. Feist drew his inspiration from ground-breaking superinsulated houses built in Canada and the United States, including the Lo-Cal house developed by researchers at the University of Illinois in 1976, the Saskatchewan Conservation House completed in 1977, and the Gene Leger house built in 1977 in Pepperell, MA. Aiming to refine North American design principles for use in Europe, Feist built his first Passivhaus prototype in 1990–1991.

Feist later obtained funding for a major Passivhaus research project called Cost-Efficient Passive Houses as European

Standards (CEPHEUS). Conducted from 1997 to 2002, the CEPHEUS project sent researchers to gather data on 221 super-insulated housing units at 14 locations in five countries (Austria, France, Germany, Sweden, and Switzerland).

THE STANDARD SETS A STRICT BAR

The Passivhaus standard is a residential construction standard requiring very low levels of air leakage, very high levels of insulation, and windows with a very low U-factor. To meet the standard, a house needs:

• An infiltration rate no greater than 0.60 ACH50;

• A maximum annual heating energy use of 15 kwh per square meter (4,755 Btu per square foot);

• A maximum annual cooling energy use of 15 kwh per square meter (1.39 kwh per square foot);

MICHIGAN PASSIVHAUS. Architects Matt O'Malia and Riley Pratt of GO Logic in Belfast, ME, successfully captured the comforts of traditional design in a cutting-edge, high-performance home in rural Michigan.

Roof
1. ⅝-in. roof sheathing
2. #30 felt paper
3. 28 in. loose-fill cellulose
4. Vent baffles
5. ½-in. ZIP System sheathing (air barrier)
6. Air-sealed rigid-foam blocking

Wall
1. 2×6 stud wall
2. Dense-packed cellulose
3. ½-in. ZIP System sheathing (air barrier)
4. 11⅞-in. I-joist Larsen truss
5. Dense-packed cellulose
6. ⅝-in. fiberboard sheathing
7. Housewrap
8. 1× furring strips

Floor
1. 2× sleeper
2. 1½ in. concrete

Foundation
1. 2×4 stud wall
2. Dense-packed cellulose
3. Continuous vapor/air barrier
4. ICF foundation wall
5. Waterproof membrane
6. 6-in. EPS rigid foam
7. Parge coating
8. 8-in. XPS rigid foam

• Maximum source energy use for all purposes of 120 kwh per square meter (11.1 kwh per square foot).

The standard recommends, but does not require, a maximum design heating load of 10 watts per square meter and windows with a maximum U-factor of 0.14.

The Passivhaus airtightness standard of 0.6 ACH50 is particularly strict. It makes the Canadian R-2000 standard (1.5 ACH50) look lax by comparison.

Unlike most U.S. standards for energy-efficient homes, the Passivhaus standard governs not just heating and cooling energy but overall building energy use, including baseload electricity use and energy used for domestic hot water.

Thick walls, thick roofs, and triple-glazed windows

Most European Passivhaus buildings have wall and roof R-values ranging from 38 to 60. Wood-framed buildings usually have 16-in.-thick double-stud walls or walls framed with deep vertical I-joists. Masonry buildings are usually insulated with at least 10 in. of exterior rigid foam. To meet the Passivhaus window standard, manufacturers in Germany, Austria, and Sweden produce windows with foam-insulated frames and argon-filled triple-glazing with two low-e coatings.

Although the Passivhaus Institut recommends that window area and orientation be optimized for passive solar gain, the institute's engineers have concluded, based on computer modeling and field monitoring, that passive solar details are far less important than airtightness and insulation R-value.

In the United States and Canada, the phrase *passive solar house* was used in the 1970s to describe houses with extra thermal mass and extensive south-facing glazing. Because of the possibility of confusing Passivhaus buildings with pas-

sive solar houses, most English-language sources use the German spelling of *Passivhaus* to reduce misunderstandings.

Gotta have an HRV

Feist recommends that every Passivhaus building be equipped with an HRV. Because the space heating load of a Passivhaus building is quite low, this load can usually be met in a mild climate by using an air-source heat pump to raise the temperature of the incoming ventilation air. Some European Passivhaus buildings use integrated ventilation systems with a heat pump evaporator coil located in the ventilation exhaust duct, downstream from the HRV, to allow the heat pump to scavenge waste heat that might otherwise leave the building. In this way, the ventilation ductwork becomes part of a forced-air heating system with a very low airflow rate.

In Europe, most non-Passivhaus homes are heated with a boiler connected to a hydronic distribution system. Because residential forced-air heating systems are almost unknown in Europe, many Passivhaus advocates declare that their

PASSIVHAUS MONTEREY. Designed by architect Justin Pauley and built by Rob Nicely, this compact farmhouse achieves home building's highest performance standard without a shred of aesthetic compromise.

houses "have no need for a conventional heating system"—a statement that reflects the European view that forced-air heat distribution systems are "unconventional."

PASSIVHAUS COMES BACK TO THE UNITED STATES

The first building in the United States that aimed to meet Passivhaus standard was a private residence built by architect Katrin Klingenberg in Urbana, IL, in 2003. The home included an R-56 foundation with 14 in. of subslab EPS insulation, R-60 walls, and an R-60 roof. Klingenberg specified triple-glazed Thermotech windows with foam-filled fiberglass frames.

Although Klingenberg's Urbana home was built to the Passivhaus standard, she didn't bother to have the home certified and registered. The first U.S. building to achieve that goal was the Waldsee BioHaus, a language institute completed in Minnesota in 2006. That building includes an R-55 foundation with 16 in. of EPS foam under the concrete slab, R-70 walls, and an

R-100 roof. The building's triple-glazed windows were imported (at a high cost) from Germany.

Klingenberg later founded a nonprofit organization, the Ecological Construction Laboratory (E-co Lab), to promote the construction of energy-efficient homes for low-income and middle-income families. In October 2006, the E-co Lab completed Urbana's second Passivhaus building: a 1,300-sq.-ft. home that resembled Klingenberg's home in many ways.

As Klingenberg devoted more and more time to promoting Passivhaus buildings in North America, she decided to found the Passive House Institute U.S.—basically, a North American outpost of the Darmstadt institute—in Urbana.

In 2011, the European institute severed relations with its U.S. satellite. The bitter divorce was accompanied by a series of accusatory press releases, and the two organizations remain estranged.

Determining the best thickness for subslab foam

In the United States, designers of cutting-edge superinsulated homes generally recommend 2 in. to 6 in. of rigid foam insulation under residential slabs. For builders who use extruded polystyrene (XPS), the most commonly used subslab insulation, that amounts to R-10 to R-30.

As Alex Wilson wrote, "Building science expert Joe Lstiburek ... argues that for any house north of the Mason-Dixon Line we should follow the '10-20-40-60 rule' for R-values: R-10 under foundation floor slabs; R-20 foundation walls; R-40 house walls, and R-60 ceilings or roofs." For reasons that are somewhat murky, however, Passivhaus builders install much thicker layers of subslab insulation than most superinsulation nerds.

PASSIVHAUS BUILDINGS HAVE VERY THICK SUBSLAB FOAM

To meet the Passivhaus standard, Katrin Klingenberg, the founder of Passive House Institute U.S., installed 14 in. of expanded polystyrene (EPS) insulation—seven layers of 2-in. foam (a total of R-56)—under the slab of her home in Urbana, IL. The Waldsee Biohaus, a Passivhaus language institute in Bemidji, MN, has 16 in. of EPS under its foundation slab.

What's the explanation for these differing recommendations?

I approached engineer John Straube in hopes of satisfying my curiosity on the surprising disparity between the subslab insulation recommendations of North American physicists and Passivhaus advocates. John Straube is a professor of building envelope science at the University of Waterloo, ON, and a very smart guy.

I asked Straube whether the differing recommendations resulted from uncertainties related to soil temperature measurements. No, Straube answered, the reason for the disparity lies elsewhere.

Is there a cheaper way to do it?

As it turns out, the PHPP software used by Passivhaus designers never considers whether the incremental cost of thicker and thicker insulation is greater than the cost of an alternative method of meeting the home's energy needs—for example, a PV array.

Straube explained that Passivhaus designers have only a few dials to turn when adjusting a home's specifications. (Straube gave credit to energy consultant Marc Rosenbaum for the control-panel metaphor.) The Passivhaus standard does not allow the use of site-generated PV to help meet the 15 kwh per square meter and 120 kwh per square meter goals. Once the designers have specified the best available windows, for example, the window dial can't be turned down any further. These houses are just about as airtight as buildings can be built, so the airtightness dial has basically been bottomed out. Once the easy dials have been turned, the only remaining variable under the designer's control is insulation thickness—so, to ensure the house meets the standard, that's what gets adjusted, even when the resulting insulation thickness is illogical or uneconomic.

The cost of PV-powered heat

Straube looked up soil-temperature data. "A slab on grade insulated to R-32 in Finland had an average heating season soil temperature of 12.5°C (55°F)," Straube wrote in an e-mail. "Hence, during the heating seasons the average temperature difference between soil and indoor air is about 15°F." In other words, the delta-T across an insulated slab is much less than the delta-T across an insulated wall—at least in cold northern climates.

If a home uses electricity to supply heat, a heat pump is obviously more efficient than a resistance heater. "If you account for a coefficient of performance of 2.5 for the heat pump over the season, the cost of PV-powered heat is no more than 60/2.5 = 24 cents per kwh." (When Straube's calculation was made, PV systems cost $8 per watt to install; the current cost for a utility-installed system is now well below $3 per watt. Current cost estimates for PV-generated electricity range from 15 cents to 20 cents per kilowatt-hour. Of course, the dropping price of PV modules strengthens rather than weakens Straube's argument.)

Straube continued, "Note that many central forms of renewable electricity production work at 25 cents per kwh, such as wind, microhydro, tidal, biomass, concentrating solar thermal, etc. So this seems like the high end of electric production costs."

Once the cost of PV-generated electricity is known, it becomes a simple matter to calculate whether the incremental cost of very thick foam insulation is cheaper or more expensive than PV. Most builders would agree that it makes little sense to invest in foam when a PV array is cheaper.

It makes sense to stop at R-15 to R-25

Straube wrote, "The cost of insulation becomes more than the cost of generating energy for the walls in a typical house in a 7,200-HDD climate at about R-60 (using the Building Science Corporation approach), and slabs [on grade] at about R-20 to R-25, depending the cost of placing EPS (which costs around 10 cents per R per square foot). Basements have less heat loss [than slabs on grade], so the cutoff point is more like R-15 to R-20 for a basement slab. Heating a slab with radiant tubes increases the temperature of the slab from around 68°F or so to 80°F or so on average, so the insulation levels need to be increased by about 50% over this for radiantly heated slabs."

Building Energy Optimization (BEopt), an energy modeling program developed in 2004 at the National Renewable Energy Laboratory in Golden, CO, shows designers the "least-cost path" to building optimization by performing calculations similar to those made by Straube. The idea behind BEopt is that no building should have a PV array until the designer has implemented every building envelope measure cheaper than PV. Once this point is reached, an investment in PV *may* make sense. Certainly such an investment would make more sense than spending additional dollars on insulation because the insulation would provide even less benefit per dollar invested than PV.

What about maintenance costs?

Those who have been following the discussion this far may have noticed a flaw in the "PV is better" argument: PV equipment and heat-pumps have a shorter life and require more maintenance than subslab insulation. In fact, this point may be enough to convince some builders to choose 14 in. of foam over a PV array. It's a defensible position, but it's one that should be made only after considering the fact that the homeowners would get more bang for their buck from a PV array than from the last 10 in. of foam.

Over the last 15 or so years, it's been exciting to see the Passivhaus standard take root in the United States, where several dozen Passivhaus buildings have already been built. But it's important to remember that superinsulated houses are not new. Canadian and American researchers and builders began building superinsulated homes in the late 1970s.

A BRIEF LOOK AT RECENT HISTORY

My own interest in superinsulation can be traced back to my years as editor of *Energy Design Update*, a superinsulation newsletter launched by Ned Nisson in 1982. I took over as editor in 2002. In 1985, Ned Nisson and a co-author, Gautam Dutt, published a landmark book, *The Superinsulated Home Book*.

The book emphasized the importance of careful air-sealing measures, and it provided details for building double-stud walls, Larsen-truss walls, and foam-sheathed walls. It described the advantages of low-e glazing, argon-gas-filled glazing, and triple-glazed windows.

By 1985, superinsulation concepts were well understood. Researchers had studied and quantified air leakage in homes. Books and magazines with superinsulation details were widely available. Builders could buy low-e windows, triple-glazed windows, HRVs, and blower doors. Builders had developed a number of techniques for building homes with very low rates of air leakage. And many successful

homes with R-40 walls and R-60 ceilings had already been built.

Eleven years after this somewhat arbitrary milestone, Dr. Wolfgang Feist founded the Passivhaus Institut in Darmstadt, Germany, to promote the newly developed Passivhaus standard.

During the 1990s, a group of Vermont builders and energy experts, including Andy Shapiro, were advocating superinsulation techniques. All over the country, builders interested in superinsulation were building similar homes. In the fall of 2001, my photo of one such house—David Hansen's house in Montpelier—appeared on the cover of the *Journal of Light Construction*. The house had double-stud walls, an R-60 ceiling, careful air sealing details, triple-glazed Canadian windows, and a Venmar HRV.

THEY AREN'T PASSIVE

Passivhaus buildings are not passive; they require active space heating systems, active hot water systems, and active ventilation systems. That's why the original German designation of "Passivhaus" is problematic. For English speakers, the two-word spelling *passive house* is even worse than *Passivhaus*, because it introduces a new confusion—the confusion between passive solar houses and buildings that meet the Passivhaus standard.

The choice of the label for this superinsulation standard (Passivhaus) influenced the European decision to market these homes as "homes without a heating system."

GOLD STARS AND A FEW DEMERITS

What I like about the Passivhaus standard:

- It is based on the concepts championed by the North American pioneers of superinsulation.
- It sets a high bar for airtightness.
- It requires high-performance windows.
- It addresses thermal bridging.
- It focuses on envelope improvements rather than fancy equipment.
- It sets an energy goal that is in the ballpark of what will be necessary to achieve required carbon reductions.
- PHPP is an extremely useful and accurate design tool.
- The Passivhaus standard is now attracting wide attention, and designers are thinking and talking about design details in a new way.
- The number of Passivhaus buildings is growing.

However, these excellent characteristics of the Passivhaus standard must be balanced against a few flaws and missteps:

- Calling these superinsulated houses passive is problematic.
- The claim that these are houses without heating systems is false.
- Delivering heat through ventilation ducts makes no sense.
- The annual space heating limit of 15 kwh per square meter per year is arbitrary.
- The PHPP software has no cost-effectiveness feedback.
- The standard has a small house penalty.
- The standard doesn't distinguish among energy sources.

THEY AREN'T "HOMES WITHOUT HEATING SYSTEMS"

In my early reporting on the Passivhaus standard, I fell hook, line, and sinker for the marketing claim that these were homes without heating systems. Based on information provided by Swedish architect Hans Eek, I reported in *EDU* that his Lindås development was "the first project in Sweden without any heating systems."

Later, I had to publish a retraction. In July 2005, I reported, "Total mean electrical energy use per apartment [at the project in Lindås] was 8,200 kwh per year, including 1,800 kwh per year for space heating." The heating requirements were very low, raising the question, Why exaggerate?

Dr. Wolfgang Feist's statements on this issue appear to be tailored to his audience.

In October 2010, Dr. Feist told a Boston audience, "In the heating climates, a Passivhaus building is not a zero-energy building—you still need to heat it." In stark contrast, however, the definition of a passive house on the official Passivhaus Institut website states, "A passive house is a building in which a comfortable interior climate can be maintained without active heating and cooling systems. The house heats and cools itself, hence 'passive.'" Yet every single Passivhaus building I have studied and reported on includes an active heating system.

Although some Passivhaus proponents say that no one ever claims that these are homes without heating systems, the claim is actually plastered all over the Web, in articles posted by writers in Germany, Ireland, Sweden, Denmark, Norway, and the United States. In fact, all Passivhaus buildings require a heating system. Such exaggerations undermine the credibility of the Passivhaus movement.

WHY DELIVER SPACE HEAT THROUGH VENTILATION DUCTS?

The next misstep made by the Passivhaus movement was the declaration that space heat should be delivered through ventilation ducts. It seems that Dr. Feist recommended this method of heat delivery to bolster his claim that these houses don't require heating systems. In recent years, Dr. Feist has rescinded this requirement, but it still appears in many Passivhaus documents.

This recommendation makes no sense, so it's worth puzzling out how it came about. The apparent rationale behind the recommendation: Because these houses are called "passive," they can't have a furnace or a boiler. If heat is added to the ventilation air, it's disguised, so proponents feel justified in claiming—albeit at the cost of straying from the truth—that these are houses without heating systems.

Why is this heat delivery method such a bad idea? Ventilation airflow requirements are quite low—often only 40 cfm to 80 cfm—while the delivery of space heat or cooling generally requires higher air flows. In a cold climate, ventilation air flow limitations and limitations on the maximum temperature of ventilation air make this heat-delivery method impossible.

Some Passivhaus documents make a fetish of requiring that all duct systems deliver 100% outdoor air, and ridicule U.S. forced-air systems that include partial recirculation of indoor air. But there is no scientific basis for preferring 100% outdoor air systems to systems with partial air recirculation. A designer striving to deliver all space heat through ventilation ducts actually has a perverse incentive to

overventilate the house, since an increase in the ventilation air flow rate may be the only way to deliver enough heat to keep the occupants comfortable. Clearly, overventilation is undesirable, because it incurs an energy penalty.

Really, who cares how space heat is delivered? The Passivhaus Institut has released contradictory statements on whether the delivery of space heat through ventilation ducts is required; the recommendation is still featured prominently on the Passipedia website.

THE ANNUAL SPACE HEATING LIMIT IS ARBITRARY

The next problem with the Passivhaus standard is that the annual space heating limit of 15 kwh per square meter per year is arbitrary. The requirement is easy to achieve in a mild climate, but tough to achieve in a cold climate. Where did this limit come from? It appears to simply represent the space heating energy required to heat a well-built superinsulated home in the climate of central Europe, with the following assumptions:

- Space heat must be delivered through ventilation ducts.

- Ventilation rate = 0.3 to 0.4 air changes per hour.

- Temperature of ducted air = no higher than 122°F.

- The best windows in Europe are U-0.14 windows; the best achievable airtightness is 0.6 ACH50.

With these limits specified, the best houses in a central European climate need 15 kwh per square meter per year for heating. The problem with an arbitrary standard like this is that building a house that complies with the standard may cost much more than can ever be justified by anticipated energy savings.

THE PASSIVHAUS SOFTWARE PROVIDES NO COST-EFFECTIVENESS FEEDBACK

The entire Passivhaus approach provides no cost-effectiveness feedback, so designers often specify very thick layers of insulation—even when energy saved by the insulation is worth so little that the investment makes little sense. These high levels of insulation are specified for a single reason: to meet the arbitrary goal of 15 kwh per square meter per year. North American designers of net-zero energy homes take a different approach than Passivhaus designers: they compare the energy savings attributable to each measure under consideration with the energy production of a PV array. For example, if $1,000 of insulation saves less energy on an annual basis than the energy produced by a $1,000 PV array, then the insulation is not worth installing.

But the PHPP software has no red flag to warn designers that they have chosen to install insulation that costs more than PV, so Passivhaus installers don't know when

to stop making their insulation thicker and thicker. The result: insulation that costs more than a PV array.

It's important to note that I'm not advocating that builders actually install a PV array; nor am I particularly interested in arguing over whether insulation usually lasts longer than PV modules. (For the record, it usually does.) I am proposing that the cost of PV is a useful benchmark representing the high limit of likely future energy costs; for this reason, it makes sense to avoid envelope measures that yield a smaller energy return than a PV array. If you add more insulation than this benchmark justifies, you are planning for a future that will never come.

Many engineers have performed calculations to show when the cost of subslab foam exceeds the cost of a PV array. According to calculations made by Gary Proskiw and Anik Parekh (published in *Solplan Review*, January 2011), you don't need much subslab foam, even in Canada. According to Proskiw and Parekh's calculations, even in Yellowknife, YT, a basement slab requires no more than R-10

DON'T BE A FOAM HOG

You can save a lot more energy by installing 2 in. of foam under seven houses than by installing 14 in. of foam under one house.

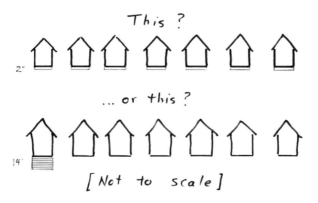

This ?

2"

... or this ?

14"

[Not to scale]

---

vertical insulation at the slab perimeter. John Straube's calculations point to somewhat thicker foam, however. Straube said that cold-climate builders should install between R-20 and R-25 foam under a slab on grade. Beyond that point, said Straube, the extra foam costs more than a PV array.

If you see a Hummer parked in someone's driveway, you might infer that the residents are energy hogs. Is there any more logic to being a "foam hog"—installing what amounts to unnecessary foam—than there is to wasting other types of materials? After all, it makes much more sense to install 2 in. of foam under seven houses than 14 in. of foam under just one house.

As with the false statements about homes without heating systems, claims that the insulation levels required to meet the Passivhaus standard are cost-effective undermine the credibility of the Passivhaus movement.

THE PASSIVHAUS STANDARD INCLUDES A SMALL-HOUSE PENALTY

The next problem with Passivhaus—the small house penalty—is shared by many other standards, including the Energy Star program. It's easier for large homes to comply with the Passivhaus standard than small homes, so the standard creates a perverse incentive to increase the size of homes. The main reason it's easier for larger houses to comply with the standard is that the ratio of the area of the home's envelope compared to the interior floor area is less for a large home than a small home, so large homes have less heat loss per unit of floor area than small homes. As Marc Rosenbaum has said, "Why should energy budgets be calculated on a per square meter basis instead of a per person basis?"

NOT ALL ENERGY SOURCES ARE DIRTY

Finally, the Passivhaus standard doesn't distinguish among energy sources. If the source of a home's energy is biomass or a wind turbine, there is less of a need to design a heroic envelope than when the source of a home's energy is coal. Again, Marc Rosenbaum is worth quoting here: "There is certainly a point where load reduction should hand the baton over to renewable generation."

If you're designing a NZE house, it's important to focus on domestic hot water and miscellaneous electrical loads

If you design a "pretty good house" with R-20 basement walls, R-31 above-grade walls, an R-49 ceiling, triple-glazed windows, a minisplit heat pump, and an HRV, what should you do next to reduce your energy bills? Maybe aim for the Passivhaus standard?

According to Marc Rosenbaum, that wouldn't make any sense—in part because a low-energy house uses more energy for domestic hot water and miscellaneous electric loads (lights, appliances, and plug loads) than for space heating and cooling. "Maybe install a heat-pump water heater or a solar water heater," Rosenbaum advised at a passive house conference in Portland, ME, in 2014. "That's what you need to do. But don't make it a passive house. Look at all energy use instead of putting 12 in. of foam under the slab."

MONITORING DATA FROM 12 HOMES

Rosenbaum's session was called "Getting to Net Zero." He began his presentation by explaining his aim: to design net-zero all-electric homes heated by minisplit heat pumps. (Rosenbaum defines a net-zero house as one that produces as much PV-generated electricity on site as it uses on an annual basis. In other words, this is a site energy calculation; it has nothing to do with source energy.)

Rosenbaum is the director of engineering at South Mountain Company on Martha's Vineyard in Massachusetts. He has helped install monitoring equipment at 12 all-electric superinsulated homes in New England, and he presented the monitoring data from these homes at the Portland conference. The homes varied in size from 1,200 sq. ft. to 1,600 sq. ft.; each house had between two and four occupants.

These homes don't meet the Passivhaus standard

The houses that have been monitored for the longest period are eight homes that are part of a small development on Martha's Vineyard called Eliakim's Way. The energy-related specifications for these homes were listed in the opening paragraph of this chapter. The homes are quite tight—a few of them passed the Passivhaus airtightness goal of 0.6 ACH50 or less—and have more insulation and better windows than most new homes. However, they fall short of meeting the Passivhaus standard. Domestic hot water is provided by electric-resistance water heaters. Each house has a 5-kw roof-mounted PV array.

Rosenbaum has monitored the homes' energy use patterns for four years, with submeters that record the electricity used for space heating and cooling, domestic hot water, ventilation, and miscellaneous electrical loads (lighting, appliances, and plug loads), as shown in the chart on the facing page.

If you want to whittle down these loads, what do you focus on? Not space heating and cooling. Here are some of Rosenbaum's observations:

Average annual electricity use per household at Eliakim's Way	
Lights, appliances, and miscellaneous plug loads	3,913 kwh
Domestic hot water	3,051 kwh
Space heating and cooling	1,790 kwh
Ventilation	307 kwh
Total annual energy use per household	9,061 kwh

- "For most of these houses, lights, plug loads, and appliances is the highest category of energy use."

- "When it comes to plug loads, people use stuff that you can't predict."

- "In almost all cases, energy used for domestic hot water is greater than energy used for space heating."

- "You have to deal with hot water, lights, plug loads, and appliances or you will not get to net zero."

- "Once you stop making boutique passive houses, you have to start thinking about real people. If this is a movement, you have to think about how people really live in their houses."

To reduce energy use in these houses, the next step would probably be to install a heat-pump water heater. "My Stiebel Eltron® heat-pump water heater keeps my basement dehumidified," Rosenbaum said. "The peak relative humidity in the basement during the summer was 60%. Yes, a heat-pump water heater steals energy in the winter, but it's good in the summer."

Rosenbaum likes LED lighting. "Every net-zero energy home needs LED or CFL lighting," said Rosenbaum. "These days, the LED light quality is so much better. I bought four of those Cree® things from the Home Depot®. They really make everything look sparkly."

A FEW MORE REMARKS ABOUT THE PASSIVHAUS STANDARD

Although Rosenbaum's presentation was focused on NZE buildings, he occasionally commented on the Passivhaus standard. He noted, "It's harder to make small houses meet the Passivhaus standard, although it is not hard to make small houses use less energy." One of the houses that Rosenbaum has helped monitor is Ted and Andrea Lemon's Passivhaus in southern Vermont. At the Lemons' house, "Heating and cooling use twice as much energy as PHPP predicts."

Rosenbaum questioned the usefulness of the PHPP default assumptions for plug loads and domestic hot water (both of which are unrealistically low). He said, "PHPP assumes 6.6 gallons [25 liters] of hot water a day per person, but that's not enough for normal Americans."

Of course, missing the target sometimes has side benefits. Rosenbaum said, "If people are using three times as much electricity for plug loads as the default value set by PHPP, that helps you hit your heating number." Rosenbaum emphasized that he isn't disdainful of the Passive House movement. "The Passive House Institute U.S. is tackling these issues, " he said.

Which design principles from the 1970s are worth retaining, and which should be discarded?

Everybody loves passive solar design. Back in the 1970s, "passive solar" was the essential first step for cold-climate builders. It was considered an approach with obvious advantages over complicated "active solar" schemes that required pumps, fans, and electronic controls.

While the definition of a passive solar house was well established by the 1980s, Wolfgang Feist muddied the waters in the 1990s when he decided to call his new superinsulation guidelines "the Passivhaus standard." Ever since that fateful day, journalists and owner/builders have confused passive solar design principles with Feist's superinsulation standard from Germany.

Rather than focusing on the confusion between passive solar design principles and the Passivhaus standard, however, I'd like to travel back in time to the 1970s, the heyday of the passive solar movement, to identify the original principles espoused by passive solar designers (see the sidebar on the facing page). Once these principles are identified, we'll examine how many of them have stood the test of time.

SOLAR VS. SUPERINSULATION

In 2009, the Passive House Institute U.S. invited me to give a presentation at the fourth annual North American Passive House Conference in Urbana, IL. In that presentation, "The History of Superinsulation in North America," I discussed the debate between solar house advocates and superinsulation advocates during the late 1970s and early 1980s. After Joe Lstiburek and John Straube saw my presentation

online, I was invited to present it again at the 14th annual Westford Symposium on Building Science in August 2010.

Here's a quick summary of the relevant history: During the late 1970s and early 1980s, advocates of superinsulation raised questions about the validity of passive solar design principles. A debate ensued, and superinsulation won.

Although I'm quite familiar with the historic debate, and I side with the superinsulation crowd, certain aspects of the passive solar approach—an emphasis on careful solar orientation, a concern for proper roof overhangs on the south side of a house, and a preference for south-facing windows over north-facing windows—seem embedded in my DNA.

Lately, however, I've begun to wonder whether there is any technical justification for these recommendations. Do these design principles result in energy savings? Or am I just dragging around the stubborn legacy of my hippie past?

FORGET THE THERMAL MASS

Some passive solar principles—especially the old belief in the near-magical effects of thermal mass—never made much sense to me. Thermal mass is expensive. Thermal mass complicates remodeling. Thermal mass makes a home unresponsive to sudden changes in the weather. By keeping a home cold when the occupants want to warm it up, or by keeping a home hot when the occupants want to cool it off, thermal mass is as likely to interfere with

- The long axis of the house should be oriented in an east–west direction.

- The rooms where people will spend most of their time should be located on the south side of the house, while utility rooms, bathrooms, closets, stairways, and hallways should be located on the north side of the house.

- There should be lots of extra glazing area on the south side of the house, and little or no glazing on the north side of the house.

- The roof overhang on the south side of the house should be designed to shade the south windows during the summer solstice, but to allow the sun to shine through the south windows on the winter solstice.

- The house should include extra interior thermal mass to soak up some of the solar heat gain that comes through windows on a sunny day.

occupant comfort as it is to contribute to energy savings.

For most cold-climate builders, the disadvantages of extra interior thermal mass outweigh any advantages. Even radiant floor designers, many of whom sang the praises of thermal mass in decades past, have mostly accepted the new consensus: Low-mass floors are easier to control, and result in higher levels of occupant comfort, than high-mass floors.

HOW MUCH SOUTH-FACING GLAZING?

My faith in another passive solar principle —adding plenty of south-facing glazing— was first shaken by Gary Proskiw's 2010 paper, "Identifying Affordable Net Zero Energy Housing Solutions." Briefly, here's what Proskiw found:

- South-facing windows are so expensive that the value of the heat gathered by the windows is too low to justify the cost of the windows.

- Money that a builder might want to spend on extra south-facing windows would be better invested in other energy-saving measures.

- The area of south-facing glazing "should be limited to that necessary to meet the

functional and aesthetic needs of the building."

It turns out that every extra square foot of glazing beyond what is needed for function and aesthetics is money down the drain. In a way, this advice is liberating: It compels the designer, secure in the knowledge that no technical or functional issues are at play, to think about aesthetic issues—and that's almost always a good thing.

PROPER ORIENTATION

What about orientation? According to conventional wisdom, the wise designer studies a site carefully, looking for a knoll with good southern exposure, and tries to align the long dimension of the house in an east–west direction.

Lately, building scientist Joe Lstiburek has delighted in puncturing this balloon. "I don't think orientation matters anymore," Lstiburek told me on the phone. "I see passive houses that are overheating in summer as well as winter—in Chicago! These houses need to reject the heat, not collect the heat."

So where did the passive solar design principles come from? What's changed since the 1970s?

TODAY'S HOUSES ARE BETTER INSULATED AND LESS LEAKY

For one thing, passive solar buildings never worked all that well. Even back in the 1970s, they were cold on winter mornings and hot on sunny afternoons. But most solar enthusiasts were so excited by the idea of "free heat" that we accepted uncomfortable conditions as a necessary part of the brave new solar future we were all busy creating.

Second, today's houses are better insulated and a lot more airtight than they used to be. That's good, because they require less energy to heat and cool than homes built in the 1970s. However, recent improvements in insulation and air-sealing standards make homes with lots of south-facing glazing more susceptible to overheating—so it's more important than ever to avoid excessive glazing area.

It's also essential that we make the right decision when choosing between high-solar-gain glazing and low-solar-gain glazing. That decision has gotten trickier lately, especially because Proskiw's calculations have called into question the entire idea that south-facing windows are heat-collecting devices. Some designers (including Lstiburek) have abandoned the idea of orientation-specific glazing specifications and now advise that all windows should have a low SHGC.

DON'T DO IT

In a 2014 article titled "Zeroing In," Lstiburek addressed passive solar design principles with his usual bluntness. "Don't bother with the passive solar," Lstiburek wrote. "Your house will overheat in the winter. Yes, you heard that right . . . You should go with very, very low SHGCs, around 0.2, in your glazing. If this sounds familiar to those of you who are as old as me, it should. We were here in the late 1970s when 'mass and glass' took on

'superinsulated.' Superinsulated won. And superinsulated won with lousy windows compared to what we have today. What are you folks thinking? Today's 'ultra-efficient' crushes the old 'superinsulated,' and you want to collect solar energy? Leave that to the PV."

WHY PASSIVE SOLAR DOESN'T WORK VERY WELL

Four salient facts undermine the old premises of passive solar design:

- In a well-designed house, the energy required for space heating represents a smaller percentage of a home's energy budget than it did in the 1970s. In many low-energy homes, domestic hot water requires more energy than space heating. For more information on this concept, see "It's Not about Space Heating" on p. 250.

- While large expanses of south-facing glass help heat up a home on a sunny day, the solar heat gain doesn't come when heat is needed. Most of the time, a passive solar home has either too much or too little solar heat gain, so much of the solar heat gain is wasted.

- At night and on cloudy days, large expanses of south-facing glass lose significantly more heat than an insulated wall.

- These days, investing in a PV array yields more useful energy than an investing in a south-facing window.

A NEW LOOK AT THE OLD PRINCIPLES

So what kind of advice would I give a young designer contemplating the five passive solar principles listed on p. 253?

The long axis of the house should be oriented in an east–west direction. I still have a sentimental attachment to this principle, even though I know it won't

WEST COAST SOLAR. This California home designed by Mariah Hodges combines traditional passive solar strategies with new-age materials.

save any energy. The reason I like to follow this principle—at least when the site allows it to be followed—is that it allows more rooms to get sun during the day. If you live in a cold climate, winter sun is cheerful. An east–west orientation is also best for any house with a roof-mounted PV array.

The rooms where people will spend most of their time should be located on the south side of the house, while utility rooms, bathrooms, closets, stairways, and hallways should be located on the north side of the house. It won't save any energy, but this is still a good principle, for the same reasons that it makes sense to orient the long axis of a house in an east–west direction. However, if you live in a mixed climate or a hot climate where the sun is oppressive and shade is your friend, this principle can be ignored.

There should be lots of extra glazing area on the south side of the house, and little or no glazing on the north side of the house. This principle is overstated. If your site has a wonderful view to the north, of course you want to include north-facing windows—and you may want your living room or dining room to face north. Moreover, there is no reason to include extra glazing on the south—only what's necessary (in Proskiw's words) "to meet the functional and aesthetic needs of the building."

That said, every house I have ever designed had more south glazing than north glazing because sunshine is cheerful and I like sunny rooms. (Up to a point; watch out for glare. Many passive solar houses are so sunny on winter afternoons that the occupants all flee to the home's dark northern corners.)

The roof overhang on the south side of the house should be designed to shade the south windows during the summer solstice, but allow the sun to shine through the south windows on the winter solstice. Although there's nothing wrong with this idea, it's worth pointing out that it has always been impossible to design an overhang that will keep out the sun when it is unwanted and admit the sun when it is wanted. At best, the designer can come up with an overhang that kind-of, sort-of, almost works, but not quite. The sun is tricky. It follows the same path through the sky in March, when sun may be welcome, as it does in September, when it may be unwelcome. Moreover, at 10:00 a.m. and 2:00 p.m., it sneaks in sideways, at an angle, and stubbornly undermines the intent of the designer's overhang.

So it's OK to shrug your shoulders and accept imperfection in this department—especially if you take Lstiburek's advice and just jump on the low-SHGC bandwagon.

The house should include extra interior thermal mass to soak up some of the solar heat gain that comes through windows on a sunny day. I'm happy to throw this principle out the window. However, if you live in a hot climate with high air-conditioning bills, you may want to build a house with a lot of interior thermal mass. Just remember that many of the benefits of thermal mass can be achieved at a lower cost by installing extra insulation.

MARTIN'S PRETTY GOOD HOUSE MANIFESTO

10 principles that green designers and builders need to keep in mind

One of the presentations I attended at the Passive House conference in Portland, ME, in September 2014 was a session called "Passive House Certifiers' Roundtable." The first speaker on the panel, Tomas O'Leary, explained that he usually charges about $2,200 to certify a residential Passivhaus project. He warned the audience that certification is "quite an effort; don't underestimate it."

O'Leary advised that anyone interested in certifying their Passivhaus should remember the following important steps:

• Prepare, collate, and submit the construction and mechanical details.

• Photograph all critical details.

• Make sure you get an HRV commissioning report.

• Remember that your blower door test has to be performed twice: under both pressurization and depressurization conditions.

• Make sure that you enter the right climate data into PHPP; data from a nearby weather station might not be good enough.

• Enter the correct U-factors for all of the window components—Uframe, Uedge, Uglass—because each component has to be modeled.

• The R-value per inch of all relevant materials has to be documented. Listing the R-values is insufficient; each R-value requires a document that justifies the listed value.

• Document a 360° panorama of the shading situation at the building site.

Is each one of these details really essential for determining whether a house can be certified as a Passivhaus? Absolutely.

If you are in any doubt about this issue, remember that one of the cited causes of the famous divorce between the Passivhaus Institut in Germany and Passive House Institute U.S. was a dispute over the details of the certification documents for a house in Canada. The dispute centered on two points: whether the efficiency calculations for a Canadian HRV met the strict efficiency calculation requirements specified by the German institute and whether an evergreen tree was tall enough to invalidate the shading calculations entered into PHPP.

GETTING STUCK IN THE WEEDS

I admire energy nerds who use THERM modeling for all kinds of complicated building assemblies. I really do. We can learn a lot from THERM modeling calculations. I'm grateful that someone has

NOT EVERY HOUSE needs to be a science project. Sometimes, "pretty good" is good enough.

made the calculations to determine that innie windows perform slightly better than outie windows. Now we know. I'm also grateful that Stephen Thwaites and Bronwyn Barry are available to explain the subtle differences between the way window U-factors are calculated in Europe and the way they are calculated in North America.

But when I hear lengthy discussions on these issues, I sometimes think we've fallen down the rabbit hole. If you are a builder or a designer rather than a building scientist, it may be time to clear the air. It's sometimes important to balance the recommendations of Passivhaus engineers with some common sense. Because it's getting hard to breathe down here, I've decided to pop my head out of the rabbit hole and write my Pretty Good House Manifesto. It's time to identify which features really matter.

1. We need to be humble

I've heard Passivhaus builders justify expensive construction details by explain-

ing, "Europeans build houses to last 200 years." Well, yes. That's kind of, sort of, true. But we should remember that 200 years ago, buildings didn't have central heating, insulation, plumbing, or electrical wiring—so you wouldn't really want to live in one. At best, a 200-year-old building is kind of like a shipping container. It's a rigid shell inside of which you can build a modern house.

It's hard to know what kinds of homes will be desirable in 2217. In 200 years, maybe everyone will be living in electric cars. Or boats. It's really hard to know whether a 200-year-old Passivhaus building will be considered desirable or a quaint relic in 2217.

My first wife's mother was raised in a solidly built 200-year-old farmhouse near Dingle, Ireland. There were 12 children in the family growing up together in the two-room stone house. The house never had running water or electricity, and it is now being used as a sheep barn—about the only purpose it is fit for.

Thousands of solidly built homes in Detroit have been abandoned, and I suspect that in the coming decades, tens of thousands of homes in Arizona will also be abandoned. In the United States, we demolish buildings at a surprisingly fast clip. Nice homes often end up too close to a busy road or in a neighborhood where no one wants to live.

How many of today's $500,000 Passivhaus homes, each of which was "built for 200 years," will end up getting an addition? Perhaps a second story? Maybe a remodeled kitchen that needs a bump-out? The fact is, we don't know. One thing's for sure: Building a house that is designed to last 200 years is guaranteed to be expensive.

All of these arguments support a building philosophy that Stewart Brand called the "low-road" approach. Sometimes, a small, inexpensive house makes sense.

2. Airtightness matters

The Passivhaus standard may have gone off the rails with its space heating energy budget (15 kwh per square meter per year), but they got the airtightness target (0.6 ACH50) just about right. If you want to build a good house, pay attention to airtightness during construction. Once your windows and doors have been installed, perform a blower door test. Reducing air leaks is the most cost-effective way there is to lower your energy bills.

3. There is nothing wrong with rules of thumb

Study buildings in your climate zone that are attractive, simple, and energy-efficient. Pay attention to their specifications. If possible, talk to the residents and find out whether the buildings are working well. If you do this, you will develop a gut instinct for what works in your climate zone. Eventually, these instincts can be codified into rules of thumb.

DESIGNERS NEED TO CONSIDER ENERGY EFFICIENCY, but it isn't the only goal to keep in mind. Aesthetics matter, too.

KEEP IT CLEAR. You don't want to have any chimneys, plumbing vents, or dormers penetrating your south-facing roof. Keep this space clear for a PV array.

A well-known rule of thumb for cold-climate builders in North America is the 5-10-20-40-60 rule developed by the Building Science Corporation: Windows should have a minimum R-value of 5 (equal to a U-factor of 0.20), basement slabs should be insulated to R-10, basement walls should be insulated to R-20, above-grade walls should be insulated to R-40, and attics or roof should be insulated to R-60.

Although some Passivhaus designers ridicule the rule-of-thumb approach as unsophisticated, it works just fine. It gives designers a guideline for good work, but it isn't set in stone. One of the implied corollaries of this type of rule is that it is somewhat flexible. After all, R-35 walls also work just fine. So does an R-55 attic.

4. We need to include PV

If your building site allows you to build a house with an unshaded south-facing roof, you should include a PV array—especially if you live in an area served by a utility that offers net-metering contracts.

Whether or not your house includes a PV array, designers need to learn how to compare the kilowatt-hours saved by any proposed energy improvement with the number of kilowatt-hours that could be generated by a PV array of the same cost. The calculation really isn't that difficult. Among the designers who use this method are Marc Rosenbaum, an energy engineer at South Mountain Company, and David Posluszny, a Massachusetts owner/builder.

Here's an example of how the method works: Posluszny knew that he could save a few kilowatt-hours each year by upgrading from double-glazed windows to triple-glazed windows. Was the upgrade worth it? It turned out that a few extra PV modules on his roof would generate more energy than the window upgrade would save—for the same investment. So he chose the double-glazed windows.

Of course, performing this type of calculation doesn't obligate the designer to always choose the option that provides the lowest-cost reduction in a home's annual

A HOUSE WITH A SIMPLE SHAPE—one without ells or bump-outs—is easier to heat and cool than a convoluted house.

energy budget. In the case of Posluszny's calculation, a designer could justifiably decide to specify triple-glazed windows, based (for example) on improved occupant comfort, even if that decision increased the construction budget. But it's important to make these decisions consciously, with an understanding of the cost and benefits of envelope improvements compared to the cost and benefits of a PV system.

5. We need to size and orient our windows with an eye to comfort and delight, not passive solar gains

Forget about specifying oversize windows for your south elevation. The bigger you make your windows, the more money you are wasting. In other words, stop thinking that south-facing windows are a good way to heat your house.

Passive solar design principles from the 1970s need to be reexamined in light of an astute analysis made by Gary Proskiw (see "Expensive Windows Yield Meager Energy Returns" on p. 181). Proskiw wrote, "The reason the two window upgrades [in his study] fared so poorly, from an economic perspective, is that the space heating load in a NZE house is very small compared to any other type of house. By adding window area or upgrading window performance, the space heating load is reduced but it is already so small that

there is little opportunity for further savings."

Proskiw concluded that "window area should be limited to that necessary to meet the functional and aesthetic needs of the building." Isn't that liberating? Just put in a window that looks good and suits your needs—no bigger. It's pretty simple. There is a side benefit to this approach: your house is less likely to overheat during the summer. Of course, it still makes sense to locate your main rooms on the south side of the house (because people like natural light) and to locate your mudroom, pantry, hallway, and mechanical room on the north side of your house.

6. All-electric homes make sense

As we make the transition to renewable energy, it makes sense to avoid appliances that burn carbon-based fuels like natural gas and propane. All-electric homes make sense, especially if you are able to include a PV array on your roof.

7. Pay attention to domestic hot water and miscellaneous electrical loads

If you have designed a tight, well-insulated home that isn't too big, you will probably find that you are using more energy for domestic hot water than for space heating. To reduce this slice of the energy pie, consider installing a heat-pump water heater and a drainwater heat recovery device. (For more information on this topic, see "It's Not about Space Heating" on p. 250.)

Limit the urge to buy new electrical gadgets for your home. Every time you specify an appliance, look for an Energy Star label. Needless to say, it's important to keep incandescent light bulbs out of your house. LED technology has now advanced to the point that you can find an LED lamp for every application.

8. Think twice before purchasing expensive building components

Every generation of designers lusts after a must-have building component. Back when I was building my first house in 1974, it was a Jøtul wood stove. Sure, it was expensive—but it was Scandinavian, and it got a good review in the *Whole Earth Catalog*. These days, the must-have building component might be a triple-glazed Zola window from Europe, or a Zehnder HRV with a glycol ground loop.

Here's the thing: If you find yourself saying, "I know it's really expensive, but it's supposed to be the best one on the market," stop and ask yourself whether you really need it. In another eight years, it's just going to be an old Jøtul stove, and there will be something else new and shiny that everyone is talking about.

A Pretty Good House can usually be put together with pretty good components.

9. We need to monitor our energy use

For most homeowners, monitoring energy use just means keeping track of our electricity, gas, and oil bills. We need to pay attention. Are we using more than our neighbors? Are our bills going up or down?

The nerdier members of our tribe will go a step further and will install electrical submeters, HOBO® sensors, and eMonitors. That's fine. We all learn a lot from paying attention to actual energy use. Energy monitoring provides data, and data matter much more than projections developed by computer modeling programs. This philosophy—monitor energy use and pay attention to what's happening—is far better than the usual approach (namely, "I got a plaque to put on my house and now I'm done").

10. Occupant behavior affects energy bills

While low energy bills are obviously desirable, we need to remember that the construction details of the house don't tell the whole story. The other side of the coin is occupant behavior. If you follow your grandmother's advice—Don't leave the water running! Turn out the lights when you leave the room!—you'll save energy. If you build yourself a new 3,000-sq.-ft. Passivhaus and install a big plasma TV and a second refrigerator, on the other hand, your energy bills are going to be higher than mine.

Some energy-obsessed designers spend weeks trying to track down a European window that will nudge their design from 16 kwh per square meter per year to 15 kwh per square meter per year—a difference that might save $12 a year in a 2,000-sq.-ft. house. When the house is completed, however, it turns out that the teenagers in the family like to take 30-minute showers in winter and dry their hair with hair dryers during summer. At that point, the $50,000 that you invested in European windows starts to look like a bad investment.

If you want to tread lightly on the planet, plan to live in a small house or apartment. Don't waste energy. If you follow these simple rules, your lifestyle is probably already greener than that of your wealthy neighbor who just built a brand-new Passivhaus—especially if you bicycle to work.